YOUR Lord HAS NOT Forsaken You

Addressing the Impact of Trauma on Faith

NAJWA AWAD & SARAH SULTAN

Foreword by Omar Suleiman

Your Lord has not Forsaken You: Addressing the Impact of Trauma on Faith

First Published in England by
Kube Publishing Ltd
MCC, Ratby Lane, Markfield
Leicestershire, LE67 9SY,
United Kingdom
Tel: +44 (0) 1530 249230
E-mail: info@kubepublishing.com
Website: www.kubepublishing.com

2nd impression, 2025

CIP data for this book is available from the British Library.

ISBN: 978-1-84774-220-9 *paperback*
ISBN: 978-0-86037-221-6 *ebook*

Editor: Shaykh Ismail Kamdar
Creative Direction, Design and Cover: Nida Khan
Illustrations and Layout: Rola El Ayoubi
Typesetting: Abdel-Minem Mustafa
Printed by: Elma Basim, Turkey

Contents

Foreword

All praise is due to Allah, and may His peace and blessings be upon the final Messenger, the Mercy to the Worlds, Muhammad and upon all those who follow his way with righteousness until the end of time.

Trauma is a topic that is very close to my heart. I spent much of my youth dealing with trauma, and my own journey of knowledge and *Dawah* has also been a journey of overcoming deep trauma and channelling it towards the production of what heals and clarifies. This amazing work by Dr. Najwa Awad and Sarah Sultan is something I wish I had access to when I was younger. Over the past few years, I have seen the hard work and long hours they spent researching this topic, and greatly appreciate all the time and sacrifice that went into writing this excellent work.

The result is a wonderful book that I believe will benefit many people around the world. This book was designed to benefit anyone who has ever had to deal with any kind of trauma, large or small. In a sense, every one of us can find benefit in the work. You will find in this book chapters covering a variety of trauma types, and how to use faith to bring us back to our best version and to our Loving Creator. We hope that no matter what trials you have faced in life, you will find comfort and a way forward through this book.

Allah revealed Islam not to bring discomfort to mankind, but to heal it. The Qur'an is a *Shifā'* (healing), and the final Messenger (blessings and peace be upon him) is a mercy. One can, therefore, find in the teachings of the Qur'an and Sunnah cures for every illness, including the various forms of trauma faced in life. This book was written in a clear and accessible way to make its ideas easy to implement.

This life is a test, and each of us are tested in different ways. Every one of us has at some point or another faced a trial that is traumatic and difficult to move past. Sometimes we get stuck in these trials and feel overwhelmed. Without the right support, it is too easy to fall into despair and lose hope.

This book is a gentle guide for dealing with so many of these traumatic trials of life. In this book, you will learn how to break cycles of negativity, move forward after grief, overcome anxiety about the future, fight negative thoughts and silence your inner critic. The authors have taken a very gentle and empathic approach to helping us deal with any kind of trial we generally face in life.

The prophetic model of this book is built upon the powerful message of Surah *al-Duha*. Reminding us that after night, there is always a dawn. This Surah calls on us to recall Allah's blessings, be optimistic about the future, and maintain positive thoughts about our Creator. "Your Lord has not forsaken you!" we are reminded in the powerful message of this Surah, and that forms the foundation of this wonderful book.

Filled with optimism and constructive advice, this is not just a manual on psychology, it is a very personal guidebook for life. The authors have taken the time to structure this book in a manner that makes it easy for anyone to follow and understand. Each section has practical activities to help inspire breakthroughs and to push us forward. The inspirational optimistic message of Islam flows through every page of this book.

I hope that this book inspires you as much as it inspires me. I hope you find even more comfort and healing in it than you ever imagined. I ask Allah to reward the authors and all those involved in putting together this book with the best of both worlds, and to make this a source of continuous reward for them.

Was Salam Alaykum Wa Rahmatu Allahi wa Barakatuhu

Dr. Omar Suleiman
Yaqeen Institute for Islamic Research
Founder, President & CEO

Introduction

Your Lord Has Not Forsaken You

Addressing the Impact of Trauma on Faith

Giving a voice to unbearable pain

When you hear the word "trauma," images of a soldier in combat, holding on to dear life while people all around him are being violently killed, may come to your mind. Or maybe you envision a refugee who forcefully left her beloved home to relocate to safety, only to have her entire family drown at sea. Trauma can provoke a wide range of ideas, but if you are like most people the clinical term feels exceptional and uncommon, and like something that doesn't happen to average people like us. But what if you don't need to travel to different corners of the world to experience trauma? What if these struggles are much closer to home—something your friend endured as a child, an event your sibling has kept to themselves, or a load that you have been quietly carrying without even realizing it?

According to the Adverse Childhood Experiences (ACEs) Study, in a sample of over 17,000 individuals, researchers found that 64% of the people surveyed had experienced something traumatic during their childhood years.[1] Contrary to the images of trauma we described at the beginning, like war and violence, these more commonly experienced traumatic incidents included emotional abuse, physical abuse, sexual abuse, domestic violence, household substance abuse, household mental illness, parental separation/ divorce, incarceration of a household member, emotional neglect, and physical neglect. When you walk down the street, two out of every three people you pass by have likely experienced at least one of these significant traumas during their childhood. These substantial traumas are sometimes called 'big T' traumas.

---

1 Felitti et al., "Relationship of Childhood Abuse."

Now imagine what the numbers would look like throughout a person's life span, especially during the tumultuous years of early adulthood when most people are experiencing intimate relationships for the first time, having children, coping with major changes like entering the workforce and adjusting relationship expectations with parents. Allah ﷻ tells us,

Do the people think that they will be left to say: We believe, and they will not be tried? But we have certainly tried those before them, and Allah will surely make evident those who are truthful, and He will surely make evident the liars.[2]

Adverse experiences and traumas are much more common than we might expect and can include conflict with family (spouse, parents, or children), extreme stress at work, natural disasters, financial trouble, unexpected illness, divorce, and legal issues. These smaller, but still significant, traumas are sometimes called 'small t' traumas. When we broaden the definition of trauma in this way, then everyone has likely been touched by trauma in one way or another.

Trauma, even trauma we may not realize has impacted us, can manifest itself in ways we may not anticipate. We may see the consequences of trauma all around us, like heightened anxiety, nightmares, irritability, and depression but completely overlook the connection between what we experienced in the past and our current day-to-day lives.

2 Qur'an 29:2–3.

The huge blow-out with your spouse that left you shaky for a day, that shame you felt as a child when your parent hit you for something you didn't do, the racial slur you heard at the supermarket when you were a teenager all invisibly piled up in your nervous system without you knowing and one day you wake up feeling really unhappy and have no idea why.

Did you know that many people's chronic depression and anxiety is actually due to residual trauma? Did you know that some individuals who appear to have ADHD or fits of uncontrollable anger are actually acting this way because of unhealed trauma? Even physical ailments like frequent headaches, stomach issues, and body aches can be linked to trauma when no physiological reasons can be found.

Many times, in trying to figure our own selves out we look to the byproducts of our trauma, like anxiety and depression, instead of the actual source itself—leaving us vexed as to why we can't heal that part of us that seems to be ever beyond our grasp.

Does it feel like your soul is tired no matter how much rest you get?

Are you overcome with restlessness and anxiety, even when you think you should feel safe?

Do you feel a sense of emptiness and struggle to connect with others in a genuine way?

Do you find yourself losing your temper over seemingly small things because a bigger cloud is overshadowing you?

Do you feel that you cannot trust anyone because nobody has your best interests at heart?

Are you numb and completely disengaged from your life and relationships?

Do you struggle to deal with stress effectively and find yourself always fighting or running away from conflict?

Are you angry with Allah ﷻ because it feels like your burden is too heavy to bear?

Do you find yourself crying frequently and unable to shake off a sadness weighing you down?

Do you struggle to find joy in your daily life or even to complete menial tasks completed?

Do you carry a deep sense of shame and feelings of unworthiness?

These painful feelings can all be residual effects of trauma, and when you begin to heal your trauma at the source, what is weighing heavily on your mind, body, and soul will begin to disappear. Healing will make space for connecting with others, experiencing joy, revitalizing your relationship with Allah ﷻ, and regaining a sense of control over your emotions, thoughts, and responses to situations. When we are overwhelmed by the circumstances that surround us, we tend to lose parts of our identities and ourselves. Through healing, we can regain the parts that have been lost and replace the puzzle pieces that trauma has removed from our minds, bodies, and hearts to allow ourselves to be whole once again.

The science behind trauma

As two therapists who have seen scores of individuals and families in our private practices over the years, we have borne witness to the tremendous impact that trauma can have on people and their communities. Trauma affects both the brain and body, altering the biological stress response system. Unbeknownst to many, 'big T' trauma and compounded 'little t' traumas can embed themselves into our bodies insidiously without us realizing it. Research shows that even when we no longer think about a trauma, it still hides in our body. So, hypothetically something that happened to you at age 7 can still be affecting how you cope with stress, and how you manage your relationships today.[3]

During exposure to trauma, our mind and body create an adaptive response necessary for our survival as human beings. In particular, the amygdala (a part of the brain primarily associated with processing emotions) causes alarm bells to start ringing, our muscles tense, we breathe faster, and our hearts begin to pump faster to ensure that more blood and oxygen can get to our muscles. This is called the "fight, flight, or freeze" response, which prepares our bodies to deal

3 Van der Kolk, "Body Keeps the Score."

with a threat or difficult situation that is happening around us. Basically, during stressful situations, we have three options: we attack and defend ourselves, run away toward safety, or freeze in place.[4] The sympathetic nervous system is responsible for mobilizing the body's resources during stressful situations, which induces the fight, flight, or freeze response.

In normal stressful situations, experiencing intense emotions and bodily sensations is a healthy response. Although symptoms can feel overpowering during and immediately after a stressful event, they are usually transitory and don't cause any prolonged negative impact on day-to-day life. Our amygdala, which warns us of impending danger and activates the body's stress response, is moderated by the frontal lobes, particularly the medial prefrontal cortex (MPFC).[5] The MPFC helps us make judgements about what is dangerous and what is not by observing what is going on and predicting what will happen depending on how we choose to respond.

Issues begin to arise when our sympathetic nervous system can't turn off. This can happen when extreme stress persists over a prolonged period of time, or an incident is so traumatic that the amygdala can't turn off, constantly reacting as though the danger has returned, when it has not. The more our nervous system is in a traumatized state, the more we will perceive threat all around us. The MPFC cannot be effective when constantly in fight, flight, or freeze mode, causing physiological imbalances and struggles in day-to-day functioning. Patterns develop that cause us to become overly focused on perceived hypothetical dangers, leading us to

4 Roozendaal, McEwen, and Chattarji, "Stress, Memory, and the Amygdala."
5 Shin, Rauch, and Pitman, "Amygdala, Medial Prefrontal Cortex."

experience powerlessness, fear, hopelessness, and a constant state of vigilance. Sometimes trauma or stress can be so overpowering that one can begin to disassociate or disconnect from feelings, identity, and memories of oneself.

In the current climate in which we have unprecedented exposure to every tragedy that unfolds in the news and on social media, most people are exposed to trauma on a constant basis without even realizing it. Indirect exposure to trauma, including viewing graphic news reports, being told a detailed traumatic story by another person, hearing that someone you care about has experienced something traumatic, and working in a field that exposes you to others' suffering, can often yield the same symptoms as experiencing a trauma yourself. This is called vicarious trauma or secondary traumatic stress.[6] In the same way as experiencing something traumatic yourself, we can get stuck in "fight, flight, or freeze" mode, when we no longer feel safe and feel like we have to defend against a threat that is no longer present. After direct trauma or vicarious trauma, our nervous system changes and relates to the world in a very different way than before,[7] with increased hypervigilance and difficulty in fully engaging in life.

Growth and healing are possible

This book seeks to address trauma from spiritual, mental, emotional, and physical perspectives. The focus will be on working through the depressive feelings, worries, and doubts that may arise as negative experiences impact our faith. There is no easy fix for trauma. However, healing is very possible. You can move past your pain. We see it in

6 Stamm, Secondary Traumatic Stress.
7 Van der Kolk, "Body Keeps the Score."

therapy all the time, and it is incredible to behold. There is even a name for it: Post-Traumatic Growth.

Although trauma can profoundly change an individual's life-narrative, thought patterns, beliefs, and ability to manage emotional distress, positive psychological changes can be experienced as well.[8] It sounds counterintuitive. However, there is growing research on this amazing phenomenon. Post-traumatic growth is defined as the ability to thrive after enduring a traumatic event and includes positive changes such as the development of new perspectives and personal growth.[9] Researchers have identified five areas of post-traumatic growth,[10] and our intent in writing this book is to help you to rediscover yourself through the lens of growth and healing in all of these areas:

A greater appreciation of life – After being buried in grief and overwhelming trauma, emergence from the rubble can lead to a changed perspective and much gratefulness, making the mundane details of life seem like extraordinary blessings.

Increased closeness in relationships – Experiencing the severance of a relationship or living through trauma can increase the appreciation we feel for significant people in our lives and allow us to be more empathetic toward them.

Identification of new possibilities – Life-changing events shift our priorities. Suddenly things can seem clearer and opportunities that may have been there all along are suddenly discernible.

---

8 Sheikh, "Posttraumatic Growth in Trauma Survivors."
9 Zoellner and Maercker, "Posttraumatic Growth in Clinical Psychology."
10 King and Hicks, "Detecting and Constructing Meaning in Life Events."

Increased personal strength – Before enduring particularly difficult circumstances, you may have thought that everything you are currently handling would have been impossible for you. Once you've been through tremendous hardships, future challenges may not seem as daunting.

Greater spiritual development – Going through suffering can result in a sense of spiritual and religious renewal and a greater sense of closeness to Allah ﷻ. When our priorities change, God becomes a more integral part of our daily lives, which adds to a sense of stability and growth.

Post-traumatic growth shows you that there is a light at the end of the tunnel, and that your trauma does not define who you are or where you can go in life. You are enough. You are capable of handling this seemingly insurmountable situation. You are perfectly equipped to deal with everything you face because you were meant to face it. And if Allah ﷻ has chosen you to face these tests, then you are guaranteed to have the ability to pass them due to His promise,

Allah does not charge a soul except [with that within] its capacity.[11]

You are resilient even if you feel like you can barely hold on right now. The strength, courage, and capacity for healing are embedded within you and we pray that this book will be a starting point to help you to achieve it.

---

11 Qur'an 2:286.

Goals of this book

We have many goals and several intended audiences for this book. First and foremost, we want this to be a resource for Muslims around the world. The chapters are easy to read and can be completed in chunks or sections at a time. We want the information to be easy to digest so that a busy mother can read it throughout the day or a professional who is working two jobs to make ends meet can read it during their lunch break. Although this book is not directly intended for clinicians, we also hope that mental health professionals can use it to supplement their therapy with clients who could benefit from reinforcement of concepts discussed during sessions. Lastly, we want this book to be a guide for imams and community leaders who are on the frontlines dealing with their congregations' individual and communal problems. Since many *imams* and community leaders are typically not trained in the field of psychology, we hope this book can be a resource to enhance the spiritual counselling they already do on a daily basis.

Before we discuss the purpose and intended use of the book further, we also would like to take a moment to discuss what this book is not. As two licensed psychotherapists who have been in the field for over 25 years combined, we know that the topic of trauma is one of the most complex and ever-changing topics in our field. Every day, new research and methodologies are being published in attempts to help those suffering from the effects of trauma. Having attended multiple trauma trainings and having worked with several hundreds of clients struggling with trauma, we also recognize the importance of pursuing psychotherapy to heal the innermost complexities of symptoms.

This book is not meant to be a substitute for therapy but only an introduction to the topic and how to begin the healing process. We will discuss, in depth, what trauma is and provide practical exercises to help address your symptoms, but please know that most individuals do not find complete relief without working with a professional. A psychotherapist will help you uncover, process, and heal the unique parts of your trauma that can never be sufficiently addressed in a workbook or by speaking to someone who doesn't have expertise in this field. If at any time you have flashbacks, feel like you are about to harm yourself or someone else, feel incapacitated by emotion or that the contents of this book are too triggering for you, stop reading and seek professional help immediately.

Now that what we have discussed who this publication is for and what it's about, let's look at its intended purposes.

1. Promote healing

The primary purpose of this book is to provide a refuge and healing for those who have silently endured trauma, perhaps not fully understanding what is happening to them and not knowing how or where to get help. Trauma is multifaceted and often carries with it very heavy and challenging emotions including deep sadness, paralyzing fear, unrelenting anxiety, and the suffocating feeling of being trapped and unsafe. Early in the process of contemplating seeking help, individuals may be cautious and would rather learn about the topic on their own. This book is a safe way to begin the healing process and a first stepping-stone for those individuals.

2. Establish the connection between trauma and faith

There is extensive research about how spirituality helps individuals cope with trauma and how trauma can deepen faith,[12] but not much literature about how trauma can negatively impact a person's faith. In our clinical experience, we have observed a strong link between trauma and faith-based doubts, which contributes to an increase in atheism and agnosticism.

In our experiences as therapists, we have seen a wide range of responses to traumatic experiences, but one fact remains true: spirituality and a connection with Allah ﷻ, whether it was present before the trauma or not, is very helpful as people strive to move forward following a tragedy. Trauma has a unique way of throwing us off balance; when the devastation of trauma spills over into an individual's belief system, it can lead to an increase in difficult thoughts and emotions, impacting spirituality even to the point that one abandons faith altogether. This is commonly seen when people ask after a trauma, "Why does God allow bad things to happen?" "If God existed, He wouldn't have allowed this," or "If God permitted this trauma to happen to me, then I don't want to have anything to do with religion." One of the best forms of armour we can equip ourselves with to protect our connection with Allah ﷻ during difficult times is to strengthen it during times of ease and stability. When we establish this connection in our thoughts and actions during good times, it is easier to tap into that resource during times of struggle.

---

12 Cornah, *Impact of Spirituality on Mental Health.*

The link between trauma and faith-based doubts is important in many ways. If our hypothesis is correct, that many Muslims are struggling with faith because of trauma-related issues, then how can healing trauma potentially affect faith? We suspect that healing trauma and challenging negative views about religion can strengthen faith. Rewiring our response to trauma can have a profound effect on every facet of our being, including the spiritual part of ourselves. One of our goals in writing this book is to help ourselves and our readers to find faith that can aid us in getting through our troubles. We call on faith-based researchers to further explore the relations between trauma and spirituality through qualitative and quantitative studies as the results may have many implications for both secular and Islamic psychology. We also want to highlight the link between trauma and faith for imams and those who give dawah (Muslim missionaries) so the subject can be broached with due diligence and sensitivity.

3. Provide a comprehensive approach and framework

The primary methodology of treating trauma around the world currently focuses heavily on alleviating symptomology through interventions for the mind and body. For Muslims and other individuals who believe in a Higher Power, this framework falls short and is incomplete from a holistic perspective. While our paradigm will be discussed in more depth in the next section, one of the purposes of this book is to address trauma in the mind and body as well as in the heart and soul.

4. Promote psychology literacy

Lastly, we hope that this book will be a means of promoting psychology literacy. The field of psychology is vast and most students around the world do not take psychology during grade school, and only a percentage of those who go to college will take an introductory class. The lack of exposure to psychological knowledge contributes to misconceptions surrounding this subject, which further deepens the stigma associated with the field of psychology and psychotherapy. While this book will barely scratch the surface of the field of psychology, one of our goals is to touch on a variety of basic psychological terms, concepts, and techniques so the average Muslim can walk away feeling more empowered about their understanding of mental health and well-being.

Paradigm used in this book

This book uses a holistic and Islamic approach to treating trauma. Secular psychology seeks to address trauma primarily through the mind and body, whereas Islamic psychology incorporates the mind as well as the heart *(qalb)*, soul *(ruh)*, and desire *(nafs)*. For the purposes and limited scope of this book, we will focus primarily on healing trauma through the mind, heart, and body.

The mind

The importance of thoughts and cognitions is evident in the Islamic tradition:

[We sent them] with clear proofs and written ordinances. And We revealed to you the message that you may make clear to the people what was sent down to them and that they might give thought.[13]

There are many additional *ayat* that emphasize the importance of thought, some of them being:

Say, "I only advise you of one [thing]: that you stand for Allah, [seeking truth] in pairs and individually, and then give thought." There is not in your companion any madness. He is only a warner to you before a severe punishment.[14]

Indeed, in the creation of the heavens and the earth and the alternation of the night and the day are signs for those of understanding. Who remember Allah while standing or sitting or [lying] on their sides and give thought to the creation of the heavens and the earth, [saying], "Our Lord, You did not create this aimlessly; exalted are You [above such a thing]; then protect us from the punishment of the Fire."[15]

Allah ﷻ teaches us that thinking is important for reflecting, observing, and believing.

---

13 Qur'an 16:44.
14 Qur'an 34:46.
15 Qur'an 3:190–91.

In the field of psychology, cognitive therapy and cognitive behavioural therapy are some of the most popular treatment modalities due to their practicality, versatility, and well-documented efficacy.[16]

Cognitive theory states that how individuals perceive and interpret the world around them influences how they feel and behave.[17] On a day-to-day, minute-to-minute basis individuals interpret what they experience by way of various types of thoughts. Many of these thoughts are 'automatic thoughts' whose content we assume to be correct, although it might actually be incorrect. Over time, thoughts are interpreted and grouped into categories of information, called 'schemas,' based on relations between the thoughts. Chronic negative thoughts can lead to dysfunctional schemas or 'cognitive distortions,' which may subsequently lead to maladaptive feelings and/or behaviours.

> ***In simple terms: Our thoughts affect our feelings, which in turn affect our behaviour, and when we modify our thoughts, we can change our emotions and how we interact with the world.***

Once thoughts become conscious, we can make a choice to keep them or alter them. If we choose healthy, positive, and Islamically congruent thoughts, then our mood and behaviour will likely follow. If we choose unhealthy thoughts (although sometimes they can be very difficult to manage and change, especially with trauma) then our mood and behaviour will likely reflect our outlook. Aaron Beck, the father of Cognitive Therapy, identified many common cognitive

---

16 Hofmann et al., "Efficacy of Cognitive Behavioural Therapy."
17 Knapp and Beck, "Cognitive Therapy."

distortions, or unhealthy ways of thinking, that we all experience from time to time. Those who suffer from anxiety, depression, and trauma, are much more susceptible to these cognitive distortions.

Each chapter in this book will address one of the ten most common types of cognitive distortions linked to common faith-based questions.[18] Through the cognitive approach employed throughout this book you will understand why you have the negative thoughts that you do and how you can change them in an effort to decrease your overall feelings of anxiety, depression, and the impact of the trauma you have experienced.

The heart

In Islamic psychology, there is special emphasis on the heart in reasoning, belief, and psychological healing. The heart is mentioned over one hundred times in the Qur'an and is central to our thinking and feeling.

> ***So, have they not travelled through the earth and have hearts by which to reason and ears by which to hear? For indeed, it is not eyes that are blinded, but blinded are the hearts that are within the chests.***[19]

The Qur'an indicates that the heart has the capacity to reason, and today scientists are discovering that our bodies have cardiac consciousness showing that the heart has a way to communicate

18 Please find a table containing definitions of each of the ten cognitive distortions at the end of this chapter.

19 Qur'an 22:46.

with the mind, although not much is known about this connection[20] The supremacy of the heart is demonstrated in the following *hadith*:

> ***There lies within the body a piece of flesh.***
> ***If it is sound, the whole body is sound; and***
> ***if it is corrupted, the whole body is corrupted.***
> ***Verily, this piece is the heart.***[21]

There are several ways to soften the heart in Islam, but in this book, we have chosen to incorporate Islamic techniques based on the Qur'an, primarily focused on how Allah ﷻ addressed Prophet Muhammad ﷺ in Surah *al-Duha* when he was sad and anxious. *al-Duha* is the Arabic word for "dawn," which is quite an appropriate metaphor for what this surah offers—a light at the end of a tunnel of darkness.

Before this surah was revealed, the Prophet ﷺ had not received revelation from Allah ﷻ in some time, which really distressed him. Furthermore, some of those who disbelieved in his message mocked him, saying that Allah was displeased with him. How did Allah ﷻ comfort him?[22]

> ***By the morning brightness***
>
> ***And [by] the night when it covers with darkness,***
>
> ***Your Lord has not forsaken you,***
> ***[O Muhammad], nor has He detested [you].***

---

20 Hassanpour et al., "How the Heart Speaks to the Brain."
21 Sahih al-Bukhari, no. 52; Sahih Muslim, no. 1599a.
22 Qur'an 93:1–11.

And the Hereafter is better for you
than the first [life].

And your Lord is going to give you,
and you will be satisfied.

Did He not find you an orphan
and give [you] refuge?

And He found you lost and guided [you],

And He found you poor
and made [you] self-sufficient.

So as for the orphan, do not oppress [him].

And as for the petitioner, do not repel [him].

And as for the favour of your Lord, report [it].

As we examined this chapter of the Qur'an, it was apparent to us that it offers an answer to the question of how to heal from psychological trauma. This chapter of the Qur'an provides us with a glimpse as to how Allah ﷻ, the One and Only God, comforted Prophet Muhammad ﷺ, the best of mankind.

What fascinated us, as professionals in this field, was the amount of clinical research we've stumbled upon in the course of writing this book that is consistent with the method that Allah ﷻ used to comfort

Muhammad ﷺ at a traumatic time in his life. While we believe that Allah ﷻ is capable of changing one's psychological state at will, perhaps the inference that even the best of humans is vulnerable to life's traumatic events was meant to provide us with a sense of comfort that we're not alone in facing life's darkest challenges.

Based on this framework, which we call *The Duha Approach,* we attempt to bring to our readers a comprehensive and Islamically sound approach to treating trauma. Let's take a brief look at a few of these interventions and how you will see them throughout the chapters in this book.

Attachment

In the third *ayah* of Surah *al-Duha* Allah ﷻ states,

> ***Your Lord has not forsaken you,***
> ***[O Muhammad], nor has He detested [you],***

comforting the Prophet ﷺ that, despite the lull in revelation, Allah ﷻ had not abandoned him. The same concept applies to you and your hardships or trauma. The traumas in your life are not because Allah ﷻ hates you or has ever stopped protecting you. Keep in mind that prior to this time of angst, the Prophet ﷺ experienced many events that would be considered traumatic to the average person; some of these included orphanhood, poverty, being a victim of physical assault and emotional abuse. He was also a war veteran. In this book we hope to regrow your attachment and connection to Allah and for you to know that your trauma is not a means of pushing you away from faith but of bringing you closer to Him. Secure attachment to a Higher Power is linked to psychological wellness.[23]

Shifting perspective

In the fourth and fifth *verses* of *Sūrah al-Ḍuḥā*, Allah ﷻ states,

> *And the Hereafter is better for you than the first [life]. And your Lord is going to give you, and you will be satisfied,*

which gives perspective to the Prophet ﷺ that, although he is in pain and experiencing distress now, matters will get better. When we experience trauma, it can feel as though we are trapped in a dark tunnel, with no way out and a sense of certainty that we will be stuck there forever. Allah ﷻ is assuring the Prophet ﷺ, and indirectly the believers, that not only will the difficulties in this world come to an end, but the Hereafter will be better and filled with contentment.

Our book addresses perspective-changing, both cognitively and through an Islamic framework. Shifting perspective is an important part of cognitive therapy as well as dialectical behaviour therapy (DBT), which are both effective in treating a myriad of psychological ailments.[24]

---

23 Leman et al., "Secure Attachment to God Uniquely Linked to Psychological Health."
24 Linehan et al., "Research on Dialectical Behaviour Therapy"; Hofmann et al., "Efficacy of Cognitive Behavioural Therapy."

Cognitive therapy

In the sixth, seventh, and eighth *verses* in *Sūrah al-Ḍuḥā*, Allah ﷻ states,

> *Did He not find you an orphan and give [you] refuge? And He found you lost and guided [you], And He found you poor and made [you] self-sufficient.*

In these *verses*, Allah ﷻ is directly working on the cognitions of the Prophet ﷺ. He gently confronts him by pointing out his blessings and reshaping how he was thinking about his current state of affairs, which is one of the most fundamental techniques of cognitive therapy. We have already discussed the value of the cognitive approach, but wanted to further point out the merit of this approach as Allah ﷻ also used it with the Prophet ﷺ.

Behavioural activation

In the ninth and tenth *verses* of *Sūrah al-Ḍuḥā*, Allah ﷻ states,

> *So as for the orphan, do not oppress [him].*
> *And as for the petitioner, do not repel [him],*

emphasizing the importance of taking action. Cognitive Behavioural Theory states that not only do our cognitions affect our behaviour but our behaviour also reinforces our cognitions.[25] Taking action strengthens the neural pathways of desired thoughts and behaviours,

25 Chartier and Provencher, "Behavioural Activation for Depression."

increasing the likelihood of repeating the same thoughts and behaviours in the future, and achieving the goal of change. It's not enough for us to simply change our thoughts, but to accompany our new thoughts with new actions. The workbook section in each chapter of this book will help prepare you to implement specific strategies in your day-to-day life so your new behaviours can strengthen your new, healthier mindset.

Cultivating gratitude

In the last *verse* of *Sūrah al-Ḍuḥā*, Allah ﷻ states,

> *And as for the favour of your Lord, report [it],*

instructing the Prophet ﷺ to acknowledge and proclaim his blessings. In this book, we will discuss the importance of identifying and reflecting on blessings, and how research has shown that these small practices have an immense impact on well-being.[26]

Additionally, at the end of each chapter, we include an inspirational Qur'anic verse and *ḥadith* section for further contemplation and remembrance, as thinking about and reflecting on Allah ﷻ is important for softening the heart:

> *...Then woe to those whose hearts are*
> *hardened against the remembrance of Allah.*
> *Those are in manifest error...*[27]

---

26 Wood, Froh, and Geraghty, "Gratitude and Well-Being."

27 Qur'an 39:22.

Has the time not come for those who have believed that their hearts should become humbly submissive at the remembrance of Allah and what has come down of the truth? And let them not be like those who were given the Scripture before, and a long period passed over them, so their hearts hardened; and many of them are defiantly disobedient.[28]

We believe that this combination of techniques will effectively address what many hearts are desperately seeking and cannot find in secular trauma treatment.

The body

In the past two decades, there has been a tremendous amount of research pointing to how trauma is stored in the body.[29] Researchers have found that trauma is kept in somatic memory and creates long-term chronic physiological alterations. The average person might figure that trauma is solely processed and kept in the brain; however, research shows that while trauma is processed in the brain, unprocessed trauma stays in the body.[30] While the mind forgets over time, the body does not, and can develop psychosomatic symptoms such as stomach aches, headaches, or other inexplicable pain and discomfort.

Psychosomatic symptoms are well documented in scientific literature and also mentioned in the Qur'an. When Prophet Yaqub عليه السلام experienced the trauma of the loss of his son, Prophet Yusuf عليه السلام,

28 Qur'an 57:16.
29 Van der Kolk, "Body Keeps the Score."
30 Van der Kolk.

he became blind; his psychological state affected his physiological state:

> *And he turned away from them and said,*
> *"O, my sorrow over Yusuf," and his eyes became*
> *white from grief, for he was distressed.*[31]

Expressive therapies, which can include art, movement, visualization and breathing exercises, are effective in supplementing other types of therapy, particularly when someone has experienced complex trauma over time.[32] While not all of our chapters will include expressive therapy techniques, the strategies we share are applicable to all of our chapters.

Book format

The chapters from Part 2 of the book are designed to be independent so that if a person wants to read about a particular issue, they can get help and relief without having to read the entire book. We do, however, recommend reading the book in its entirety as important information and different interventions will be interwoven throughout it. Most interventions are described in detail in separate chapters, but some important ones do resurface.

Each chapter has a specific topic (such as death, infidelity, or chronic toxic relationships) and addresses one of the ten most common cognitive distortions from the cognitive behavioural framework. Additionally, each chapter is paired with one of the most common questions that comes up in the midst of the trauma and faith crisis today, such as:

31 Qur'an 12:84.

32 Dunphy, Mullane, and Jacobsson, "Effectiveness of Expressive Arts Therapies."

Why does Allah hate me?
Why does Allah allow these things to happen?
Why do bad things happen to good people?
My **iman** *should be stronger.*
Why else would I be feeling this way?

Other chapters address basic questions related to trauma such as:

Why do only bad things happen to me?
Why bother living if the future is filled with pain?
The world would be better without me.
Why is everybody's life better than mine?

Each chapter has the same format and includes:

→ A Case Study
→ Why is this Happening to Me?
→ Understanding your Thoughts and Emotions
→ Changing Your Mind, Body, and Heart
→ Inspirational Hadith and Ayat for Reflection
→ Practical Exercises
→ The Case Study Revisited

Part 3 contains common coping skills from the chapters and additional coping skills we thought would be useful for readers to know as well. The coping skills are written in an easy-to-access fashion for quick reference while reading or after completing the entire book.

Part 4 contains resources and tips on how to get help beyond the book.

Opening *du'aa*

As you are about to begin the primary section of this book, we encourage you to identify your intentions to help guide you in the best way. Intentionality is an important concept in Islam, mindfulness, as well as healing.

'Umar ibn al Khaṭṭāb reported the Messenger of Allah ﷺ as saying "Actions are to be judged only by intentions and a person will have only what he intended..." [33]

33 *Sunan* Abi Dawud, no. 2201.

We thought it would be helpful to begin our journey with a *du'aa*. You may decide to use it or not. Feel free to modify the *du'aa* however you like to suit your needs.

O Allah, please reward me for seeking the first steps in my healing journey so that I can become the best possible version of myself I can be. Allah, please accept my attempts in seeking nearness to You and building a stronger relationship with You. Allah, please open my heart to receive the contents of this book in the best way and make it easy for me to work through and implement the strategies. Allah, please grant me healing in every form; only You truly know the healing I need. Allah, please count me as those who seek knowledge for the betterment of myself, my faith, and those around me.

Allahumma āmin.

As you begin to internalize the messages within this book, we pray for healing that will allow you to feel like your best self, and that the past will no longer hold the same power over you. We ask Allah ﷻ that the daily struggles that come your way will be met with resilience and that you will feel empowered to face the present moment with serenity and strength. We pray that through a strengthened connection with yourself and Allah ﷻ, you will find yourself at peace once again.

We sincerely hope you will benefit and enjoy growth from this book. Best wishes in starting your healing journey.

10 Most Common Cognitive Distortions

What is a cognitive distortion?

An unhealthy thinking pattern or belief that is inaccurate, and often perpetuates to a negative bias in how we interact with our environment and those in it.

Cognitive Distortion: Filtering

(Chapter 1)

Definition:

Life experiences go through a sieve that filters out the good and only what is negative remains and is brought to one's attention. As a result, the world is perceived from a negative bias.

Cognitive Distortion:
Should Statements

(Chapter 2)

Definition:

Using "should," "ought," or "must" statements, which can set up unrealistic expectations of ourselves and others. They involve rigid rules and do not allow for flexibility.

Cognitive Distortion:

Black & White Thinking or All-or-Nothing Thinking

(Chapter 3)

Definition:

Seeing things in black-and-white categories. Falling short of perfection is viewed as a total failure. This involves the inability to see grey in between the two extremes.

Cognitive Distortion: Overgeneralization

(Chapter 4)

Definition:

Coming to a general conclusion based on a single event or one piece of evidence. A single negative event leads to assuming a never-ending pattern of negativity.

Cognitive Distortion:
Emotional Reasoning

(Chapter 5)

Definition:

Assuming that your negative emotions reflect reality. It is the assumption that because you feel something, it must be true.

Cognitive Distortion: Magnification & Minimization

(Chapter 6)

Definition:

Magnification:
Occurs when you look at your own errors, fears, or imperfections and exaggerate their importance. This also includes overly focusing on negative events in your life.

Minimization:
Occurs when you look at your strengths or positive things in your life as small and inconsequential.

Cognitive Distortion:
Self-Blame or Personalization

(Chapter 7)

Definition:

Seeing yourself as the cause of a negative external event that you were not primarily responsible for.

Cognitive Distortion: Labelling

(Chapter 8)

Definition:

Overgeneralizing by taking one incident or characteristic of a person and applying it to the whole person rather than considering the situation or behaviour objectively.

Cognitive Distortion:

Disqualifying the Positive

(Chapter 9)

Definition:

Rejecting positive experiences by insisting that they "don't count." Only negative beliefs are maintained due to not allowing positive experiences to play a role in determining your reality.

Cognitive Distortion: Jumping to Conclusions

(Chapter 10)

Definition:

Creating a negative interpretation about something even though there are no definite facts that convincingly support that conclusion. Jumping to conclusions can occur in two ways:

1

"Mind-reading" involves a person thinking that others are negatively evaluating them or have bad intentions toward them.

2

"Fortune-telling" involves predicting a negative future outcome or deciding that situations will turn out for the worst before the situation has even occurred.

Chapter 1
Why Do Bad Things Always Happen to Me?
Breaking the Cycles of Negativity

We cannot solve our problems with the same level of thinking that created them.

ALBERT EINSTEIN

Case study

Muadh is a 52-year-old man who is very well respected in his local Muslim community. From the outside looking in, he has many good things going for him: a prestigious job working for a Fortune 500 company, a nice home, and a beautiful sports car. The walls of his home tell a different story, however. Muadh is currently separated from his third wife and his children are struggling with behavioural issues at home and school. When Muadh got married this time around he thought it would be different but the same relationship patterns persisted as before: constant bickering, big fights about insignificant things and feeling totally alone. "How could this happen again?" and "Why do bad things always happen to me?" were questions Muadh would ask himself often. He couldn't help but take this most recent divorce personally as he was the common denominator in all his failed relationships. Muadh could feel that his self-esteem was low, and he had difficulty seeing positives in his life outside of his relationships. Muadh felt like he was a good person overall but was convinced there must be something wrong with him because he kept getting involved in bad relationships over and over again.

What is happening to me?

Feeling trapped within the confines of the same problem over and over again is both soul-crushing and overwhelming. Whether the issue is never-ending conflict with a family member, recurring feelings of defeat, or something holding you back from living the life you envisioned for yourself, it's emotionally exhausting to face the same issue day in and day out, sometimes year after year. A difficulty that keeps resurfacing, sometimes under different guises, can feel like pushing a huge boulder up a hill; you expend so much energy trying to make progress only to be met with more resistance.

Over time you might wonder:

> ***"Is there something wrong with me?"***
>
> ***"How could so many bad things happen to one person?"***
>
> ***"Why do bad things keep happening to me?"***

Or you might take a different approach and think:

> ***"How could the world be such a bad place?"***
>
> ***"There are so many evil people out there."***
>
> ***"Why is everyone out to get me?"***

No matter how you interpret your experience, it becomes increasingly difficult to see good in anything or anybody through the pain. The more negative things you experience, the more negative the world looks. The worse people treat you, the worse you feel about yourself. And the more difficult your trials are, the more impossible it feels to change.

Understanding your thoughts and emotions

The filtering phenomenon

When unfavourable things happen back-to-back or repeatedly, it's easy to get discouraged and begin to look at the world through a pessimistic lens or filter. Filtering is a cognitive distortion, or unhealthy way of thinking, that skews how a person views the world and causes everything to be perceived from a negative bias.[1] Life experiences go through a sieve that filters out the good and only what is negative remains and is brought to one's attention.

1 Burns, *Feeling Good*.

Common everyday examples include:

> ***Getting angry with your child when he or she generally gets good grades but slips up and gets a poor grade.***
>
> ***Becoming upset with a friend, who is generally reliable and kind, when they make a mistake.***

When a person has a history of trauma, an internalized filter can be even more painful than it is for the average person. Traumatic events leave bigger impressions on the mind and body and cut into the soul in a deeper way. Some of these examples include:

> ***A person might generally have good relationships, but after feeling betrayed by a loved one begins to fear that most people are out to hurt them.***
>
> ***Someone who was physically attacked because of their religion may begin to think all negative interactions with others have to do with their faith, although most experiences in their day-to-day life are neutral or positive.***

Cognitive biases

Over time, the filtered thoughts develop into more intricate frameworks, which impact how the overall environment is experienced. A filter blocks positive stimuli and allows only the negative to come through. This filter, along with each person's individual temperament, experiences, and circumstances lead to the development of *biases*. Biases are patterns of thinking that form over a period of time and impact how the world is seen.

Some of these biases include:

> ***Failure is inevitable regardless of hard work or effort—therefore, there is no point in trying.***
>
> ***Humans are selfish, and you should never let your guard down because people will hurt you.***
>
> ***Humans are unreliable and you can't depend on family and friends for anything.***
>
> ***Patience is the best recourse no matter what even if others hurt or abuse you.***
>
> ***When more than one person hurts you it's because there is something wrong with you and not them.***
>
> ***It's better to be with others who hurt you than to be by yourself.***

Once a filter and biases are in place it can be difficult to break free from those thought patterns. These cognitive and emotional biases are like colored glasses and can affect how we see everything unfolding in our lives, ultimately influencing our decision-making. Before we delve into how biases affect our decision-making, let's discuss why or how people form filters and biases in the first place.

Contributors to the development of filters and biases

Learned pessimism

Disappointment is uncomfortable, and sometimes very painful. When a person is let down often, whether through events or people in their life, the healthy thing to do is to adjust expectations, try something new, or view the situation differently. Another option is to stop expecting good things to happen altogether—this prevents future disappointment since one is not hopeful that good things will happen in the first place. The logic is: If I don't expect good things to happen to me, then I won't be disappointed when I don't succeed, or good things don't come my way.

This unhealthy and maladaptive way of looking at the world is initially developed to protect oneself; however, long-term it does much more harm than good. Over time, this way of thinking builds deep-rooted pessimism and a very reactive (instead of proactive) way of addressing concerns.

Childhood invalidation

Parents, teachers, and caregivers play major roles in how we view and interact with the world. When we have role models who are pessimistic or have unhealthy ways of looking at things, we are susceptible to internalizing the same ways of thinking.

Let's take a very common example of striving for good grades. Imagine a child who worked hard all quarter to get good grades. This child did their homework, tried their best in class, and looked forward to coming home to show their report card to their parents. This child was successful in making the honour roll with all As and one B. They are excited and happy with the results of their hard work, but when they show the report card to their parent, the first thing the parent says is, "Why do you have that B?" This unexpected reaction instantly deflates the child's pride in their hard work over the course of weeks in just seconds. This reaction not only teaches a child to focus on negatives and shortcomings, but that their efforts, feelings, and thoughts are not valid or valuable. When a child thinks or feels something only to have an adult say their experience is wrong (not just about school but any life experience) it creates self-doubt, anxiety, and a lack of security.

Genetics

A study conducted by Todd et al. in 2013 suggests the inclination towards pessimism may be partially genetically based.[2] Researchers are exploring whether a person's genetic makeup may make them more susceptible to perceiving the glass as half empty. If this is the case, then individuals with this predisposition may have to try a little harder than others to practice looking on the brighter side of things.

---

2 Todd et al., "Genes for Emotion-Enhanced Remembering."

Implications of having a negative filter

According to cognitive behavioural theory, thoughts impact our feelings, which in turn influence how we behave, ultimately having significant implications for our filters and potential biases. If a person has a skewed way of thinking about the world, whether through a particular filter or bias, it's inevitable that feelings and behaviours in that subject area will be affected as well. If someone thinks they will not succeed, they will feel as though they have already failed, and will not take the appropriate steps to become successful. As a consequence, they will not be successful. This is called a self-fulfilling prophecy.

There are two kinds of self-fulfilling prophecies: self-imposed and ones imposed by others (also known as the Pygmalion effect). Self-imposed prophecies are internal, coming from within ourselves, and can be about ourselves or about other people. If a man thinks all women are irrational, he will behave in ways that will substantiate this through his interactions with women; he will speak to women in a condescending and offensive manner and will interpret their responses as irrational when they get upset, ultimately validating his initial perception. Similarly, if a woman thinks poorly about herself, she will interact with others in a way that will eventually cause them to view her in the same light, thereby substantiating her low self-esteem (e.g., she will be overly critical of herself when speaking with others).

The Pygmalion Effect occurs when a person behaves in ways that meet others' expectations of them. In the famous Rosenthal and Jacobson (1966) study, researchers described certain students as "ready to bloom" and realize their potential.[3] Unbeknownst to their teachers, the students were labelled in this way at random, rather than based on their intellectual abilities. Students believed to be on the verge of academic success by their teachers performed in accordance with these expectations as seen by substantial gains in their IQ at the end of the study. Students not labelled as "ready to bloom" did not have similar IQ gains. Further research has supported the conclusion that teachers' expectations can have a substantial effect on students' academic performance due to children fulfilling the expectations of those around them—in essence, a self-fulfilling prophecy.[4]

Beginning to change a filter or bias

Once you have identified a negative filter and unhealthy biases, it's important to look at what learned responses you have developed as a result of your cognitions. If you are seeing a pattern in life problems or interpersonal conflict, meaning the same problem keeps coming up in different ways, it's important to reflect not just on the biases contributing to your thoughts, but on your learned behaviour as well.

Why do certain people end up being in the same situation over and over again? Why do some women keep finding themselves in abusive relationships? Why do some men keep losing their jobs over and over? Why are some families in one financial hardship after another? Most of the time these situations do not happen coincidentally, but due to a negative filter and learned maladaptive patterns of behaviour. Let's look at some theories as to why we sometimes find ourselves in the same predicaments over and over again.

---

3 Rosenthal and Jacobson, "Teachers' Expectancies."

4 Boser, Wilhelm, and Hanna, "Power of the Pygmalion Effect."

The cognitive perspective

Cognitive theory suggests that individuals make the same mistakes over and over because those mistakes are learned responses. Theorists believe that we have neural pathways in our brains that are reinforced by habit. A good way to visualize this is a dirt road. The more you travel on the dirt road, the more well-established it becomes, and the less likely you will travel on the grassy or wooded area. It is much easier to tread a well-worn path than one covered in rocks and branches.

There is also a physiological explanation of the Islamic principle that the more you practice anything, the easier it becomes. The more you do good deeds or bad deeds, the easier they become. The more often you get up for night vigil (*tahajjud*), the easier it becomes, just as the more you look at pornography, the easier it becomes an ingrained habit. This is because the relevant neural pathways get strengthened any time a behaviour is repeated.

Cognitive theory also suggests that bad things keep happening to you because you are trapped in a cycle of making the same mistakes over and over. This does not mean that you are not a smart or good person, but that you don't know how to break the cycle yet. If you are trapped in a room and the only way you know how to get out is through the door you will spend all your time trying to break the lock free, when perhaps the only way to get out is through the vent in the ceiling. It is possible that the solution is outside what you may be comfortable with or know exists.

An example:

A lonely teenager feels hopeless and begins to engage in pleasurable self-destructive behaviour through the party scene (drinking, clubbing, and casual sex). His negative filter makes him feel that there is no good in his life and his bias makes him think he may as well do whatever he wants, good or bad, because it doesn't matter. As he engages in risky behaviour, he temporarily feels better and learns that his actions provide relief, although he feels exponentially worse from the consequences of his actions later. He internalizes the idea that it's better to feel good for short periods of time followed by feeling bad, rather than feeling bad all the time. Over time, he gets stuck in a cycle and doesn't know how to feel better without engaging in self-destructive behaviour.

Cognitive behavioural theory suggests that individuals can learn maladaptive ways of coping with their problems, and over time these coping behaviours become habitual. The more someone gets into the pattern of making the same mistake over and over, the more difficult it will be to change the behaviour.

The psychodynamic perspective

Psychodynamic theory offers a different perspective on why we fall into the same patterns, especially in relationships. According to one theory, individuals keep making the same mistakes over and over because they are trying to heal unmet needs from early childhood development. A person will keep putting themselves into the same predicament because, subconsciously or unconsciously, they want to use the current situation as an opportunity to resolve what happened in the past. Unfortunately, since the person has not learned better ways of dealing with the situation, they keep making the same decisions over and over, leading to even more unresolved struggles.

This perspective is useful for those who tend to get in the same types of toxic relationships over and over but do not understand why.

An example:

A girl grows up in a household where her father abuses her mother, which makes her feel insecure and vulnerable. She develops biases that the world is unsafe and that she needs to be protected by others in order to get by. When she gets older, she finds herself attracted to very strong men who carry themselves with a lot of bravado because this makes her feel safe. This initially makes her feel good but over time she realizes these men are also sometimes controlling and violent towards her. She finds that these men are actually very much like her father, although this was exactly what she was trying to escape in the first place.

In cases like this, there are oftentimes two major forces contributing to the individual's decision-making.

1. ***Humans are attracted to what they are used to because it feels most familiar and comfortable. A person who grows up in an abusive household may hate it, but may find themselves being part of one as an adult because that is the dynamic and treatment they are accustomed to.***

2. ***Humans have an innate need to resolve conflicts and when they are unable to do so, will create similar future conflicts to resolve previous issues. These conflicts are not created on purpose but subconsciously to help heal past wounds.***

Changing your mind, body, and heart

If you feel that you are a magnet for bad things happening to you, it's likely that you are struggling with a combination of a negative filter and unhealthy learned ways of adapting to stress in your environment. Don't worry, filters and biases are not permanent, unless you let them be. The nice thing about learning different psychological theories is that you can gain the tools needed to change thoughts, feelings, and behaviours with reflection and practice.

The most logical thing to do if you have biases is change them; however, if you are like most people, you probably aren't sure what biases you have in the first place. The tricky thing about biases is that when unexamined they appear logical, healthy, and like other thoughts you might have. A filter or bias may have been present for so long that you don't remember what it's like to see the world without it. In order to help reveal some of your biases you have to work backwards from repetitive cycles of conflict in your life.

Take a moment to reflect:

1. ***What causes me the most distress in my life on a regular basis? Don't think of specific stressors or individuals, but***

themes in your life. Is what bothers me conflict with others? Not feeling good enough? Fear of what others might think? Abandonment? Feeling attacked?

2. ***Do you have themes in your emotions? Are you chronically angry, sad, or anxious? What environmental stressors are usually present when you experience these emotions?***

Once you have the answers to these questions you can begin to work backwards and reflect on whether there are fallacies in your thinking contributing to your distress. Let's look at a few examples:

If you notice a theme in your life that other people have ill will towards you then it's possible that you have a bias in your views of other people. Let's say you are finding yourself having the following thoughts:

"I was called on in the meeting because my boss knew I didn't know the answer and he wanted to embarrass me."

"My husband came home late on purpose today because he intentionally didn't want to spend time with me."

"My friend takes a long time to text me back because deep down she actually doesn't like me."

Can you spot the filter and bias? A negative filter is preventing you from seeing good things in other people and focusing on the negative, while your bias is impacting your ability to objectively see and interact with others. This bias can be something you learned from your environment over time, or it could be the result of a trauma (for example, someone betrayed your trust).

Let's take another example. Upon reflection, you might have come to the realization that most of your distress comes from yourself. You are your own worst critic. You have perfectionist ways and can't stand when you do things incorrectly. It may be that you have thoughts like:

> ***"I can never do anything right."***
>
> ***"How did I mess this up again?"***
>
> ***"God, I'm so dumb!"***

Can you see the filter and bias here? You might be filtering out all the good things about yourself and just looking at the negative. Your bias is that you are flawed and that there is something wrong with you. This could be something you came to think on your own or that others have said to you. It can also be a result of trauma, such as emotional abuse in childhood.

Once you have identified the negative filters you have, you can begin to work on them by using counter thoughts. If you have a filter that others are out to get you, practice the *sunnah* of having *husn ad-dhan* (having a good opinion of others) and giving others many excuses. If you have a filter that you are worthless and not good at anything, counter those thoughts with positive qualities about yourself. Try to have 1–3 counter thoughts for every thought derived from your negative filter. It might take work and not feel genuine at first, but the more you practice replacing those thoughts, the more those new thoughts will become a part of your belief system. Keep practicing every day until you get the results you want. If it takes weeks, don't get discouraged—it took years and years to develop and maintain those unhealthy biases so undoing that work will not happen overnight.

Also notice how it feels in your body when you experience negative thoughts. During this exercise close your eyes, breathe deeply and notice where the tension lies (your forehead, your chest, your stomach, your shoulders, etc.). When you are ready to counter your negative thought, imagine the thought leaving that place in your body and letting it float away in a balloon drifting toward the sky. Don't forget to breathe deeply throughout. Imagine the balloon being released, drifting out your door, lingering near the ground, and then propelling itself with the wind to the horizon. Don't rush the balloon leaving and let it take as long as you need until you feel that the negative thought has left you.

When you are formulating your counter thought, imagine gently placing it on the part of your body where the negativity has left. Continue to breathe deeply. Imagine placing something therapeutic and reparative like a bandage or compress to heal that area. Cover that area gently until you start to feel yourself heal underneath. This visualization exercise might sound silly, but it taps into the mind-body connection, reinforcing a healthy cognitive shift and releasing trauma stored in the body. Using visualization can have powerful effects on your healing process and has been substantiated through a systematic review of numerous studies.[5]

Below are some additional exercises to try if you are feeling that only bad things happen to you.

1) Through the Prophet's eyes ﷺ:

This exercise taps into your negative filter. Prophet Muhammad ﷺ had some incredibly difficult times in his life when he had no food, people were trying to kill him, and he had no sense of physical security. People abused him, attempted to sully his reputation, and rejected the words of Allah ﷻ. He ﷺ also did not have any of the modern luxuries we have today like running water in the home, internet, electricity, etc. If the Prophet ﷺ had a negative filter it would have been very easy for him to be overcome by his trauma, fall into depression, and stop sharing the message of Islam.

Reflecting on your life now, as difficult as it may feel, what are positive things that you have that he ﷺ didn't? What are good things about you? What are positives you have in your life or things you have the potential to look forward to? Imagine sitting down with the Prophet ﷺ and conversing with him. Write those blessings down on sticky notes and post them on your mirror so you see them often.

5 Wahbeh et al., "Complementary and Alternative Medicine."

2) Follow the pattern:

This exercise is for helping explore behaviours resulting from your filter and biases. In the field of psychology there is a process called *transference*, which occurs when a person subconsciously or unconsciously interacts with another person in a certain way because that person reminds them of someone else. You have likely experienced this at some point; e.g., when a waitress at a restaurant has a similar voice to a friend you had in elementary school, or a person's tone reminds you of the boss you struggled with at your first job. Transference can be a part of a person's bias(es).

If you notice that you are getting in the same types of unhealthy relationships repeatedly, try to find a common thread between all those people and reflect on if they remind you of a trauma you experienced, perhaps from childhood.

Ask yourself:

> ***Do these individuals remind me of a caregiver or someone I struggled with in the past?***
>
> ***Who had the biggest impact on my negative emotions growing up?***
>
> ***Who made me feel anxious, stressed, or depressed in my early development?***

Reflect on whether the people from your recent toxic relationships have similar characteristics and remind you of a person who might have hurt you in the past.

If a pattern becomes clear, and you find the original source of pain, then know that working on that relationship where the pain first started is imperative to healing. You do not, and sometimes should not, work on the relationship directly with the person; rather, this can be done within yourself. One effective way of trying to repair damage from previous relationships is writing candid letters to that person venting all your feelings and frustrations about what happened. This is very cathartic and brings a feeling of resolution for many people, which can be useful for future relationships. Once you have finished releasing all of your feelings into the letter, burn it, shred it, or throw it away.

Spiritual inspiration for reflection

The Messenger of Allah ﷺ said:

> *"Whoever among you wakes up in the morning secure in his dwelling, healthy in his body, and having his food for the day, then it is as if the world has been gathered for him."* [6]

---

6 *Jāmiʿ al-Tirmidhī*, vol. 4, bk. 10, hadith 2346.

"No disaster strikes except by permission of Allah. And whoever believes in Allah, He will guide his heart. And Allah is Knowing of all things."[7]

Ibn Kathir said about this verse:

Whoever suffered an affliction, and he knew that it occurred by Allah's Judgement and Decree, and he patiently abides, awaiting Allah's reward, then Allah guides his heart, and will compensate him for his loss in this life by granting guidance to his heart and certainty in faith. Allah will replace whatever he lost for Him with the same or what is better. Ali ibn Abi Talhah reported from Ibn Abbas: "... and whosoever believes in Allah, He guides his heart." Allah will guide his heart to certainty. Therefore, he will know that what reached him would not have missed him and what missed him would not have reached him.[8]

"And We will surely test you with something of fear and hunger and a loss of wealth and lives and fruits, but give good tidings to the patient who, when disaster strikes them, say, 'Indeed we belong to Allah, and indeed to Him we will return.' Those are the ones upon whom are blessings from their Lord and mercy. And it is those who are the [rightly] guided."[9]

7 Qur'ān 64:11.
8 Ibn Kathīr, *Tafsīr Ibn Kathīr*, 10:24–25.
9 Qur'an 2:155–57.

Practical exercises

A. Through the Prophet's eyes ﷺ:

Step 1: Imagine sitting with Prophet ﷺ. What are positive things (amenities, luxuries, blessings, etc.) he might say you have that he didn't?

Step 2: Write those blessings down on sticky notes and post them on your mirror so you see them often. Write one good thing per note. Say your blessings out loud once a day with intention and mindfulness (paying attention to what you are saying, not being hasty). Saying the blessings out loud has a stronger effect than just saying it in your head.

B. Following the pattern

Step 1: Examine the relationships in your life and see if you notice any patterns in the people you are in conflict with (certain characteristics, behaviour patterns, fight patterns). Write down patterns you see below.

Example: *I keep getting fired. All my bosses are rude, aggressive, and inconsiderate. When I'm with them I feel combative and insubordinate. This pattern has happened with my last 3 jobs.*

____

____

____

____

Step 2: Once you have identified the current patterns, go back to earlier in your life and see if there are any difficult situations or people that remind you of the current conflict you are going through. If you see a connection to someone or something traumatic in your past write it below.

Example: *My boss reminds me a lot of my father. My father was very aggressive, authoritarian, and sometimes violent. I never felt understood by him and felt that he always came first.*

____

____

____

Step 3: Identify how you may be contributing to the problem through transference (treating someone a certain way because they remind you of someone in your past). Write down your specific behaviours before, during, and after the problem at hand and describe how others are affected by your actions.

Example: *Because my bosses remind me of my father, perhaps I'm disrespectful and have a poor attitude. This outlook might put off my employers and make them not want to keep me long-term.*

Step 4: Visually break down the problem so you can see your pattern more clearly. Using a 3–5 step chart, break down the pattern of your problem.

My boss asks me to do something I don't want to do, and this reminds me of my father.

I develop a poor attitude.

My boss develops a poor attitude and acts harshly towards me.

I resent my boss for how he treats me, and I start to become stubborn and rebellious.

↓

I get fired.

↓

↓

↓

↓

Step 5: Go back to the original source. On a separate piece of paper write a letter with all your thoughts and feelings towards the person for whom you have unresolved feelings from the past. Do not hold back. Tell them how their actions have upset and impacted you. This activity can be done in more than one sitting. Keep writing until your anger and sadness is released.

Step 6: Now that you have a better handle on the past, you can alter your incorrect beliefs about your current situation. Identify maladaptive thoughts and biases you currently have because you were holding on to your past so you can begin to change them. Write down all your unhealthy beliefs/thoughts and replace them with more appropriate ones. Then begin to apply the healthy thoughts in day-to-day life, especially when you feel triggered. Over time, your unhealthy thoughts will be replaced by your new healthier ones.

Unhealthy thought	Healthy thought
When my boss asks me to do something it's because he wants to put me down and make me feel like I have no control (transference from my father).	My boss is not the same as my father. It's my boss's job to make sure the company runs smoothly. He asks me to do tasks because we are all a team, and everyone has a certain role to play.
My boss thinks he is better than me.	As my employer, my boss has the right to give me directions on how he wants tasks completed. This does not mean he thinks he is better than me.

Case study revisited

Muadh didn't understand why he kept getting into the same toxic relationships over and over. He tried the Follow the Pattern exercise and noticed that all the women he had married were aggressive and reminded him a lot of his mother. As a child, Muadh never felt that she loved him although he did everything in his power to try to be close to her. When Muadh thought more and more about the connection between his ex-wives and his mother, he realized that perhaps he was trying to heal the relationship with his mother by marrying people similar to her.

Furthermore, Muadh realized that he had pretty negative biases about women and that this was also contributing to some of the conflict with his wives. Since Muadh expected women to be hurtful, disloyal, and irrational, he acted in ways to unconsciously facilitate this, thereby creating a self-fulfilling prophecy.

Muadh realized that he needed to better understand and overcome what had happened with his mother in order to have healthier relationships in the future. He wrote a letter to his mother about all the feelings he had experienced during childhood. The letter was unfiltered and didn't leave any negative feelings or thoughts unaddressed. Sometimes a few days would pass and Muadh would have more to say so he would add a P.S. at the end of the letter. When he felt like he had nothing more to write, he burned the letter and decided to forgive his mother for everything. He didn't feel what she did was right but didn't want to hold on to the negative feelings anymore.

After putting the difficult parts of his childhood to rest, Muadh felt like he had more clarity in his life. He realized that bad things didn't happen to him more than the average person—he was filtering out the good things in his life. Muadh decided he was going to take a break for a year from thinking about marriage and shift his focus to other aspects of this life. Muadh decided he needed to work on his and his children's well-being. He bought several self-help books for himself and invested heavily on spending more quality time with family. As a result, his children began to respect him more and started doing better at home and at school. Muadh understood that if/when he met the next person he wanted to marry, premarital counselling would be a very important step to prevent him from repeating the same mistakes of the past.

Chapter 2
I Should've Gotten Over it by Now

Surviving the Impact of Grief on Faith

Should you shield the valleys from the windstorms, you would never see the beauty of their canyons.

ELISABETH KÜBLER-ROSS

Lincoln, Reclaiming Banished Voices, 95.

Case study

Khadeejah's best friend, Amina, passed away in a sudden car accident one month ago. They attended college together and had been friends for over 20 years. After Amina's sudden death, Khadeejah felt unable to cope with the grief she was enduring. Every time she picked up her phone, she remembered she couldn't call her best friend. She couldn't imagine a future without the friend who had enriched so much of her past.

Khadeejah found herself changing as the days went on. Her temper flared up and she found herself feeling angry about seemingly minor issues. She also cried often and struggled to get out of bed for days at a time. She tried to drag herself to the restroom to make wudu for each salah *but sometimes the despair was so overwhelming that it felt impossible to lift her head off the pillow. Khadeejah continually felt guilty about her feelings of sadness, so she decided to talk to a friend about her struggles. When she approached her and explained what was happening, her friend replied, "It's been a month so it's time to get back to regular life. Have you tried praying and reading Qur'an? When your* iman *increases, you won't feel like this anymore. Be grateful that you'll be reunited with Amina in* jannah.*"*

Khadeejah returned home feeling even more depressed and was convinced that her relationship with Allah ﷻ wasn't strong enough. She already felt devastated and now she felt like a terrible Muslim. At this point she began to question her ability to connect with Allah ﷻ, telling herself: "My friend was right. I should've gotten over it by now. I must be a bad Muslim. My iman *should be stronger. Why else would I still be feeling this way?"*

What is happening to me?

Experiencing grief can feel like you're caught in a storm in the middle of an endless, dark ocean. As the storm strengthens, you are pulled under by huge waves and barely able to catch your breath. The rain pounds while the waves seem relentless. Suddenly, the waters calm and you catch a breath, not realizing this is the eye of the storm—an illusion of calmness before the waves begin to crash over you again. Sometimes you don't know what will trigger the revival of the storm—a memory, a scent, or an old text message.

Traumatic experiences, sudden life changes, and the loss of someone you love can be incredibly overwhelming. The pain can feel so intense that you may wonder how a person can experience such torture and still be capable of living and breathing. There will be days when you cry and can't seem to stop and then there will be days when you feel guilty because you haven't cried. Whether you have lost someone, your home, your job, or the life you imagined you would have, grief can be so painful that you feel it in your bones.

Grief and loss can transform our daily lives, the way we face the world, and our views of ourselves. Loss is often a form of trauma and can, therefore, cause a significant shift in things we previously considered unquestionable. You may start to question your capabilities, strengths, and relationships. The parts of your life that previously seemed the most certain may suddenly seem unclear.

While you used to consider yourself a person with good judgement, your view of this quality might change drastically after a financial investment has been completely lost. While you used to consider yourself a strong person, you may now feel broken after the unexpected death of a family member. While you may have considered yourself a successful person, you may start to doubt this after being fired from your dream job. Along with changes in your perception of yourself, the perception of your faith may change following an intense loss.

What you're feeling right now, as you struggle through tremendous pain, is a feeling that has touched the lives of people from the beginning of time. Furthermore, these feelings have even impacted the best of humanity—the Prophets of Allah عليهم السلام. Consider the example of Prophet Yaqub عليه السلام. He had twelve sons, one of whom was the Prophet Yusuf عليه السلام. When Yaqub was separated from his son Yusuf, he grieved so deeply that his eyes turned white due to how much he cried. His intense grief is expressed in the Qur'an,

> ***And he (Yaqub) said, "Oh, my sorrow over Yusuf," and his eyes became white from grief because of the sorrow that he suppressed.***[1]

People often misinterpret the grieving process as a sign of discontentment with the decree of Allah جل جلاله. When things in your life are not going in the direction you anticipated or a sudden event causes you to feel hurt or devastated, feeling this way does not indicate a weakness in your relationship with Allah جل جلاله or in your ability to accept what He has written for you.

---

1 Qur'an 12:84.

Consider what happened when Ibrahim, the young son of the Prophet Muhammad ﷺ, passed away:

> ***Allah's Messenger ﷺ took Ibrahim and kissed him and smelled him and later we entered Abu Saif's house and at that time Ibrahim was breathing his last breaths, and the eyes of Allah's Messenger ﷺ started shedding tears. `Abdur Rahman bin `Auf said, "O Allah's Apostle, even you are weeping!" He said, "O Ibn `Auf, this is mercy." Then he wept more and said, "The eyes are shedding tears and the heart is grieved, and we will not say except what pleases our Lord. O Ibrahim! Indeed, we are grieved by your separation."*** [2]

If the greatest human beings to walk the earth—those who were the most beloved to Allah ﷻ—experienced such sadness, then how can we attribute our feelings of grief to a lack of *iman*? Allah ﷻ did not reprimand the Prophet Muhammad ﷺ when he grieved for the loss of his son because grief, sadness, and difficult emotions do not indicate doubt in Allah ﷻ nor a weakness in our relationship with Him. Emotions were created by Allah ﷻ and serve a purpose. Therefore, telling yourself that you **"shouldn't"** feel a certain way denies an essential part that Allah ﷻ has placed within you.

2 *Sahih al-Bukhari*, no. 1303.

Understanding your thoughts and emotions

When we create unrealistic rules and expectations for ourselves and others, we are engaging in an unhealthy thinking pattern called **"Should Statements."** This is a type of cognitive distortion in which we use words such as "should," "ought," and "must" to create ideas that lead us to feel pressured and resentful. These statements can set up unattainable standards for ourselves and others. Should statements involve operating by rigid rules and do not allow for flexibility.[3]

Should/must statements are similar to the concept of *"if only"*—the idea that you or your life is missing an essential component, with which everything would be better. This is a thought pattern that leads to constant dissatisfaction, discontent, and regret. This thought pattern also leads to other cognitive distortions that can yield a negative self-image and negative interactions with others.

Consider these examples:

> ***"I shouldn't have eaten that. I just can't control myself. I should be thinner. If only I could lose those extra 20 pounds, I'd find someone to marry. No one would find someone like me attractive."***

3 Burns, *Feeling Good*.

"He shouldn't be so inconsiderate and self-centred. He should be on time instead of being late constantly. If only he wasn't late, I wouldn't feel resentful toward him."

"I shouldn't yell at my children so much. I must be a horrible mother and a failure. If only I were a better mother, everything would fall into place."

The Prophet ﷺ said,

> *... Seek help from Allah and do not lose heart, and if anything (in the form of trouble) comes to you, don't say: If only I had not done that, it would not have happened, but say: Allah did that what He had ordained to do. Your 'if' opens the (gate) for Satan.*[4]

When things aren't going the way we anticipate, our minds try to make sense of what is happening. We believe that our lives, our minds, and our emotions **should** function a certain way. When any of these get off track, we draw certain conclusions. We may start thinking about the things we **should** have done differently or the negative qualities we, or others, **must** possess to have caused this to happen.

"My best friend passed away one month ago. I should be able to get back to my day-to-day life by now. I must be doing something wrong to still be crying every day."

---

4 *Sahih Muslim*, no. 2664.

"Everyone says a Muslim shouldn't feel sad. Maybe my faith is the problem here."

"I should have stronger iman. *I must be a bad Muslim for feeling this way."*

Or

"Why is she still looking so sad every day? She wasn't even engaged for long. She'll find someone else. She should be over it by now."

"She should understand that Allah decreed this. If she's still sad about it, she must be doubting Allah. She must have low iman.*"*

Unhealthy ways of coping with difficult emotions

As human beings, we attempt to cope with negative emotions in different ways. We often attempt to push away our difficult emotions or the difficult emotions of others. They make us feel uncomfortable and it's painful to sit with these feelings. You may find that you try to distract yourself, put on a fake smile, or even self-medicate through the use of drugs or alcohol to alleviate the pain you are feeling. You may find that others invalidate your emotions because they don't understand or don't know how to deal with them.

Another way we may try to reject these difficult emotions is through *rationalization*. Our minds always seek to make sense of the world, particularly when things seem chaotic. Our brains naturally try to make connections even when a realistic connection doesn't exist. We may connect two events or thoughts that occur around the same time, whether or not there is an actual relationship between them. When you're feeling down, you may find that you feel further away from Allah ﷻ and Islam. This may result in connecting feelings of sadness, hurt, or pain with a lack of faith even though the two are not necessarily connected.

When people around us are uncomfortable seeing us in pain, they may engage in something called *spiritual bypassing*,[5] a process through which spiritual ideas and practices are used to sidestep or avoid facing emotional issues and psychological wounds. During times of stress or sadness people may tell us, "You should pray more. You must not be praying enough." There is absolute merit and truth to the idea that prayer can bring a sense of comfort, as Allah ﷻ tells the Prophet Muhammad ﷺ in Surah *al-Hijr*,

> ***We know how your heart is distressed by what they say. But celebrate the praises of your Lord and be of those who prostrate themselves in adoration.***[6]

Along with this, we have to also understand that trauma and fleeting feelings of sadness are not the same thing. And while

5 Cashwell, Bentley, and Yarborough, "Only Way Out Is Through."

6 Qur'an 15:97–98.

prayer is healing, Allah ﷻ provides us with many means through which we can journey toward healing, alongside our connection with Him. While a cancer patient can be encouraged to pray for health, chemotherapy is also a means that is necessary to heal the underlying issue. In the same way, someone who is struggling due to an emotional or psychological wound needs to heal the wound through appropriate treatment as the Prophet Muhammad ﷺ said,

> ***Allah has sent down both the disease and the cure, and He has appointed a cure for every disease, so treat yourselves medically, but use nothing unlawful.***[7]

What's happening in your brain

Every trauma tends to involve loss, whether it is the loss of safety and security after a natural disaster, the loss of a relationship, or the loss of the future you had anticipated after an accident that causes long-term health issues. While it is safe to say that trauma nearly always involves loss, the reverse is not true: loss is not always traumatic. Grief is a healthy response to loss—it is the natural experience of a wound that is in need of healing. Therefore, there is nothing inherently problematic about grieving the loss of someone or something.[8] However, when we do not have the opportunity to fully grieve and adapt to the loss we have experienced, it will continue to affect us, often in subtle ways, even years later. Without proper grieving and adaptation, the impact of the loss can be a traumatic experience.

---

7 *Sunan Abi Dawud*, no. 3874.
8 Worden, *Grief Counseling and Grief Therapy*.

George Engel, M.D. related mourning the loss of someone or something to the healing of physical wounds, implying that the loss of a loved one is psychologically traumatic in the same way that being severely wounded would be physiologically traumatic.[9] Both of these types of wounds need to heal; otherwise, further complications ensue, such as the manifestation of trauma.

When we are unable to grieve fully and an experience becomes a source of trauma, our central nervous system becomes dysregulated and hyper-activated. When this happens, we are thrust into survival mode, which shuts down the executive functioning part of our brain and prevents us from thinking clearly. This is why we may react to situations in unhealthy ways or do things during times of stress that we would not have done during times of ease.

If you've ever yelled at a loved one when you're particularly overwhelmed or if you've ever done something that you know takes you further away from Allah ﷻ when you're feeling like a wreck, consider what's happening in your brain during these moments. In the same way that we may do things we know are unhelpful during these moments, we may also avoid doing things that can potentially provide us with a little bit of respite.

This is one reason why some people struggle to worship Allah ﷻ during times of extreme stress. Our prefrontal cortex, the decision-making part of our brain, rationally knows that prayer, making *du'aa* or reflecting on verses from the Qur'an, will likely be helpful during difficult times but this part of our brain tends to shut down in response

---

9 Engel, "Is Grief a Disease?"

to trauma.[10] When the "danger activation centre" (including the amygdala in the picture below) part of our brain is dominant, there is a decrease in self-awareness, our capacity to self-evaluate, and our ability to establish goals. All of these require advanced thought processes, which are very difficult to sustain during times of extreme stress.[11]

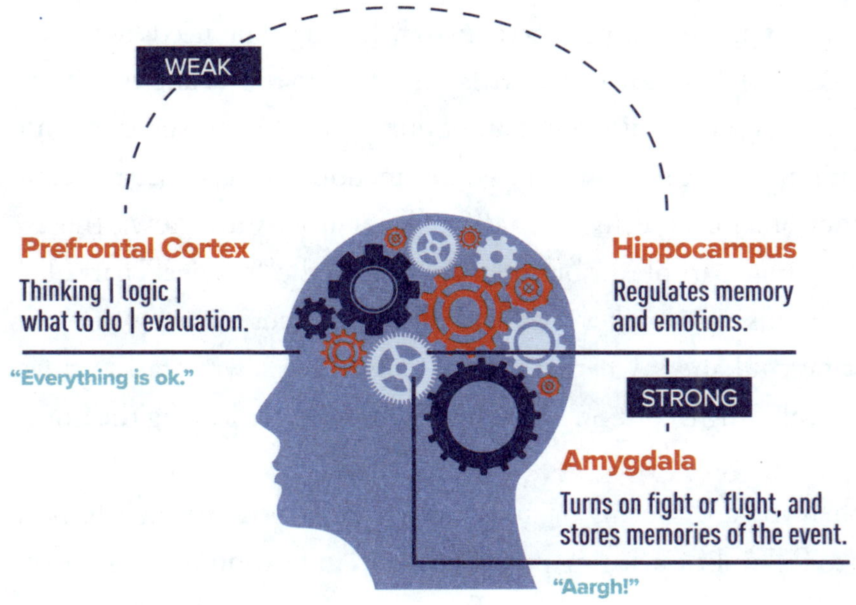

You may also think:

> *"Even during really hard times, I continued praying but prayer felt different. I couldn't focus and I couldn't get relief through it. Shouldn't prayer bring me comfort during my struggles?"*

---

10 Shin et al., "Regional Cerebral Blood Flow."
11 Buades-Rotger, Beyer, and Krämer, "Avoidant Responses to Interpersonal Provocation."

Prayer can bring us immediate relief when we are able to completely focus on our words, our movements, and the feelings within our body while praying. This is called mindfulness and is also very similar to the concept of *khushoo'*, or focus in prayer. This type of concentration activates our prefrontal cortex and can help us to shift away from stressed survival mode to a calmer, more mindful state.[12]

However, in order for any activity to help, our brain needs to register it. Research has shown an association between prayer and the ability to re-engage the "thinking" part of our brains.[13] However, traumatic reminders cause increased amygdala function and decreased prefrontal function. This means that a difficult memory shuts down the "thinking" part of our brains and turns on the "survival" part of our brains. This makes it difficult for us to focus our attention on the task at hand,[14] whether it's our daily prayers, work tasks, or even remembering to put on your child's shoes before leaving the house.

When you are grieving or surviving a trauma, your struggle to pray or to feel uplifted during prayer is not an indication of the state of your heart. It's an indication of the state of your brain—a brain that has endured trauma is a brain that will have trouble focusing on anything other than the pain that it is currently experiencing.

12 Lazar et al., "Meditation Experience."
13 Newberg et al., "Cerebral Blood Flow during Meditative Prayer."
14 Semple et al., "Higher Brain Blood Flow."

Changing your mind, body, and heart

If you are feeling as though your emotions indicate that you aren't a good Muslim, that thought can be changed. Let's consider the trajectory this thought pattern might lead to:

"I shouldn't be feeling sad. My iman *must not be strong enough."*

↓

"If I have weak iman, *then my relationship with Allah is weak."*

↓

"If my relationship with Allah is weak, then Allah must be upset with me."

↓

"If Allah is upset with me and hates me, then I must be doomed."

↓

"If I'm doomed, what's the point in trying to change things?"

Here, we see the connection between emotions, thoughts, and behaviours. When we are in pain and we set unrealistic standards about overcoming these emotions, these unhealthy thoughts propel us into a hurtful cycle. These negative thoughts lead to negative emotions, which eventually yield negative behaviours.

Negative view of self

Examples:

"I'm worthless."

"I'm unworthy of Allah's Mercy."

"I'm not capable of doing anything good."

"I'm ungrateful."

Failure to achieve the impossible

Examples:

"I missed one of my prayers so I've failed. I can't accomplish a goal I set my mind to. It's obvious I'm not capable of anything good."

"I can't get past this depression so I must be an ungrateful person. I knew I was worthless."

Should statements/ Unrealistic standards

Examples:

"If I never make a mistake then maybe I'll be worthy of Allah's Mercy."

"I should push away any feelings of sadness and worry so I can be grateful to Allah."

If you or others around you are enforcing a set image of what it means to be a good Muslim and this image involves not grieving or allowing yourself to feel uncomfortable emotions, you may start to expect that Allah ﷻ wants the impossible from you. And if you can't fulfil the *impossible*, what's the point of trying to fulfil the *possible*? This can have a profound impact on your relationship with Allah ﷻ.

You can find some helpful definitions below.[15]

Please note: A lot of Islamic literature utilizes the words "guilt" and "shame" interchangeably. It is difficult to translate Arabic terminologies directly into English so although some Islamic

15 The National Institute for the Clinical Application of Behavioural Medicine, *Guilt vs. Shame.*

publications may describe shame as a positive attribute, the way they typically use this term is in line with the definition of healthy guilt below. Whatever terminology is used, our main goal is to propel ourselves forward in strengthening our connection with Allah ﷻ and not to hold on to an emotional experience that pushes us further away from Him.

Healthy guilt, unhealthy guilt, and shame

Healthy guilt is a feeling of psychological discomfort about something we've done that is not in line with our personal values. We can use this to hold ourselves accountable and work toward positive changes. The key here is identifying the *behaviour* as inappropriate, rather than identifying *yourself*, as a person, as the problem. Healthy guilt is similar to what the Prophet ﷺ described when he said,

> ***Consult your heart. Righteousness is that about which the soul feels at ease and the heart feels tranquil. And wrongdoing is that which wavers in the soul and causes uneasiness in the chest...***[16]

Unhealthy guilt is a feeling of disproportionate psychological discomfort about something we've done against our irrationally high standards. This could be about something sinful or something completely benign like asking someone for help.

16 *40 Hadith al-Nawawi*, no. 27.

Shame is an intensely painful feeling of being fundamentally defective. We feel this because we see ourselves as unworthy and deeply flawed.

Consider the different implications of these statements:

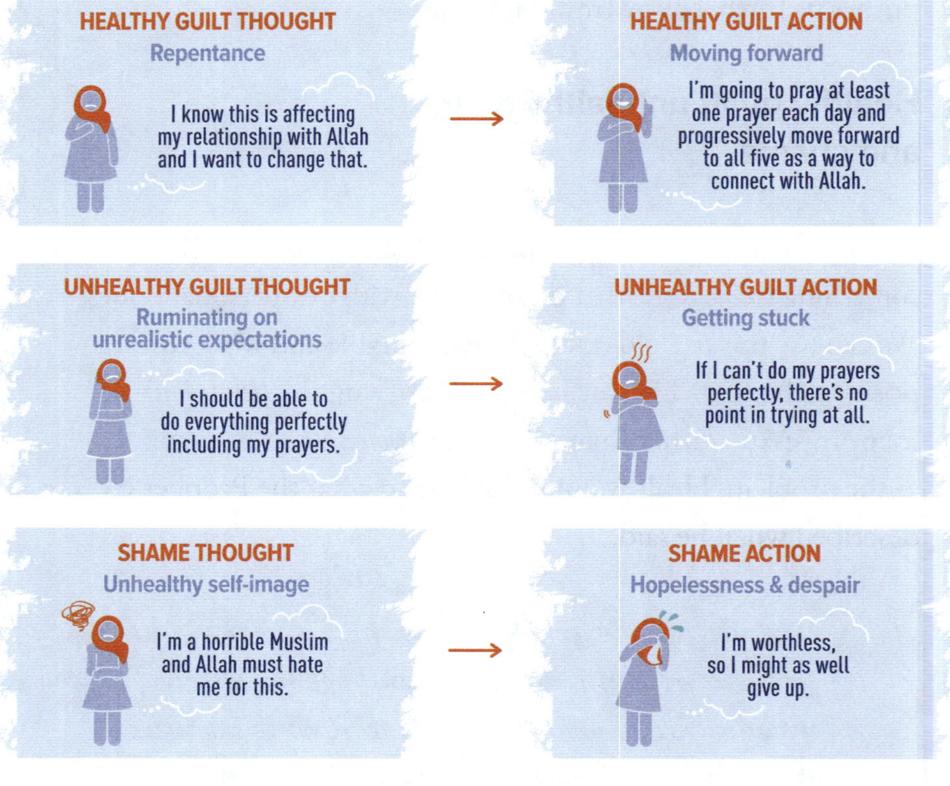

A balanced, healthy feeling of guilt is an asset that helps us hold ourselves accountable. 'Umar ibn al-Khattab said,

> *Call your souls to account before you are called to account and weigh your souls (actions) before you are weighed, for it will make the accountability easier for you tomorrow if you call yourselves to account today.*[17]

17 Ibn Ḥanbal, *al-Zuhd*, 2:30.

Healthy guilt functions as a compass for our hearts and minds. Furthermore, healthy guilt reminds us of the benefits of repentance following mistakes and questionable choices. Allah ﷻ says in *Surah al-Zumar*,

> ***Say: O My slaves who have transgressed against themselves! Despair not of the Mercy of Allah, verily Allah forgives all sins. Truly, He is Oft-Forgiving, Most Merciful.***[18]

Here, we see a promise that Allah ﷻ forgives every sin and that we are commanded to never despair of His Mercy. He does not expect perfection from us. He reminds us that things are not hopeless and that He believes us to be worthy of His Forgiveness even if we struggle to forgive ourselves.

While being human necessitates imperfection, it is incredibly liberating to realize that it is not so much about our sins or our good deeds, but rather it is fundamentally about who Allah ﷻ is. We are hopeful, not because our shortcomings are small, but because Allah's ﷻ Mercy is so great. And we are hopeful, not because our repentance is so sincere that we deserve forgiveness, but because Allah's ﷻ Compassion is so vast and His Promise of forgiveness is true. Sometimes overemphasis on our mistakes causes us to forget the Magnificence and Mercy of the One who has promised to forgive these same mistakes when we sincerely turn to Him.

18 Qur'an 39:53.

Dismantling "should" statements

Ask yourself these questions as you try to dismantle your "**should**" statements:

> ***What rule or assumption are you struggling with right now?***

Example: I believe that my feelings of sadness mean that I must have weak *iman*.

> ***How does it affect your daily life?***

Example: I feel ashamed to ask Allah for help because I'm not good enough to deserve it. I can't pray anymore because I feel worthless in the eyes of Allah and no matter what I do, I don't think it will ever be enough.

> ***When did you first realize that this unspoken rule became a part of your life? How did you learn about it? What was happening when you first adopted it?***

Example: When I was younger, I was always told that Muslims never feel sad because they are always grateful to Allah, no matter what happens. My Sunday school teachers told me, "*Iman* and sadness cannot coexist in one heart." So, when I felt sad, I assumed my *iman* had disappeared.

What are some of the advantages of this assumption? What are some of the disadvantages? (How does believing this "should" statement help you and how does it hurt you?)

Example: Sometimes thinking this way pushes me to pray more, fast more, and read more Qur'an but I always end up slipping backward after a little while. Believing that my negative feelings mean that I have weak *iman* usually leads me to stop praying and stop making *du'aa* because I don't feel like I'm worthy of being heard by Allah.

What is a potential alternative rule/assumption/ statement that would better suit you?

Example: Allah created us with emotions for a purpose. Feelings of sadness are normal and acceptable. My emotional state does not define my spiritual relationship with Allah nor my ability to worship Him.

How can you put this new and improved rule into practice in your daily life?

Example: I can remind myself that the prophets all experienced difficult emotions and Allah loved them; therefore, I can be loved by Allah too. I can still be close to Allah even when experiencing feelings of sadness.

It can be a struggle to move past the negativity you're experiencing—so much so that you may begin defining yourself based on your struggles. Consider how you want to be defined. Do you want to define your relationship with Allah ﷻ based on your current struggle or based on the potential closeness you can achieve? Your relationship with Allah ﷻ does not need to be defined by how you are feeling right at this moment.

We often identify with our imperfections and the negative occurrences in life rather than focusing on our positive qualities and the things that are going right in our lives. Trials afflict good people too. And doubts, dips in *iman*, and negative thoughts affect good people as well. Don't let the things that are going wrong define you. Never believe that you are beyond forgiveness; never underestimate the Mercy of Allah ﷻ. Allah ﷻ sees you and knows your heart, mind, and circumstances better than you know them yourself. He knows your struggles. Allow your positive choices moving forward to define you and to define your relationship with Allah ﷻ.

Spiritual inspiration for reflection

The Prophet Muhammad ﷺ said,

> ***"Verily, Allah has recorded good and bad deeds and He made them clear. Whoever intends to perform a good deed but does not do it, then Allah will record it as a complete good deed. If he intends to do it and does so, then Allah the Exalted will***

record it as ten good deeds up to seven hundred times as much or even more. If he intends to do a bad deed and does not do it, then Allah will record for him one complete good deed. If he does it, then Allah will record for him a single bad deed."[19]

The Messenger of Allah ﷺ said,

"Allah Almighty says: Whoever comes with a good deed will have the reward of ten like it and even more. Whoever comes with an evil deed will be recompensed for one evil deed like it or he will be forgiven. Whoever draws close to Me by the length of a hand, I will draw close to him by the length of an arm. Whoever draws close to Me by the length of an arm, I will draw close to him by the length of a fathom. Whoever comes to Me walking, I will come to him running. And whoever meets Me with enough sins to fill the earth, not associating any idols with Me, I will meet him with as much forgiveness."[20]

While Allah ﷻ counts our sins once and multiplies our good deeds at least 10 times, we tend to do the opposite. The "shoulds" that dictate our lives tend to erase the efforts that we put forth and focus solely on the end results. Yet, as we see in these *hadiths*, Allah ﷻ rewards us tremendously for our efforts and, rather than emphasizing our shortcomings, emphasizes our perpetual ability to get closer to Him and receive His Forgiveness.

---

19 *Sahih al-Bukhari*, no. 6491.
20 *Sahih Muslim*, no. 2687.

Practical exercises

A. Identifying a damaging thought trajectory

The first step in addressing our negative thought processes is identifying them. Use this template to consider the "should" statement you are saying to yourself and how it impacts your thought patterns.

"Should" Statement: I should... or I shouldn't...

Example: *I should never snap at my children.*

Example: *My wife shouldn't complain all the time.*

If I don't achieve this, then that would mean....

Example: *If I snap at my children, it would mean I'm not a good mother.*

Example: *If my wife complains, it means she's an unhappy person.*

If that is true, then it would mean this about me...

Example: *If it is true that I'm not a good mother, then I am a complete failure.*

Example: *If it is true that my wife is unhappy, then I'm incapable of making her happy which means we should get divorced.*

____

____

____

B. Differentiating shame, unhealthy guilt, and healthy guilt

Consider the "should" statement you wrote above. Does your thought trajectory lead you to toward shame that makes you feel hopeless and worthless, unhealthy guilt that is due to unattainably high standards or healthy guilt that propels you toward positive change? Write down your "should" statement and write down how it can be interpreted through the different lenses of shame, unhealthy guilt, and healthy guilt.

"Should" Statement:

____

____

____

____

Shame: An intensely painful feeling of being fundamentally defective. We feel this because we see ourselves as unworthy and deeply flawed.

Example: *I can't believe I yelled at my friend in the middle of our disagreement. She must hate me now since I showed her what a horrible person I am. I'm hopeless and I'll never be able to keep a friend.*

Unhealthy Guilt: A feeling of psychological discomfort about something we've done against our irrationally high standards.

Example: *I should be able to manage my emotions 100% of the time. It doesn't matter if my friend said hurtful things, I must always be composed. I just ruined our friendship for good.*

Healthy Guilt: We can use this to hold ourselves accountable and work toward positive changes. The key here is identifying the behaviour as inappropriate, rather than identifying you, as a person, as the problem.

Example: *I would have liked to handle that conversation with my friend better than I did. Next time, I'll try to keep my cool and not yell by taking a short bathroom break to calm down.*

C. Dismantling "should" statements:

Ask yourself these questions as you try to dismantle your "**should**" statements:

What rule or assumption are you struggling with right now?

How does it affect your daily life?

____

When did you first realize that this unspoken rule became a part of your life? How did you learn about it? What was happening when you first adopted it?

What are some of the advantages of this assumption? What are some of the disadvantages? (How does believing this "should" statement help you and how does it hurt you?)

What is a potential alternative rule/assumption/ statement that would better suit you?

How can you put this new and improved rule into practice in your daily life?

Case study revisited

As Khadeejah's grief continued to impact her ability to function on a daily basis, she reached out to a therapist and finally had the opportunity to process her emotions in a safe, non-judgemental space. As she began to feel validated, she realized that the sudden loss of her friend had been a traumatic experience for her and she had never allowed herself to fully explore it.

Khadeejah also discovered that her thought processes surrounding her expectations of how she "should" feel in response to Amina's death were causing her to suffer even more. She realized that her "should" statements were preventing her from grieving fully and that she couldn't move forward without addressing them. Khadeejah also realized that her "should" statements were causing her to pull away from her relationship with Allah ﷻ, which was something she used to rely on for support. Through exploration with her therapist, she realized that her "should" statements resulted in a sense of unhealthy guilt and shame. Khadeejah thought, "My iman *should be stronger. I'm still feeling sad so I must be weak and a bad Muslim. I should suck it up and move on." Khadeejah had been holding herself to an impossible standard—the idea that it is not okay to feel sad anymore is unrealistic for anyone who has lost someone important to them. Furthermore, she viewed her grief as an indication that something was wrong with her, as a person and as a Muslim. This caused her to move further away from Allah ﷻ due to shame and exacerbated her depression.*

Through understanding the impact her negative thoughts were having on her emotions, spirituality, and functioning, Khadeejah chose to dismantle her "should" statements. She realized she had been taught that sadness indicated a lack of contentment and a questioning of Allah's ﷻ decree. After changing her expectations to more realistic ones, Khadeejah realized that accepting Allah's ﷻ decree and feeling sad are not mutually exclusive and she worked to create new rules and expectations for her life moving forward. Khadeejah determined that Allah ﷻ provided her with emotions and that experiencing strong emotions during important moments in her life was okay. She also decided that she would no longer allow unrealistic expectations of herself to dictate her relationship with Allah ﷻ and began to view her struggles as opportunities to gain closeness to Him.

Chapter 3

"Why Bother Living if the Future is Filled with Pain?"

Reclaiming our Thoughts

In the depth of winter, I finally learned that within me there lay an invincible summer.

ALBERT CAMUS

"Return to Tipasa"

Case study

Aliya was in her last year of college and lived at home with her parents. Silence in her home always meant that something must be horribly wrong because the norm was constant yelling, threatening, and screaming. Her parents fought with each other all the time and she also fought with them—about her grades, how she dressed, and what she should be studying. Some days it felt like they fought about everything and nothing at the same time. It was just a never-ending feeling of walking on eggshells and feeling doomed rolled into one. Aliya used to try and please her parents but now she was just fed up and tired. She changed her degree from something she loved to pre-med, she sacrificed her social life by rarely going out with friends, and tried to do whatever her parents asked of her, but nothing was ever good enough for them. Aliya felt manipulated, taken advantage of, and guilt-tripped about everything. It felt like no matter what she did they were going to be perpetually unhappy with her and everyone else in the home. She just wanted a "normal" life in which she could be free of feeling anxious and sad all the time but there seemed to be no end in sight to her misery. She felt alone and hopeless about what to do. She found herself constantly thinking, ***"Why bother living if the future is filled with pain?"***

What's happening to me?

There are crossroads in life where trauma and the desire to keep going intersect. It's a busy intersection where on the outside everything seems to be whizzing past you, almost crashing into you, yet on the inside there is a numbness that has developed after feeling stuck between a rock and a hard place for so long. In this overwhelming pain it may feel like it takes too much effort to continue. You might ask yourself questions like:

"How much longer can I hang on?"

"How am I supposed to keep carrying such a heavy load?"

"When will this pain stop?"

On your bad days, the questions may be less exploratory and more emphatic, like:

"I hate my life."

"Nothing ever works out for me."

"Everything about me and my existence is terrible."

Thoughts about not wanting to continue life during times of adversity can alternate between feeling strangely right and feeling very scary. Many people get worried not just about experiencing thoughts of death, but also what those thoughts mean:

> ***"If I think about ending my life, does this mean I'm crazy?"***
>
> ***"What would others think about me if they found out I had these thoughts?"***
>
> ***"Will these thoughts ever go away? Am I going to feel this way forever?"***

If you've had these thoughts, know that you are not alone. There are people all over the world, including other Muslims who are reading this chapter just like you, who feel stuck with no way out. Studies shows that the lifetime prevalence rate for thinking about ending one's life in the average population is about 18.5%[1] and that those who have experienced trauma have an even higher likelihood of experiencing these feelings.[2]

You may think to yourself, "Well I bet they weren't good Muslims because even just the thought of ending your life before its time is *haram*!" How would you feel to know that that one of the best Muslims of all time had thoughts about dying when suffering from intense pain—someone who was promised heaven and was dear to Allah ﷻ? How would you feel to know that this person was Maryam عليها السلام In Surah *Maryam*, in which we are told about the conception and birth of Isa عليه السلام, Allah ﷻ tells us about the difficulties of birth Maryam عليها السلام experienced:

---

1 Lee et al., "Prevalence of Suicidal Ideation."

2 Panagioti, Gooding, and Tarrier, "Post-Traumatic Stress Disorder."

And the pains of childbirth drove her to the trunk of a palm tree. She said, "Oh, I wish I had died before this and was in oblivion, forgotten."[3]

The example of Maryam ﷺ shows that being overwhelmed with anguish and having thoughts about dying do not make you a bad Muslim. Ideas of death don't make you "crazy" and oftentimes these thoughts are just slivers of time in your life—not something that you will continue to experience indefinitely.

Unbeknownst to many, these types of thoughts are a type of cognitive distortion called **black-and-white thinking**.[4] In order to know how to cope with thoughts about not wanting to continue living, it's important to understand more about where these types of thoughts come from. When medicine helps heal the body, the sufferer doesn't need to know how or why the medicine works—the cure just needs to help the person feel better. The mind is different, however, in that gaining insight and understanding plays a crucial role in healing psychological pain in the long-term.

Understanding your thoughts and emotions

Black-and-white thinking is one of the most common unhealthy ways of thinking and occurs when a person develops extreme views about people, objects, or ideas—including religion. It is the inability to see grey in between the two extremes. This type

---

3 Qur'an 19:23.
4 Burns, *Feeling Good*.

of polarized thinking can happen at any time and for some people it happens often when they are experiencing continuous distress.

Common everyday examples include:

All-good or all-bad thinking:

Example: "I yelled at my kids again—I'm the worst mother in the world." or "My wife never cleans up—she's the worst wife ever."

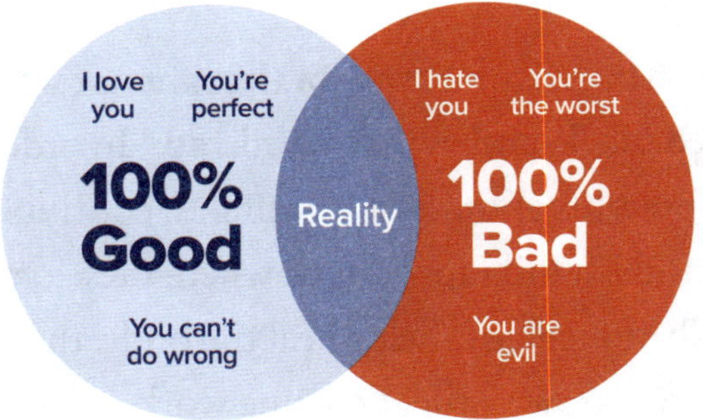

All-or-nothing thinking:

Example: "I cheated on my diet by eating two cookies, so I might as well eat the whole bag." or "I missed *fajr* prayer today so what's the point in praying the rest of the day."

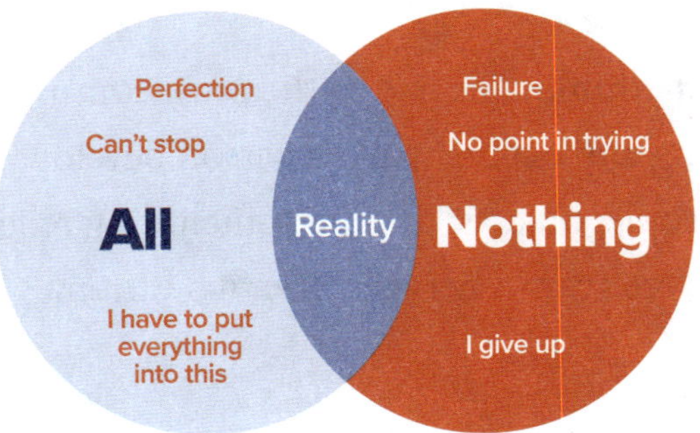

Black-and-white thinking starts all the way back in infancy. In the early stages of development, infants can only hold one good or one negative thought at a time. When an infant's caregiver is unavailable or does not meet the baby's needs (e.g., not comforting when they are upset, not feeding them when they are hungry, not changing them when they are wet, etc.) the infant will associate negative feelings with the caregiver. When the caregiver is present and meeting the infant's needs, the baby will associate positive feelings with the caregiver. As time progresses and cognitive abilities improve, the growing child will be able to hold the two views simultaneously if the caregiver is caring and consistent.[5] For example, the child might think (within their limited abilities): "My mother is away, but she still cares for me and will come back soon. I know this because she always comes back and shows how much she cares about me."

In situations in which a caregiver is neglectful, unpredictable, and/or abusive then it will be difficult for the child to reconcile the two opposing views at the same time and black-and-white thinking will persist over time. This is because when the caregiver is inconsistent, the child will never know what to expect next so it's easy to go from one extreme to another at any given time. For example, the child might think (within their limited abilities): "My mother has abandoned me. There was a time when she left and didn't come back for a very long time, so she is probably not coming back this time."

Black-and-white thinking in healthy, typical development gradually disappears from infancy through adolescence, but it's not unusual

5 Boag, "Psychodynamic Approaches to Borderline Personality Disorder."

for even healthy adults to fall into black-and-white thinking on occasion. Common examples include:

> ***"I got all Cs for my midterm grades so there is no point in continuing on with the semester."***
>
> ***"My boss gave me an unsatisfactory review so I want to quit my job immediately."***
>
> ***"My friend didn't respond to my text for two days; I'm totally done with the friendship."***

In high-pressure situations, the fight, flight, or freeze instinct can make black-and-white thoughts even darker and harder to ignore. The flight response is not always about physically leaving; it can also involve impulsively removing yourself from the picture. You might have had thoughts like:

> ***"What's the point in continuing with life?"***
>
> ***"If I knew my illness would be over soon, I could wait it out, but I don't know if it will ever go away—and so my life is already over."***
>
> ***"I'm a burden, perhaps others would be better off without me."***

It should be noted here that there is a big difference between passive thoughts of death and active thoughts of death. Passive thoughts are temporary feelings with no intent of following through, whereas active thoughts, or feeling suicidal, warrant immediate help. If you ever feel suicidal, it's important to get help right away by calling 911 or having someone take you to the nearest hospital emergency room for immediate attention. The next sections of this chapter address how to cope with *passive* thoughts of death that result from black-and-white thinking.

Changing your mind, body, and heart

Overcoming black-and-white thinking is no easy feat, but it can be done with self-compassion, commitment, and a lot of practise. You matter. Your feelings matter and your future matters. Allah put you on this earth for a reason and does not want you to end your life. He wants you to stay and find your way back to Him when the time is right.

If you have had this type of thinking all your life, then understand it cannot be undone with the flick of a switch. Looking at the world in black-and-white can not only deeply embed itself in your way of thinking, but in how your body responds to the environment around you as well. Some days your physical and mental urges to get caught up in the fight, flight, or freeze response will be stronger than others, and that is okay. The more you practise riding out those emotional waves, the easier it will be to tame them. Over time, you will notice that the black-and-white thinking still exists, but the feelings will be less intense, less frequent, and less impactful.

Building distress tolerance

Distress tolerance is the ability to experience stress without being completely overcome by it and is a great way to start practising coping with black-and-white thinking. It involves being able to take a step back, pausing, and then acting. The pause can be a few moments or a few days, but it's enough time to allow you to recentre yourself. Maintaining calm doesn't mean suppressing your feelings or pretending that a problem doesn't exist; it means that you are stressed, but that you feel in control of yourself—instead of your emotions controlling you.

The Messenger of Allah ﷺ said: "[Real] patience is at the first stroke of the calamity." [6]

The first step in building distress tolerance is to know what stress feels like in your body. Humans experience emotional overwhelm in different ways, but individuals tend to experience similar symptoms within themselves in distressing situations. The next time you feel distressed, pay attention to your body and reflect on where you feel tension or pain. Notice if you have:

- A racing heart
- Laboured breathing
- Feelings of wanting to yell
- Feelings of wanting to throw something
- Sweating
- Clenched fists

6 *Jami' al-Tirmidhi*, vol. 2, bk. 5, hadith 988.

- Tension in other parts of the body, like your neck or back
- A sense of hastiness and wanting to take immediate action
- Heat on your face, chest, or other parts of your body
- Feeling like your body is shutting down

These are signs our bodies manifest before we take action. The unrest, although uncomfortable, is actually a blessing in that it gives our bodies a signal and the ability to recognize that we have an opportunity to decide what happens next. Taking a pause in between the feeling and the action is the space where you can regain control of your body and thoughts and decide how to proceed.[7] This is also the space where black-and-white thinking can be modified. Those who succumb to black-and-white thinking usually do it here, sometimes making snap decisions that end relationships and have catastrophic effects on opportunities and achievements. Some keywords to listen for in your mind during this time are *always*, *never*, and *hate*.

"I hate my life."

"You are never there for me."

"I always fail."

7 Covey, *7 Habits of Highly Effective People*.

The Stimulus-Response Mode

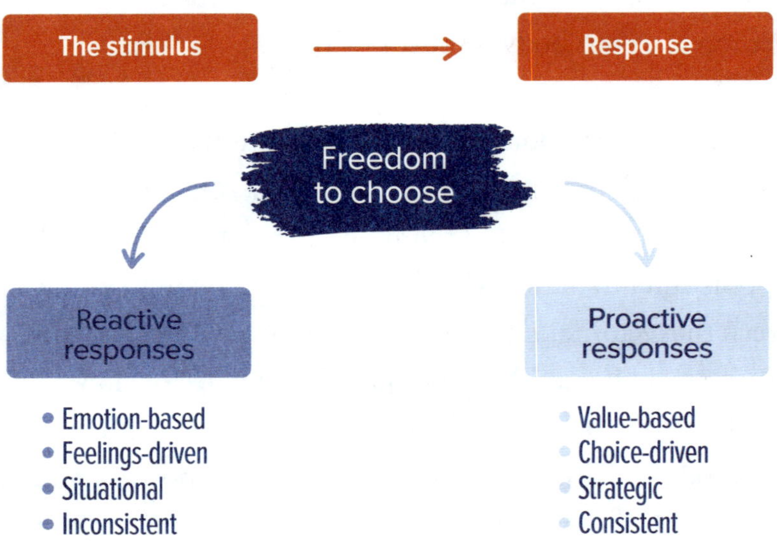

Bahaundin & Mujtaba, 2008

Practising the pause in between stimulus (what you are responding to) and response (how you act) is where all your power lies to modify your black-and-white thinking and change the course of your future.[8] You can decide if you want to act based on temporary emotions and feelings or if you want to act in accordance with healthy logic, your values, and what is in your long-term best interests. During this pause, try some of these effective exercises from the Dialectical Behaviour Therapy (DBT) model to make better choices:

8 Covey, *7 Habits of Highly Effective People*.

According to Dialectical Behaviour Therapy (DBT), we have four options when facing a calamity or hardship:[9]

1. Stay miserable
2. Solve the problem
3. Change your perception of the problem
4. Radically accept the problem

Staying miserable

The first option is to stay miserable, a common path that many people take without even realizing it. The reason so many people take this path is because they think that not taking action is a way to avoid having to make a decision; but, in fact, **not** making a decision **is** a decision.

Let's take staying in an extremely unhappy marriage, for example. Staying silent about one's feelings, participating in futile fighting, and not getting marriage counselling are all choices. Avoiding meaningful action to change is, in effect, a decision to stay unhappy. Being miserable is probably the easiest of the four options but it still takes a lot of time and effort to maintain this unhealthy state.

When people realize that being miserable is a choice, the first instinct is to think, "Well, I don't want to be miserable on purpose!" But they often continue to feel stuck because they don't know what to do next or how to change. This is okay as awareness is the first step to change.

---

9 Linehan, *DBT Skills Training Manual*.

Solving the problem

Behind every black-and-white thought there is usually a larger, big-picture issue at hand. Solving the problem is not always an option in cases involving trauma and calamity, but when possible, it's best to try to solve the problem directly. Let's look at a few examples:

If you are so upset at your parents for never letting you leave the house that you want to self-harm, the immediate issue is that you want to hurt yourself, but the big-picture issue is that there are significant communication, trust, and relational issues with your parents.

If you are so stressed out at work or school that you just want your life to end, the immediate issue is wanting to die but the big-picture issue is how you are relating to and coping with the demands in your life.

Although you may be faced with uncomfortable circumstances, addressing the problem at the root is the best way to reduce difficult emotions in the long term. An excellent way to solve a problem is to turn it into an action item and then create a basic pros and cons list associated with that idea. Writing out the pros and cons will help organize your thoughts, get more clarity on the situation, and ideally build insight into the best way to move forward. In the first example, the teen's action item may be to ask her parents to go to family therapy or to speak with her guidance counsellor about getting help. In the second example, one action item may be to consider changing from a full-time work/school schedule to part-time.

If you would like to take your pros and cons list one step further, you can use the Motivational Interviewing technique below.[10] This technique involves a more advanced pros and cons list that will help you think in a multidimensional way, whereas the traditional chart is simpler. The decision matrix looks like this:

	Benefit	Cost
Decision to change		
Decision not to change		

10 Lundahl and Burke, "Effectiveness and Applicability of Motivational Interviewing."

Example: *Should I leave my spouse?*

	Pros	Cons
Leaving spouse	Less Fighting Might find someone better Cure Situational depression	Will have to start over again Children will be negatively affected
Staying with spouse	More financial security keep same circle of friends	Emotional cost of long-term bickering Feel unfulfilled

The quicker you are able to complete the pros and cons list and act on it with due diligence, the better. The Prophet Muhammad ﷺ encouraged us to perform a prayer called *istikhaara* when making a decision. This prayer will help affirm your decision or deter you from it as Allah ﷻ knows variables affecting your situation that you may not be aware of. It can also provide a sense of calmness in knowing that you have consulted with your Creator, who knows you and your life better than anyone. Please see the end of this chapter for details about the *istikhaara* prayer.

Changing perception of the problem

If you can't change your problem, then the next best thing is to change how you view it. Perhaps the problem is not as bad as you originally thought? Or maybe it's not a problem, but could represent an opportunity? Perhaps you have more control over the problem than you think, or you play a bigger role in the problem than you think? After all, most positive changes in life start out as something difficult.

Looking at the silver lining, making excuses for people, and deriving positive meaning from adversity are key ways of looking at the situation differently. Let's take the example of someone who is suffering from a serious long-term illness. If you have ever met someone with a chronic disease, you know that there can be many setbacks at various points in their medical journey. A person who is overcome with emotion and gives into black-and-white thinking might say:

> ***"Everyone in this hospital in incompetent."***
>
> ***"There is no hope for me!"***
>
> ***"If I'm in this much pain, I might as well be dead."***

The same person who pauses and tries to reframe their pain might say:

> ***"I'm blessed to be able to get treatment for this illness even though it's not perfect."***

"I'm scared and I don't know how this disease will play out, but I trust Allah. He is the Best of Planners and everything good in my past, present, and future comes from Him."

"To Allah we belong, to Allah we must all return—when it's my time, Allah will take me. My pain now will lead to less pain in the* ākhirah.*"

The circumstances are identical, but reframing the problem completely changes the outlook of the person experiencing the difficulty. When you reframe a problem, you are taking ownership of how the problem is presented to you which, in turn, gives you power. You are exemplifying that, while you may not have control over your circumstances, you do have control over how you view them, which is more important.

A good example of changing one's views about a problem can be seen in the words of Ibn Taymiyyah ﵀, a well-known 13th-century Muslim scholar:

> *What can my enemies do to me! My garden and my paradise are in my breast; wherever I go, they are with me. If my enemies kill me, I become a martyr and if they banish me from my country, I go abroad as a tourist, and by imprisoning me, they allow me to have solitude (so that I can worship Allah).*[11]

11 Al-Qarni, *Don't Be Sad*, 120.

For the average person, these circumstances may be very traumatic and terrible, but Sheikh Ibn Taymiyyah ﷺ found a way to genuinely look at these circumstances in the best light so they had no power over him whatsoever.

Another way one can change their perspective on a problem is to imagine how the situation could be worse. Sheryl Sandberg, in her famous University of California at Berkeley 2016 commencement speech, talked about how this technique helped her with the immense grief she experienced when her husband suddenly died of complications due to a heart condition:

> *One day my friend Adam Grant, a psychologist, suggested that I think about how much worse things could be. This was completely counterintuitive; it seemed like the way to recover was to try to find positive thoughts. "Worse?" I said. "Are you kidding me? How could things be worse?" His answer cut straight through me: "Dave could have had that same cardiac arrhythmia while he was driving your children." Wow. The moment he said it, I was overwhelmingly grateful that the rest of my family was alive and healthy. That gratitude overtook some of the grief*[12]

When you feel like you have hit rock bottom, it seems that there is nowhere else to go; however, rock bottom is relative. When you imagine that your difficult situation could be worse, you can gain perspective and gratitude that it is not as bad as it could be.

---

12 O'Dea, "Transcript: Sheryl Sandberg."

Originally, Sandberg thought that the worst thing that could happen to her was her husband dying; however, when she realized that her children could have died as well if they had been riding in the car with him, she had a big shift in how she viewed the situation. This does not take away from the legitimacy of the pain you are experiencing; however, it helps to shift some of the focus away from everything that has gone wrong to what you can be grateful for.

Radical acceptance

A final option is radical acceptance. Radical acceptance involves completely accepting in one's mind and body the situation at hand so there is no longer any bitterness in the heart.[13] Radical acceptance is not giving in or giving up. It's also not complacency with matters that can be changed or should be changed. Domestic violence, for example, is not something radical acceptance would be appropriate for, whereas the death of a child would be. In the case of domestic violence, a person has options even if one isn't ready to pursue them, whereas nothing can really change the death of a loved one.

Radical acceptance also doesn't mean accepting the stressor itself; rather, it means that you have accepted that this is the decree of Allah ﷻ. Let's take terminal cancer, for example. Radical acceptance doesn't mean that you are okay with cancer or that you will not take steps to fight cancer, but it means that you accept that this is a trial that you have to face. Radical acceptance is coming to peaceful terms that you might have cancer for a long time or may even die from

13 Linehan, *DBT Skills Training Manual*.

cancer. In accepting the trial, you are not living in denial, but acknowledging the truth of your circumstances with no ill feelings in your heart or soul. Radical acceptance involves riding the wave instead of fighting it.

Radical acceptance in Islam is eloquently expressed in this *hadith*:

> *The Messenger of Allah ﷺ said, "How wonderful is the case of a believer; there is good for him in everything, and this applies only to a believer. If prosperity attends him, he expresses gratitude to Allah and that is good for him; and if adversity befalls him, he endures it patiently and that is better for him."*[14]

There is no easy way to achieve radical acceptance. This psychological concept is probably one of the most difficult achievements in one's journey with trauma. Many people can accept bad things that happen to them, but not without bitterness or despair. Radical acceptance takes a lot of reflection, talking through, and faith. For some individuals it may also take working with a professional, sometimes for many years, to get to this place of acceptance; but it is possible.

Radical acceptance is the antithesis of black-and-white thinking. It's being able to tolerate and accept something undesirable but still have hope, peace, and optimism. Instead of thinking, "I'm ill and there is no point in living," it's thinking, "I'm ill and in pain, but I have more to offer the world." Instead of saying, "I'm in so

---

14 Al-Nawawi, *Riyad as-salihin*, The Book of Miscellany, bk. 1, hadith 27.

much misery right now I should end my life," it's saying, "I'm in so much despair, but I will hang on and make the most of my situation."

Black-and-white thinking does not allow us to see the good and bad at the same time, while radical acceptance involves accepting the whole picture and being able to tolerate the good and bad simultaneously. Acceptance may involve being upset with others without ending relationships, being upset with oneself without resorting to self-harm, and even having extremely difficult life circumstances while still believing in Allah ﷻ.

Self-soothing coping skills

Pausing before falling into black-and-white thinking, changing your perspective on the problem, and radical acceptance are not easy tasks but can be made easier by practising self-soothing activities at the same time. These types of activities also help take the sharp edge off of anxiety, agitation, anger, and depression. The next time you are experiencing intense emotions, consider the following self-soothing activities to help you practise the pause longer.

Affirmations: Affirmations are brief and often powerful sayings you tell yourself to help shift your thoughts towards something positive. The nice thing about affirmations is that you don't have to believe the thoughts (at least initially) to practise them. The more you use them, however, the more you begin to alter your thoughts and begin to believe them.

"This is not what I would have chosen, but I'm at peace with it."

"Hasbi Allaho wa naima Al Wakeel *(Allah is sufficient for me and is the Best Trustee of affairs)."*

"I don't have control in this situation, but I have control over myself and that is enough."

"I accept what has been ordained for me and I know Allah will bring something good from this."

"I trust Allah and His Plan and His Wisdom."

Deep breathing: When you get upset, your breathing automatically becomes more rapid and shallow. This sends ongoing messages to your brain that you are upset and, in turn, your brain will continue to send back messages to the rest of your body that result in constricted breathing. Taking deep breaths will help counter this and make you feel more stable. Breathe in through your nose for 4 seconds, hold your breath for 4 seconds, and then exhale through your mouth like it is holding a straw for at least 6 seconds. Practise this 10 times or as long as you need to.

Tawakkul & practising hope: Have you ever driven around in really thick fog and were taken aback that you could not see the road, the usual buildings, and everything else you typically observe on your commute? Everything looks like it is covered and you cannot see past what is right in front of your car. Although it might be anxiety-provoking, you know with certainty that despite not being able to see anything, all those objects are still there. The same is for *tawakkul* (reliance on Allah ﷻ). You may not readily see Allah ﷻ in the fog of your distress, but you can constantly remind and affirm to yourself that He is still there, loves you and wants what is best for you. Intentionally practising and looking at situations with optimism can also remind you that although you are in very difficult circumstances now, relief will eventually come and that good things lie ahead.

For indeed, with hardship [will be] ease.
Indeed, with hardship [will be] ease.[15]

Additionally, practising hope and *tawakkul* during times of ease will help good thoughts come to mind more quickly when in distress. Abu Zayd al-Balkhi, a pioneer of Islamic cognitive psychotherapy in the 9th century, indicates that similar to the healthy person who keeps medicine readily at hand in case an unexpected ailment occurs, the same should be done with thoughts. Healthy thoughts should be stored during a tranquil state so they can be easily accessible when emotional distress occurs.[16]

Replace thoughts with cognitive activities: If you are feeling consumed with your thoughts, put them to the side and distract yourself with

15 Qur'an 94:5–6.
16 Badri, *Abu Zayd al-Balkhi's Sustenance of the Soul.*

other thought-based activities like doing a puzzle, learning a new task, or building something new. Distracting yourself in a healthy way can help keep your mind off the problem until you calm down.

Replace thoughts with grounding physical activities: In psychosomatic literature, which focuses on how psychological ailments manifest themselves through the body, triggering thoughts that jump-start the fight or flight response can be minimized through positive physical touch and pressure.[17] Simple physical activities may include wrapping yourself in a blanket (what Prophet Muhammad ﷺ did when distressed at first receiving revelation), lying flat on the floor (a recommended sunnah for when angry), or placing your hand on your heart. These small gestures are very simple but can profoundly help you feel safer, in control, and more secure.

Spiritual inspiration for reflection

Narrated Abu Hurairah: Allah's Messenger ﷺ said, "The example of a believer is that of a fresh tender plant; from whatever direction the wind comes, it bends it, but when the wind becomes quiet, it becomes straight again. Similarly, a believer is afflicted with calamities (but he remains patient till Allah removes his difficulties.) And an impious wicked person is like a pine tree which keeps hard and straight till Allah cuts (breaks) it down when He wishes."[18]

Narrated Abu Uthman: Usama bin Zaid said that while he, Sa'd, and Ubai bin Ka'b were with the Prophet ﷺ, a daughter of the

---

17 Wong, "Somatic Approaches to Healing Trauma."
18 *Sahīh al-Bukhārī*, no. 5644.

Prophet sent a message to him, saying. "My daughter is dying; please come to us." The Prophet sent her his greetings and added, "It is for Allah what He takes, and what He gives, and everything before His Sight has a limited period. So she should hope for Allah's reward and remain patient." She again sent a message, beseeching him by Allah, to come. So the Prophet got up and so did we (and went there). The child was placed on his lap while her breath was irregular. Tears flowed from the eyes of the Prophet ﷺ. Sa'd said to him, "What is this, O Allah's Apostle?" He said, "This is Mercy which Allah has embedded in the hearts of whomever He wished of His slaves. And Allah does not bestow His Mercy, except on the merciful among His slaves."[19]

Narrated 'Aisha: I asked Allah's Messenger ﷺ about the plague. He said, "That was a means of torture which Allah used to send upon whomsoever He wished, but He made it a source of mercy for the believers, for anyone who is residing in a town in which this disease is present, and remains there and does not leave that town, but has patience and hopes for Allah's reward, and knows that nothing will befall him except what Allah has written for him, then he will get the reward of a martyr."[20]

19 *Sahīh al-Bukhārī*, bk. 70, hadith 559.

20 *Sahīh al-Bukhārī*, no. 6619.

Abdullah ibn Mas'ud reported: I entered the home of the Messenger of Allah ﷺ while he was suffering from fever. I said, "O Messenger of Allah, you are suffering from a strong fever." The Prophet said, "Yes, for I am afflicted with fever like two men among you." I said, "Is it that you have a double reward?" The Prophet said, "Yes, it is so. Likewise, there is no Muslim who is afflicted with pain as much as the prick of a thorn or more except that Allah will expiate his sins just as leaves fall from a tree."[21]

21 *Sahīh al-Bukhārī*, no. 5324.

Practical exercises

A. Distress tolerance

To address black-and-white thinking, it's important to increase tolerance for difficult feelings. Instead of making snap decisions and statements, working on the space between a trigger and response helps with coping and the ability to make healthy decisions.

Identify your personal triggers when you are feeling like you are about to lose your cool:

1. ____
2. ____
3. ____
4. ____
5. ____

What are coping skills or activities you can use before you jump to black-and-white thinking? Think of ways to stay in the pause or grey-zone as long as you can:

1. ____
2. ____
3. ____
4. ____
5. ____

If you can't shake off your black-and-white thinking, try this exercise in your journal:

> ***"I know this is black-and-white thinking and I feel..."*** (write black-and-white statement here):

Example: "Everyone hates me and I'm worthless."

> ***"I know this is black-and-white thinking, but my rational self knows that the truth is..."*** (affirmation):

Example: "Allah cares about me and people in my life do love me."

Repeat these affirmations to yourself 3 times in the morning and evening, or as often as you need to.

B. Changing your perception of the problem: reframing

Problems are sometimes masked opportunities for learning and growth. Reframing is a powerful tool for viewing obstacles in a different or more positive light. Below, write down your top 3 obstacles and then next to them reframe them, keeping the following questions in mind:

How can I use this issue to end up in a better place than where I started?

How can I take this issue to propel me closer to my life goals?

Masked problem	Reframed opportunity
My marriage is in a terrible place right now.	We have generally not been good with communication or affection. This can be an opportunity to seek marriage counselling and learn tools to make our relationship better than it ever has been.
I am dying of cancer.	I've been aimlessly getting by in life, just doing the bare minimum in everything. Now that I have a more defined time limit, I should live life to the fullest by consistently telling my family how important they are to me, living with more intention and purpose, and taking a more active role in my spiritual development.

Masked problem	Reframed opportunity

C. Solving and radical acceptance

You have four options anytime you are facing a problem. Fill out the graph below with how life would be if you tried each option:

Example: My wife says she has met someone else she wants to marry and wants to get a divorce.

Stay miserable	Solve the problem
Perhaps my wife is going through a phase. We all make mistakes. I'll try being patient and maybe her relationship with the other man will run its course on its own.	I will try to convince my wife that the marriage can be salvaged by going to marriage counselling.
Change your perception of the problem	**Radical acceptance**
My wife committed adultery and wants to dissolve the marriage amicably. Perhaps this is a gift and an opportunity for me to find someone else who will actually respect and love me.	I accept that my wife is leaving me for another man. Although our marriage didn't end well, there were many good things that came from it, like our children. I'm not going to judge her; that will be up to Allah. After our divorce, I will stay on the best terms with her as humanly possible for the sake of co-parenting our children. I will be okay *insha Allah*.

Stay miserable	Solve the problem
Change your perception of the problem	**Radical acceptance**

Are there truths you are fighting and refusing to accept? What are they?

Example: I don't want to accept that my marriage might be over after 10 years.

____

____

What are the pros and cons of continuing to fight?

Pros	Cons
Maybe we can reconcile.	What kind of dignity and self-respect can I have by staying in a relationship like this?

What are the pros and cons of radical acceptance (not giving in, but accepting reality)?

Pros	Cons
This chapter of my life will finally be over and I can now rebuild the next one on my terms.	I have to cope with the idea of restructuring my life and family.

What affirmations will help you in your radical acceptance?

1. **Example:** Allah is the Best of Planners.
2. **Example:** I don't have control over others, but I have control of myself and that's what's important.

3. **Example:** Everything is going to be okay insha Allah.

4. ______

5. ______

6. ______

Radical acceptance is not something you can turn on like a light switch. Think about it, journal about it, and debate it in your head. When you are ready to make a commitment to accept your reality, write it down here.

Example: I accept that my marriage is over. It was a good chapter in my life while it lasted and now I'm ready for the next one. It's not exactly how I envisioned it would be, but I will have *tawakkul* in Allah and look forward to what's ahead.

Case study revisited

Aliya learned about the four options to approaching a problem (solving it, changing perception of it, radical acceptance, and staying miserable) and decided that staying miserable was not an option for her. It's not that she truly wanted to die—she just wanted the conflict and pain to stop. She thought about changing her perception of the problem but knew that this was not going to work unless she tried to work on the problem first.

Aliya decided that she wanted to go to therapy. Her parents were reluctant to accept her going to treatment, so she decided to utilize the free therapy sessions at her college. Aliya learned that she had developed depression as a result of her family dynamics and that the extreme yelling, name-calling, and fighting were actually forms of verbal abuse. Aliya consulted with her local imam *and he agreed with Aliya's therapist that her current living situation was very unhealthy.*

Aliya decided to move in with her aunt nearby and work on developing healthier boundaries with her parents from a distance. She understood that vilifying her parents was not going to get her the results she wanted long-term and so she made efforts to build a better relationship with them; when her parents acted inappropriately, however, she would try to change the subject or leave without making a scene.

With the help of her therapist, Aliya began to work on addressing her black-and-white thinking and depression. If she began to think too negatively of her parents, she would try to focus on their good qualities and the fact that they had raised her. If she became overwhelmed and started to have thoughts of wanting to shut down, or that she didn't want to continue living, she would use self-soothing activities to calm down. Over time, she realized that the quicker she started her coping skills the less she experienced black-and-white thinking. As her black-and-white thinking decreased, so did her depression.

Istikhaarah Prayer

Use this prayer when you want to make a decision about a difficult matter (or any matter). Pray two *rakat* voluntary prayer and, after completing the prayer and saying *salām* (*taslim*), say this *du'aa*.

It was narrated that Jabir bin 'Abdullah said:

> *"The Messenger of Allah ﷺ used to teach us Istikhaarah, just as he used to teach us a surah of the Qur'an. He said: 'If anyone of you is deliberating about a decision he has to make, then let him pray two rak'ah of non- obligatory prayer, then say:* Allahumma inni astakhiruka bi 'ilmika wa astaqdiruka bi qudratika wa as'aluka min fadlikal-'azim, fa innaka taqdiru wa la aqdir, wa ta'lamu wa la a'lam, wa Anta 'allamul-ghuyub. Allahumma in kunta ta'lamu hadhal-amra (then the matter should be mentioned by name) ma kan min shay'in khairan li fi dini wa ma'ashi wa 'aqibati amri, aw khairanli fi 'ajili amri wa ajilihi, faqdurhu li wa yassirhu li wa barik li fihi. Wa in kunta ta'lamu *[O Allah, I seek Your guidance (in making a choice) by virtue of Your knowledge, and I seek ability by virtue of Your power, and I ask You of Your great bounty. You have power, I have none. And You know, I know not. You are the Knower of hidden things. O Allah, if in Your knowledge, this matter (then it should be mentioned by name) is*

good for me in my religion, my livelihood and my affairs, or both in this world and in the Hereafter then ordain it for me, make it easy for me, and bless it for me. And if in Your knowledge, (then saying similar to what he said the first time, except: Wa in kana sharran li fasrifhu 'anni wasrifni 'anhu waqdur li al-khair haithuma kana thumma raddini bihi *(If it is bad for me, then turn it away from me and turn me away from it, and ordain for me the good wherever it may be and make me pleased with it)."* [22]

حَدَّثَنَا أَحْمَدُ بْنُ يُوسُفَ السُّلَمِيُّ، حَدَّثَنَا خَالِدُ بْنُ مَخْلَدٍ، حَدَّثَنَا عَبْدُ الرَّحْمَنِ بْنُ أَبِي الْمَوَالِ، قَالَ سَمِعْتُ مُحَمَّدَ بْنَ الْمُنْكَدِرِ، يُحَدِّثُ عَنْ جَابِرِ بْنِ عَبْدِ اللَّهِ، قَالَ كَانَ رَسُولُ اللَّهِ ـ ﷺ ـ يُعَلِّمُنَا الاِسْتِخَارَةَ كَمَا يُعَلِّمُنَا السُّورَةَ مِنَ الْقُرْآنِ يَقُولُ «إِذَا هَمَّ أَحَدُكُمْ بِالأَمْرِ فَلْيَرْكَعْ رَكْعَتَيْنِ مِنْ غَيْرِ الْفَرِيضَةِ ثُمَّ لْيَقُلِ اللَّهُمَّ إِنِّي أَسْتَخِيرُكَ بِعِلْمِكَ وَأَسْتَقْدِرُكَ بِقُدْرَتِكَ وَأَسْأَلُكَ مِنْ فَضْلِكَ الْعَظِيمِ فَإِنَّكَ تَقْدِرُ وَلاَ أَقْدِرُ وَتَعْلَمُ وَلاَ أَعْلَمُ وَأَنْتَ عَلاَّمُ الْغُيُوبِ اللَّهُمَّ إِنْ كُنْتَ تَعْلَمُ هَذَا الأَمْرَ - فَيُسَمِّيهِ مَا كَانَ مِنْ شَىْءٍ - خَيْرًا لِي فِي دِينِي وَمَعَاشِي وَعَاقِبَةِ أَمْرِي - أَوْ خَيْرًا لِي فِي عَاجِلِ أَمْرِي وَآجِلِهِ - فَاقْدُرْهُ لِي وَيَسِّرْهُ لِي وَبَارِكْ لِي فِيهِ وَإِنْ كُنْتَ تَعْلَمُ - يَقُولُ مِثْلَ مَا قَالَ فِي الْمَرَّةِ الأُولَى - وَإِنْ كَانَ شَرًّا لِي فَاصْرِفْهُ عَنِّي وَاصْرِفْنِي عَنْهُ وَاقْدُرْ لِيَ الْخَيْرَ حَيْثُمَا كَانَ ثُمَّ رَضِّنِي بِهِ»

22 *Sunan Ibn Majah*, vol. 1, bk. 5, hadith 1383.

Chapter 4

"How Can I Trust Again?"

Navigating Betrayal

Vulnerability sounds like truth and feels like courage. Truth and courage aren't always comfortable, but they're never weakness.

BRENE BROWN

Daring Greatly

Case study

Kathleen had never loved anyone the way she loved Mustafa. They met when they were in college and quickly realized there was something worth pursuing. They dated for a while and soon started to get into serious relationship territory. When they started to discuss marriage, Mustafa told Kathleen he wanted the future mother of his children to be a Muslim.

Kathleen began to study Islam and found that a lot of the tenets and values resonated with her. She may never have explored the religion if she hadn't met Mustafa but she felt comfortable converting. They had a small marriage ceremony in a local masjid and were happily married for 10 years. During these 10 years, they had 3 children and both gradually learned more about Islam.

Mustafa started to become more involved in the community, particularly through teaching classes. His schedule started to get busier and Kathleen found herself spending more time alone with the children. When she broached this subject one day, Mustafa reluctantly admitted that he had been having an affair for some time but didn't tell her due to fears of upsetting her.

Kathleen was stunned. It never crossed her mind that infidelity was a possibility, especially from someone who portrayed himself as a spiritual and practising person. Suddenly, she was plagued with doubts, including unsettling questions surrounding her faith in her religion. Mustafa was the one who had introduced her to Islam all those years ago yet he had betrayed her. If this was what Islam was about, she didn't want to have anything to do with it! She found herself thinking, "If someone I loved, looked up to, and invested so much time in could betray me, how can I ever trust again?"

What is happening to me?

When someone you trust betrays you, it hurts tremendously. The pain can be so intense that it can be felt physically. People often describe it as a "punch in the gut," where it feels as though all of the breath has been completely knocked out of you. Whether you are double-crossed in a business deal, or a person in a position of authority abuses their power, or you have unexpectedly discovered that you've been lied to, betrayal is soul-crushing.

When a betrayal occurs, the blow you experience is two-fold. First, you experience a breach of the trust that you so tenderly gave to another person—so much so that the relationship is often changed in a permanent way. Secondly, you suddenly realize that you've been lied to for an extended period of time but didn't know until this moment. You may start to doubt yourself and wonder how you hadn't seen it before. You may question if you're gullible because you trusted someone who had been lying to you for so long. You may feel inadequate—as though something or someone else has been prioritized over you. You may even wonder if you've done something to bring this upon yourself and whether you deserve this type of treatment.

Betrayal and the accompanying breach of trust is a unique type of trauma. No one has died but in many ways the emotions you experience can be even more difficult than other types of loss. A large part of your life has died after a betrayal and can never be revived fully. You may even feel as though a part of yourself has passed away in the process. It's important to grieve the loss of the relationship you thought you had.

Understanding your thoughts and emotions

After experiencing trauma associated with a betrayal you may suddenly find yourself scanning the world for threats all around you. If your husband could have kept his porn addiction a secret for so long, what would stop something just as shocking from happening in another relationship in your life? If your uncle, who is supposed to care for you, touches you inappropriately, what would stop someone else from doing the same? And, even scarier, your fears might start to extend to Allah ﷻ. You might be thinking, "If the person I trusted more than anyone in my life was capable of hurting me so badly, how can I trust anyone at all? If nobody can be trusted, what if I feel like I can't trust Allah?"

What you're feeling—and even what you're thinking—is normal after experiencing betrayal. These passing thoughts are so common that there is even a hadith about them: The Prophet ﷺ said,

> *Allah has forgiven my followers the thoughts that occur to their minds, as long as such thoughts are not acted upon or uttered.*[1]

This hadith can alleviate a lot of the shame many of us may feel when doubts surface related to our faith and our relationship with Allah ﷻ. However, these thoughts can still increase our anxiety and may result in distancing ourselves from Allah ﷻ if they begin

---

1 *Ṣaḥīḥ al-Bukhārī*, no. 5269.

to impact our actions and the way we view ourselves. Therefore, we need to proactively address them.

With a little bit of information and effort, you don't have to spend your life struggling with these thoughts. Remember, just because one person (or even more than one person) has hurt you, doesn't mean that everyone is unworthy of your trust.

Why does betrayal hurt so much?

Recovery from a betrayal can be a long journey. There are several steps in the process and everyone walks the road to healing at a different pace. Betrayal traumas involve the perpetrator being in a close relationship with the victim. Due to this, the violation of trust feels deeply personal, rather than random. If someone pushed you as you were walking down the street, you would experience a sense of shock and fear, but it wouldn't cause you to doubt any of your closest relationships. Betrayal trauma is different because it jeopardizes the safety of the very relationship you would normally turn to for comfort when distressed, which causes an increased sense of vulnerability at a time when support is most needed. When a person who is supposed to love, respect, and support you betrays you, your world can feel like it's shattering.

Why does experiencing betrayal impact my ability to trust Allah ﷻ?

Along with the general instability you may be experiencing, another type of instability may take root: instability in your relationship with Allah ﷻ. Just as you now scan the world for ways you might get hurt, you may start scanning the skies for ways you feel disappointed by God.

Why does this happen? Logically, we know that Allah ﷻ isn't comparable to human beings but emotionally we may fear risking closeness to anyone, including Allah ﷻ. There is something called "attachment theory," which began with John Bowlby who devoted extensive research to the concept of attachment, describing it as a "lasting psychological connectedness between human beings."[2] This is first created through our childhood experiences with our parents/caregivers and can influence our relationship patterns and behaviours later in life.

Attachment is a human need. Allah ﷻ created us as social creatures that are in need of belonging, closeness, and caring. Allah ﷻ says,

> ***O mankind! We have created you male and female, and have made you nations and tribes, that you may know one another...***[3]

Even our brains are wired for sociality. Research suggests that we are born with innate abilities for facial recognition and language acquisition.[4] However, the ability to move forward in these developmental stages is dependent on a child being stimulated by interactions with other people. Brain structures activate and mature during interactions with attachment figures.[5]

---

2 Bowlby, *Attachment and Loss.*

3 Qur'an 49:13.

4 Otsuka, "Face Recognition in Infants"; John-Steiner, Panofsky, and Smith, *Sociocultural Approaches to Language and Literacy.*

5 Avants et al., "Relation of Childhood Home Environment."

The brain area associated with trusting people is the same brain area needed to trust Allah ﷻ. This brain area is called the amygdala.[6] It is the core of emotion processing and assesses our experiences for safety or danger. When an emotionally charged experience transpires, such as a spouse cheating or a family member being abusive, our brain registers this experience to be remembered long-term. Our brains cannot differentiate the feeling of trusting a human being and the emotion associated with trusting God. After a betrayal trauma, the amygdala signals "danger" whenever you begin to trust someone. However, don't lose hope: The amazing thing about the brain is that it's flexible. We may struggle to trust Allah ﷻ now but that doesn't doom us to struggle forever.

Changing your mind, body, and heart

Now that you understand why you might struggle with trusting Allah ﷻ after you've had your trust betrayed by someone close to you, we can work toward changing this thought process. When you think, "How can I ever trust again?" you are engaging in a form of cognitive distortion called **overgeneralization**.

Overgeneralization means coming to a general conclusion based on a single event or one piece of evidence. Therefore, when something bad happens, you expect it to happen over and over again. Thinking that you will never be able to trust again creates a permanent umbrella over your entire life based on one rainy day.

---

6 Koscik and Tranel, "Human Amygdala."

A thought trajectory based on overgeneralization may progress like this:

I thought we were close friends but now she's ignoring me.

I shared so much with her and now she's gone. I didn't matter to her.

I don't really matter to anyone.

There's no point in investing in relationships since they always end this way.

As we can see here, overgeneralization causes us to see a single event as a never-ending pattern of negativity, defeat, and pain. This causes us to search for evidence that goes along with this worldview. We see people in our lives as a part of this overgeneralized pattern of tragedy and disappointment. We focus on the times when we notice negativity and it further validates our overgeneralized perception of reality. We find what we look for: If you believe that people will hurt you, you will search for any indication that this is true rather than being able to view situations objectively.

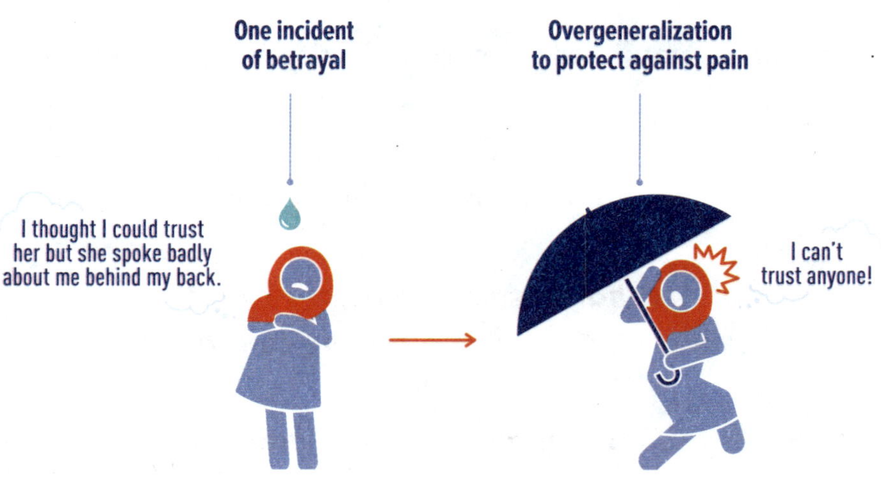

Overgeneralization can impact our ability to fully trust Allah ﷻ just as it can impact our ability to be vulnerable in our relationships with people. When we overgeneralize, we may lose sight of who Allah ﷻ truly is. Consider the impact overgeneralization can have on our faith:

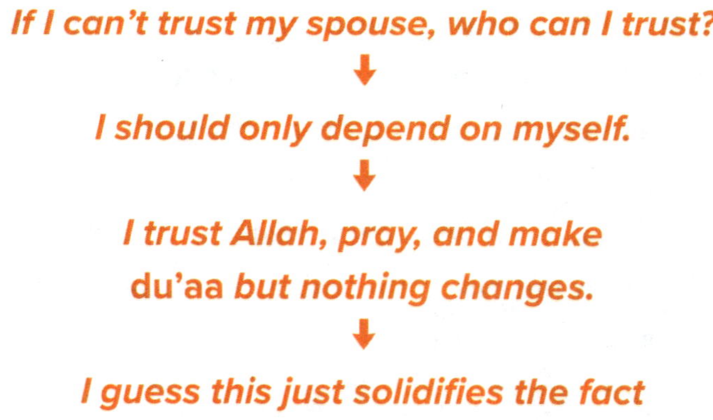

It's important to realize that we often model our relationship with Allah ﷻ after our relationship with attachment figures. Therefore, our relationship with Allah ﷻ often mirrors our relationship with others in our lives. So, when we've been hurt by people close to us, we also assume that we will be hurt by Allah ﷻ. When we ask a friend for help and she doesn't follow through, we feel disappointed and may start to expect the same from Allah ﷻ. When we ask Allah ﷻ for something we want or for help in a situation and we don't get the response in the way we anticipate, we feel disappointed and concerned that we are being ignored and are beyond help. This can be a very lonely and painful feeling.

Transforming your overgeneralizations

Consider these questions to identify and combat the overgeneralizations that are dictating the way you live and perceive your life:

> ***What overgeneralization are you struggling with? What overarching perception of the world/people/ Allah ﷻ do you have?***

Example: There is no point in investing in relationships since they all end in me feeling hurt and disappointed.

> ***How has this overgeneralization impacted you and the way you live your daily life?***

Example: No expectations mean no disappointment. But realistically, I am always disappointed and sad. I tend to avoid calling people and then I get upset that they don't reach out to me. It just proves that I shouldn't bother investing in relationships. It's safer to just depend on myself.

How has this overgeneralization impacted your relationships with others and relationship with Allah ﷻ?

Example: I tend to distance myself from people in my life even when they want to get close to me. I don't always support people since I imagine that they won't support me in the future. I don't open up to or seek help from anyone since I feel like I'm alone and I can't trust anyone. I also feel distant from Allah; I stopped asking Allah for help since I feel sure that I'll be disappointed.

What was the starting point of this overgeneralization?

Example: I told my best friend everything. We used to talk on the phone for hours every day. She knew everything about me and I trusted her with the deepest parts of myself. She gradually started distancing herself from me once she found a new friend group and eventually stopped answering my calls and texts. I was so hurt that I promised myself I wouldn't allow myself to ever feel pain like that again.

What evidence do you have that shows the inaccuracy of this overgeneralization?

Example: I guess I rationally know that not everyone will hurt me in the same way that my best friend did. There are other people in my life who I've known for a long time, and they have never betrayed my trust. My childhood friends have been there for me, and my parents have always had my best interests at heart. There are a lot of relationships that have been valuable to me that would never have existed if I had chosen not to invest in them.

What is a more realistic assumption?

Example: There is always a risk of getting hurt when we trust others; however, there is a greater risk in choosing not to invest in relationships. I may have been hurt but this does not mean that I will always be hurt if I allow myself to get close to someone.

The cost of avoiding pain

The more distressed we are at any point in our lives, the more we want relief from pain and despair and the more we fear removing the armour we imagine is protecting us from experiencing more hurt. This fear presents itself in different ways including anger toward the one who betrayed you and anyone else who crosses your path, including God; numbness in every relationship to prevent yourself from investing in something that may potentially cause pain; and creating distance from anyone who may disappoint you.

This is called *avoidance coping*. This is a maladaptive form of coping that involves avoiding thinking, feeling, or doing things that are uncomfortable. We avoid stressors rather than dealing with them. Although it may seem logical to avoid things that feel stressful and it may feel as though avoiding problems is working well for you, in reality avoidance of discomfort usually yields more stress.[7]

What we resist tends to persist. When we avoid things that yield uncomfortable emotions, the same emotions and situations we fear have an interesting way of reappearing in our lives at inopportune

7 Holahan et al., "Stress Generation, Avoidance Coping, and Depressive Symptoms."

times. When we overgeneralize, we think we are protecting ourselves from getting hurt again but, in fact, we usually end up creating situations where we do end up getting hurt. For example, you may avoid getting close to others due to fears that they may hurt you; however, in the process of avoiding connection with people in your life, relationships deteriorate, which eventually causes you pain. The cycle of avoiding discomfort often yields even more discomfort in the end.

Conquering avoidance

Avoiding problems feels like it works for us, which is why we do it. However, what we really need is to build up the ability to tolerate discomfort and stress. Avoiding anything that can be a threat feels safer because it prevents uncomfortable feelings from ever surfacing. However, difficult emotions have a function; they encourage us to figure out the source of the issue and take action to address the problem.

False refuges

We all seek to feel "protected and safe... loved and at peace... to feel at home in [our lives]."[8] We pray for a sense of refuge yet, in reality, we often turn toward *false refuges*. They provide temporary relief from discomfort and provide us with a false, temporary sense of comfort and security.

Maybe your spouse texts you, "We need to finish the discussion we were having last night. It's still bothering me." And you respond with,

8 Brach, *True Refuge*, 7.

"Sure." But you end up finding extra work to do and stay at the office late that night. Avoiding the discussion feels safer and more comfortable but it's a false refuge and the longer we live in a false refuge, the more suffering and damage we'll find once we leave it.

Maybe you're scared of being rejected and you worry that any assertion of your needs will result in others disliking you, so you avoid taking that risk and always strive to please others, allowing resentment to build up within. Maybe you're worried that you are unworthy of being cared for, so it feels safer to avoid asking for anything, even asking anything of Allah ﷻ.

Identifying your false refuges is a great step in breaking down the walls that prevent you from gaining a true sense of peace and safety. When we avoid situations, people, and thoughts that may lead to discomfort, we are falling into the trap of overgeneralization: We are operating under the assumption that we have to hide from everything in order to prevent the risk of getting hurt by anything. In the process of protecting ourselves, the shields of avoidance end up preventing us from accessing the good things in life as well.

Think about what you've been avoiding and ask yourself: What is one small thing I can do today that I haven't felt willing to do in a long time? It can be as small as looking at a picture from a happier time, picking up the Qur'an and reading one *ayah*, or gently telling yourself, "I am worthy of being loved." It can be turning off your video stream and responding to a message you've been dreading or reaching out to someone you've been avoiding due to a fallout you had years ago. Try one small change and see if you can slowly step away from your false refuge and into the true refuge of living life more fully.

How to experience safety and security through Allah ﷻ

After the end of a meaningful relationship, opening yourself up to trust again can feel incredibly overwhelming. When overgeneralization takes over, you are naturally going to assume that since one person has hurt you, every person in your life is capable of being inconsiderate, untrustworthy, and unfaithful. As mentioned earlier, this mindset can extend to an inability to trust Allah ﷻ. However, in reality, in your journey toward healing, there is no better place to gain a sense of security than in your relationship with Allah ﷻ.

It is important to keep in mind that Allah ﷻ is above and beyond what our minds are capable of imagining. We imagine that we can no longer make *du'aa* because the prayers we have fervently been making have not yet come to fruition or because we blame Allah ﷻ for allowing someone to betray us.

However, realistically, we trust in Allah ﷻ every single moment of every single day. We trust in Allah ﷻ with every breath we take—we trust that He will allow that inhalation to reach our lungs. We trust Allah ﷻ with every bite we eat—we trust that He will allow the nourishment to access the parts of our body that need it most. Every blessing we encounter is by the will of Allah ﷻ and they are innumerable. So, when we say that we can never trust again—that we can't even trust Allah ﷻ—realize that the way we live every second of our lives contradicts this thought.

The guarantees of human beings are not always guarantees. However, the promise of Allah ﷻ is always a guarantee. Allah ﷻ says,

> ***[It is] the promise of Allah. Allah does not fail in His promise, but most of the people do not know.***[9]

We assume that when our prayers are not responded to exactly in the way we hope or expect, that Allah ﷻ has chosen to overlook us. However, realize that we often ask for what we *want*, not what we *need*. We assume that our wants are best for us but Allah ﷻ knows us better than we know ourselves. He says,

> ***But perhaps you hate a thing and it is good for you; and perhaps you love a thing and it is bad for you. And Allah knows, while you know not.***[10]

There is a difference between wanting something and needing something. If what we are asking for is not given to us, then we don't truly need it.

Also realize that every prayer is heard but the answer to each prayer may come in a different form than what we anticipate. We assume that our *du'aa* can only be answered in one particular way—the way we envision the response. However, the Prophet Muhammad ﷺ said,

---

9 Qur'an 30:6.
10 Qur'an 2:216.

There is no Muslim who supplicates to Allah without sin or cutting family ties but that Allah will give him one of three answers:

He will hasten fulfilment of his supplication,

He will store it for him in the Hereafter,

He will divert an evil from him similar to it.

They said, "In that case we will ask for more." The Prophet said, "Allah has even more."[11]

Try to take an objective look at your life. The prayers you have been asking for that you feel have not yet been responded to—could the answers possibly have come in a different form? Could the hurt you've experienced actually be a form of protection from something else that may have come your way?

You may have prayed for your dream home for years and once you finally purchased it, flooding ruined what you worked so hard to build. Imagine for a moment that this hurt could have been a form of protection from something else that could have afflicted you? While assessing the damage, remind yourself, "This is painful, but this is all replaceable. The lives and health of those I love is not. Maybe this is a lesser struggle than I would have otherwise faced. *Alhamdulillah*."

11 *Musnad Aḥmad*, no. 10749.

You may have prayed for a marriage filled with love and mercy and just found out that your husband has been with someone else. The pain you are enduring feels unbearable but, as you process it, consider the fact that the children you have were meant to be yours through your marriage with him. Despite his betrayal, there are certain aspects of your marriage that can never be taken away—your children, your experiences, and the lessons you learned during your time in this relationship. After processing your hurt, when you're ready to shift your focus away from the pain of the betrayal, consider the fact that you are no longer in an unhealthy relationship and realize that your *du'aa* may have been responded to by Allah ﷻ granting you a clear way out of this relationship and the ability to move on with your healing journey sooner rather than later.

Instead of thinking, "I've been hurt so deeply, I can never trust anyone again," reframe this thought to encompass an understanding that there is One Being who will never betray you: "I've been hurt so deeply. I know I'm afraid to trust because that makes me vulnerable to being disappointed. However, Allah will never disappoint me. I trust that even when things happen that seem negative on the surface, there is something good in it because Allah always takes care of my needs."

Getting to know Allah ﷻ as a means of regaining trust

While overgeneralization and the weight of betrayal trauma can impact our relationship with Allah ﷻ, one of the best ways to reconnect with Him is through getting to know Him, His Names, and His Attributes. We cannot realistically trust someone we don't know so, naturally, learning more about who Allah ﷻ truly is will be an important step in reconnecting with Him.

Consider a story that illustrates some of the beautiful Names and Attributes of Allah ﷻ that remind us of the fact that even though we may struggle to emotionally open ourselves up to trusting Him, He is still our Protector every step of the way.

The Prophet Yusuf عليه السلام was described as,

> ***The honourable is the son of the honourable, the son of the honourable, i.e., Joseph, the son of Jacob, the son of Isaac, the son of Abraham.***[12]

The story of Yusuf عليه السلام is one filled with danger and betrayal yet is also inspirational as the culmination of it shows us the one stable force in his life (and in our own lives): the presence and care of Allah ﷻ. One thing to remember is this: even one so beloved to Allah ﷻ experienced tremendous betrayal so it is not an indication of Allah's ﷻ love and care that those around us choose to hurt us.

Yusuf عليه السلام experienced the betrayal of his own brothers who intended to kill him, of an employer who attempted to seduce him and then wrongfully accused him of sexual violation, and of high-ranking officials who jailed him despite his having not committed a crime.

12 *Ṣaḥīḥ al-Bukhārī*, no. 3382.

Throughout all of this, Allah ﷻ was, *"closer to him than [his] jugular vein"* and protected him by giving him ways to dodge physical and spiritual danger.[13] While plotting to kill him, one of Yusuf's brothers suggested placing him in a well instead. When he was accused of rape, physical evidence to the contrary was presented. When constant temptation to engage with women sexually was offered to him, Allah ﷻ positioned Yusuf in prison to save him from spiritual danger. Through experiencing constant betrayals, Prophet Yusuf عليه السلام realized that he only had Allah ﷻ. We learn from his example that even when those closest to you betray you, Allah ﷻ can raise your status and open doors for you in the most difficult and darkest of times.

From the outside looking in, it appears as though Yusuf عليه السلام was moving backward and his life was falling apart while, in reality, he was actually being positioned to become who Allah ﷻ destined him to be. If even one small step had been missing in his journey, it would not have resulted in the finale in which Yusuf عليه السلام was given a high-ranking position in the government and was reunited with his family in a position of nobility and honour. This is the hidden hand of God. At the end of his story, Yusuf عليه السلام reflects on his deep understanding of the Lord who brought him through such arduous challenges, protected him, and shaped him into the person he had become.

Yusuf عليه السلام raised his parents upon the throne, and they bowed to him in prostration. And Yusuf عليه السلام said,

13 Qur'an 50:16.

*O my father, this is the explanation of my vision of before. My Lord has made it reality. And He was certainly good to me when He took me out of prison and brought you [here] from Bedouin life after Satan had induced [estrangement] between me and my brothers. Indeed, my Lord is Subtle in what He wills (*al-Lateef*). Indeed, it is He who is the Knowing, the Wise.*

*My Lord, You have given me [something] of sovereignty and taught me of the interpretation of dreams. Creator of the heavens and earth, You are my protector (*Wali*) in this world and in the Hereafter. Cause me to die a Muslim and join me with the righteous.*[14]

Here we see that Yusuf عليه السلام calls Allah جل جلاله by two of His Names, *al-Lateef*, the Subtle and Gracious, and *al-Wali*, the Protector:

Al-Lateef: The One who is Kind, Gracious, and Understanding, with regard for the subtle details of individual circumstances.[15] He knows what is in your heart and mind. He knows exactly what you're going through. He knows where hidden goodness lies and His approach to addressing this can be so subtle that it's imperceptible to us and beyond our comprehension.

14 Qur'an 12:100–101.

15 Shelquist, "Beautiful Names of Allah: Al-Latif."

You can see this Name in action during moments when you're feeling down and a friend randomly sends you a meme that makes you laugh. Or when you open the Qur'an and suddenly come across an *ayah* that resonates with you in a way it never had before. Or when you're stuck in traffic and the bumper sticker of the car in front of you has a message that strikes you as inspirational. It's not simply your friend who is comforting you, it is Allah ﷻ who sent that friend, that statement on that bumper sticker, or that verse to uplift you. That is *al-Lateef*.

Al-Wali: The One who is the loving Defender, the nearby Guardian, and a constant Supporter.[16] He is the One who lovingly supports us in paving the way toward that which we most need in every moment of our existence. He is the One who defends us from potential harms of which we are completely unaware. He is the One who guides us and turns us toward that which is most needed, despite it sometimes not being what we want for ourselves.

You can see this Name in action when you are running late to work and caught in traffic when suddenly you see a horrible car accident in the lane you normally drive in every day, realizing that could have been you. Or when you find out a new friend you've quickly grown to love has been saying horrible things about you to others, causing you to witness her true colours and end the friendship before you've shared too much of yourself with her. Allah's ﷻ protection often comes in forms we may not notice but we can be confident that *al-Wali* is constantly defending us.

---

16 Shelquist, "Beautiful Names of Allah: Al-Wali."

Opening ourselves up to trusting again, even trusting Allah ﷻ, can be a terrifying step. However, in choosing to take action rather than avoiding anything that reminds us of the betrayal we have faced, we reclaim the power we have given to those who have hurt us and choose to thrive despite them. This power you reclaim, this ability to trust again and expand your world to include new experiences, is a gift from Allah ﷻ and another demonstration of His Mercy, His Protection, and the amazing plan He has for your life.

Spiritual inspiration for reflection

A *hadith* of the Prophet Muhammad ﷺ states, "Allah will grant whoever recites this seven times in the morning or evening whatever he desires from this world or the next: 'Allah is sufficient for me. There is none worthy of worship but Him. I have placed my trust in Him, He is Lord of the Majestic Throne.'"[17]

This *du'aa* is an excellent reminder to implement into our daily morning and evening routines. By saying this each day, while truly giving thought to the meaning of the words, the brain area involved in interpersonal trust can be gradually soothed. By saying this each day, you are actively reminding yourself that, although someone may have hurt you deeply, Allah is always worthy of your trust. And through this, the healing process can begin.

17 *Ḥiṣṇ al-Muslim*, no. 83; *Sunan Abi Dāwūd*, 4/321; *Ibn al-Sunnī*, no. 71.

Practical exercises

A. Mindfulness exercise for inspiring trust

We discussed the fact that we inherently trust in Allah ﷻ when we expect our bodies to function as they normally do. Try this guided mindfulness activity as a reminder of this fact and notice how you feel afterward:

Close your eyes. Take a deep, encompassing breath and allow it to flow out of your mouth slowly. As you allow your body to become still, bring your attention to the fact that you are breathing. And become aware of the movement of your breath as it comes into your body and as it leaves your body, without manipulating the breath or trying to change it. Simply be aware of your breath entering your lungs. Observe the breath deep down in your belly. Feeling the abdomen as it expands gently as you breathe in, and as it falls back as you breathe out.

Imagine each breath filling your lungs with the air that it needs. Allow yourself to experience the feeling of knowing that Allah ﷻ is ensuring that each breath reaches your lungs. Allow yourself to trust that each breath will be allowed in and each breath will be allowed out. Remind yourself that every breath is an exercise in trusting Allah ﷻ to take care of you and your body.

As you feel your limbs relax, tell yourself, "Right at this moment, I am safe. Others might disappoint me; I might even disappoint myself—but Allah will always be there for me." Remind yourself of the verse in Surah al-Baqarah where Allah ﷻ says,

> ***So whoever... believes in Allah has grasped the most trustworthy handhold with no break in it. And Allah is Hearing and Knowing.***[18]

Slowly open your eyes and take note of how you feel physically and emotionally.

B. Transforming your overgeneralizations

Ask yourself these questions to reconsider the overgeneralizations that are dictating the way you live and perceive your life:

What overgeneralization are you struggling with? What overarching perception of the world/people/ Allah ﷻ do you have?

How has this overgeneralization impacted your emotions and the way you live your daily life?

---

18 Qur'an 2:256.

How has this overgeneralization impacted your relationships with others and your relationship with Allah ﷻ?

What was the starting point of this overgeneralization?

What evidence do you have that shows the inaccuracy of this overgeneralization?

What is a more realistic assumption?

C. False refuges

In order to feel safe, we often turn toward false refuges. They provide temporary relief from discomfort and provide us with a false, temporary sense of comfort and security.[19] This can come in the form of distractions, avoiding difficult conversations through increasing our workload, focusing solely on others instead of working on ourselves, etc. Unfortunately, false refuges can prevent us from gaining a true sense of peace and safety.

What types of false refuges have you noticed in your life? What have you been avoiding due to your personal fears?

Think about what you've been avoiding and ask yourself: What is one small thing I can do today that I haven't felt willing to do in a long time?

19 Brach, *True Refuge*.

D. Getting to know Allah ﷻ as a means of regaining trust

While overgeneralization and the weight of betrayal trauma can impact our relationship with Allah ﷻ, one of the best ways to reconnect with Him is through getting to know Him through His Names and Attributes. We cannot realistically trust someone we don't know so, naturally, learning more about who Allah ﷻ truly is will be an important step in reconnecting with Him.

Pick a Name of Allah ﷻ and read a little more about it. What resonates with you about this Name? How have you seen this Name of Allah manifest in your life?

Case study revisited

Kathleen endured something incredibly traumatic upon the discovery of her husband's infidelity. His actions resulted in a spiral of negative thoughts that eventually affected her faith. Kathleen could not wrap her head around the fact that the man she had loved, trusted, and devoted herself to for over 10 years would hurt her so cruelly. Furthermore, her husband had been her initial introduction to Islam so, as her relationship with Mustafa ended, she thought it was the end of her relationship with Allah ﷻ. After all, if Mustafa could do this, despite being a Muslim, Kathleen began to doubt everything about Islam.

Kathleen began to experience symptoms of trauma, such as flashbacks to her discovery of Mustafa's affair, hopelessness, negative thoughts about herself, withdrawal from family and friends, difficulty sleeping, and angry outbursts. She realized she needed to do something to address what she was dealing with and sought out a therapist. Through therapy, Kathleen began to differentiate her husband's choice to betray her trust from her ability to trust other people in her life. She also explored the connection between her faith in Allah ﷻ and her faith in her husband, realizing that Allah ﷻ is beyond comparison to any human being and that her relationship with Him could be a source of soothing, rather than pain. Kathleen began to feel empowered by being able to separate and remove her husband from her faith—she began to feel a sense of ownership of her life and her ability to have a strong relationship with Allah ﷻ without her husband's presence in her life.

Kathleen realized that her overgeneralization, "I will never be able to trust anyone again" led her to distance herself from people in her life who were her supporters and from Allah ﷻ, which only amplified her pain. As she explored her negative assumptions, she realized that she was painting everyone with the same brush and basically saying that no one is capable of being a good person, which was unfair to the people who cared about her. As she learned to accept that her husband's hurtful choices did not negate the fact that others had consistently been there for her, Kathleen was able to reconstruct healthy relationships with others.

Chapter 5
"Why Does Allah ﷻ Hate Me?"
Rescripting Negative Thoughts

Be ~~with~~ someone who makes you happy.

ANONYMOUS

Case study

Ever since Rula was a young girl, she thrived in close relationships—mostly because she lacked connection at home with her parents. Her parents fought all the time and were consumed with their own issues, leading her to seek out connection with her peers at school. Her first close relationship was with a best friend in elementary school. The friendship lasted 7 years until her friend slowly began distancing herself from Rula as she fell in with a different crowd at school. The same thing happened frequently in her other friendships: Rula became very close to friends quickly and trusted them wholeheartedly, but the relationship always ended with Rula feeling confused, needy, and unwanted. As Rula got older she also noticed the same patterns as she was trying to get married. Rula would put ads on matrimonial sites and put her all into trying to make things work, but nothing ever materialized. In fact, sometimes Rula felt like she was being used or taken advantage of. Relationships for Rula seemed like trying to jam a square peg into a round hole—everything felt forced, and no matter how hard she tried she couldn't make relationships work long-term. As all of Rula's friends got married, she increasingly felt alone and unworthy. Eventually Rula also began to feel this way in her relationship with Allah ﷻ. She would pray and desperately make du'aa to Allah ﷻ for things she wanted, but she felt disconnected in that relationship as well. Rula wondered: Was He ignoring her? Did He not care about her? Was her constant du'aa *annoying and pestering Him? She didn't understand why her prayers were unanswered when she tried so hard to connect with Allah* ﷻ*. In the same way Rula felt rejected by everyone else in her life she also asked herself,* ***"Does Allah*** ﷻ ***hate me too?"***

What is happening to me?

When we experience love and fulfilment in relationships, we feel secure in how we see ourselves and relate to the world around us. Kindness, vulnerability, and loyalty are some of the best parts of our inner selves, and when we share those qualities with the people closest to us, it makes us feel good to receive those gifts in return. On the contrary, when we put a tremendous amount of effort into trying to make a relationship work and do not have the same affection and love reciprocated, we experience a great deal of emotional upheaval. Feeling rejected is probably one of the most painful experiences in life and studies indicate that the neural pathway of rejection in the brain is the same as physical pain.[1] In other words, if you feel like you are in physical pain when someone puts you down, treats you badly, or invalidates you, it's because you are.

When you experience rejection repeatedly, whether by the same person over and over or by many different people, it is not unusual to internalize the heartache and wonder if there is something wrong with you. You might ask yourself:

> ***"Why am I so unlovable?"***
>
> ***"What is it about me that no matter how hard I try it never works?"***
>
> ***"How come what I do is never good enough?"***

---

1 Kross et al., "Social Rejection."

Suffering rejection by family and friends can also spill over from your interpersonal relationships into faith and spirituality. When you are trying your best and believe Allah ﷻ has the power to help you but are not seeing the results you want, then you might start to wonder if there is a disconnect. You might question if Allah ﷻ likes you, or if He is ignoring you like others in your life. Or perhaps you might consider that you are so unworthy that Allah will abandon you as well.

The thought that Allah ﷻ, the Owner and Controller of the whole universe, dislikes you feels catastrophic for a Muslim. When a family member or friend hates you, you can attempt to try to smooth things out directly in person, but how can you do that with Allah ﷻ? You cannot see Him or talk to Him face-to-face to assess the situation. He is so powerful, and you may feel so small. Also, what are the implications of being hated by Allah ﷻ? If He hates you, will you be rejected by Him and His creation in this *dunya* and in the *akhira*? Does that mean nothing in your life and the Hereafter will work out for you?

Understanding your thoughts and emotions

Meaningful relationships are undoubtedly an integral part of life, and everyone experiences interpersonal conflict every once in a while, but why is it that some people struggle much more in maintaining relationships than others? Difficulties can involve patterns of intense connection followed by a huge falling-out, ongoing fighting, or perpetual fear of being alone and abandoned. Unstable relationships feel like coming home to find out that the locks have been unexpectedly changed; they cause a tremendous amount of stress because they involve people we love, trust, and expect to be there consistently.

If you struggle with relationships, it's important to look at three elements of your life: **(i)** how you view the world; **(ii)** how you view yourself; and **(iii)** how you value yourself in relation to others.

Cognitive perceptions of the world

When a relationship falls apart or doesn't go as planned, you want to know why. You might contemplate: "What did I do wrong for this relationship to not work out?" or "Is there something wrong with me that I can't keep a good friend or get married?" Trying to answer these questions is a way for your brain to sort through and process all the information. It's a way of synthesizing thoughts and emotions by trying to make sense of what feels like a puzzle with many missing pieces.

During these reflective times, it can be easy to go down a slippery slope in terms of making negative associations with things around you. Places, people, and things that are neutral might begin to appear negative or bad because of the difficult circumstances you are in. This is because the feelings we have on the inside colour how we see ourselves, our environment, and the people around us. If you are not feeling good about yourself, you might begin to think others don't like you as well. Similarly, if you are feeling pessimistic about life, then how you experience circumstances around you will also reflect that. When we start to make decisions based on how we are feeling, instead of using logic or facts, we begin to engage in a psychological process called **emotional reasoning**.[2] Emotional reasoning occurs when a person makes conclusions about reality based on their feelings, not facts.

"I feel ugly so therefore I must be."

"I feel like nobody loves me and so I must be unlovable."

"I feel like everyone hates me—I need to close myself off and protect myself from the world."

The same unhealthy logic we use in applying internal negative feelings to objects around us can also be applied to our relationship with Allah ﷻ. Not everyone who thinks Allah ﷻ hates them arrived at that feeling with the same thoughts, but the cause is likely the same: emotional reasoning.

---

2 Burns, *Feeling Good*.

"Everyone hates me, so Allah ﷻ must hate me too."

"Bad things keep happening to me—this is Allah's ﷻ way of showing me that He is upset with me."

"My sins are so big that Allah ﷻ just wishes bad for me."

Emotional reasoning is very dangerous. As Aaron Beck, the American psychiatrist who is considered to be the founder of cognitive behaviour therapy, stated: "If our thinking is straightforward and clear, we are better equipped to reach these goals. If it is bogged down by distorted symbolic meanings, illogical reasoning, and erroneous interpretations, we become in effect deaf and blind."[3] It's impossible for any human being to be devoid of emotion but when a person uses emotion instead of intellect to make decisions, he or she truly becomes impaired in judgement. Emotional reasoning prevents a person's ability to hear information clearly without misunderstanding or misinterpreting it. Allah ﷻ states,

> *So have they not travelled through the earth and have hearts by which to reason and ears with which to hear? For indeed, it is not eyes that are blinded, but blinded are the hearts that are within the breasts.*[4]

Emotional reasoning can be catastrophic for general mental health as well as for relationships because it creates illusions of problems and dynamics that aren't actually there. When one person engages in emotional reasoning in a relationship, whether platonic or

3 Beck, Love Is Never Enough.

4 Qur'an 22:46.

otherwise, he or she is operating on an emotion-based reality that is not only unstable but untrue, likely alienating the healthier person in the long-term. When two people in a relationship participate in emotional reasoning, then neither party is engaging rationally, making the likelihood of having a healthy and stable relationship impossible.

Cognitive perceptions of yourself

How we view ourselves dictates how we see and interpret the world. Emotional reasoning is not just a byproduct of faulty thinking but can also be a result of how we feel about ourselves. Sometimes emotional reasoning stems from psychological projection, which in simplistic terms is when a person blames another for doing or feeling what they themselves are doing/feeling. For example, a woman who has really low self-esteem might continuously blame her husband for not thinking highly of her, when in fact it's she who feels that way about herself. Another common example is that a man who is unfaithful to his wife might accuse her of infidelity when there is absolutely no evidence to substantiate his claim. Projection is subconscious and not an intentional way of manipulating someone. When something is too painful to accept about oneself, it's psychologically easier to accuse someone else of doing it.

How we view ourselves also impacts how we relate to the people we seek to have meaningful relationships with. If you have low self-esteem and feel undeserving of love, you are going to bring those feelings into how you interact with friends and family on a day-to-day basis. This can be seen in how you treat others, how you think others perceive you, and how you allow others to treat you. If you think badly about yourself, you will likely also assume others think badly of you. If you think that your ideas are stupid or are of no value, you will also expect others to feel the same.

All relationships have an equilibrium and low self-esteem can disrupt healthy equilibrium in three major ways:

1. If you think you are unlovable and less deserving than the other person of happiness, relationship satisfaction, and reciprocity, then you will inevitably withdraw because you don't perceive yourself to be worthy of experiencing the benefits of a relationship with someone good. When you emotionally withdraw from the other person, they will naturally withdraw over time as well and eventually, the relationship will end.
2. If you think you are unlovable and less deserving than the other person of happiness, relationship satisfaction, and reciprocity, then you may cling to the other person to compensate for all the ways you feel you are lacking. You might be needy and possessive, fear abandonment or think that you will never find someone else who wants to be with you. You might even give too much in a way that feels smothering. When this happens, the healthy person will flee the relationship because it's too much for them to handle such high needs and expectations.
3. If your self-esteem erratically fluctuates, then this can affect your relationships through highs and lows with attachment and unpredictability in behaviour. This might be seen in tumultuous relationships in which friends or spouses are extremely close one minute and then extremely distant the next.

Cognitions about Allah

In the same way that you think others don't like you because you don't like yourself, you might make similar inferences about your relationship with Allah ﷻ. Allah ﷻ is consistent in His message and attributes, and so if you feel that He hates you, wants bad for you, or has abandoned you, this is likely from internal turmoil. In other words, if you feel that Allah ﷻ hates you, it's very likely that you feel bad about or hate yourself. Spiritual emotional reasoning might lead you to think:

"I'm not worthy of His Mercy."

"He is not listening to me."

"He doesn't want what's best for me."

"He doesn't care about me."

Additionally, some emotional reasoning about Allah ﷻ might come from a deeper part of your unconscious, as many people project negative feelings and experiences with their parents onto Allah ﷻ. There is a fair amount of literature that suggests people project their views of their parents onto God.[5] So, for example, if you have a history of your parents being unavailable to you in childhood, it would not be unusual for you to think (incorrectly) that Allah ﷻ will not be accessible to you during times of difficulty. If you have trust or abandonment issues because of deception on the part of your

---

5 Dickie et al., "Parent-Child Relationships"; McDonald et al., "Attachment to God and Parents"; Aifuwa, "Effects of Child-Parent Attachment."

parents, you might feel that Allah ﷻ is not a consistent Provider of your needs. Lastly, if you feel unworthy of attention and love due to how your parents treated you, you may suspect the same from Allah ﷻ and think that He doesn't care about you.

Changing your mind, body, and heart

During times of distress, it might feel like it's impossible to change oneself and how one relates to others but with awareness, insight, and dedication, it is possible to change. In order to address emotional reasoning about yourself and the world, you will need to rectify three areas: how you view yourself, how you view others in relation to yourself, and how you view Allah ﷻ in relation to yourself.

Transforming how you see yourself

If you feel empty, lonely, and negative about who you are, this may not just stem from lack of self-esteem but could also be from a lack of a sense of self. When someone knows who they are as a person, has strong connections to others, has passion, drive, and purpose, then life feels full and worth living. A lack of sense of self leads to the opposite—when a person doesn't really know who they are as an individual, their mood, purpose, and goals can drastically fluctuate with their changing circumstances.

Our sense of self develops during childhood when there is a heavy dependence on our parents to take care of us and help us navigate the world. In healthy homes, a parent's love, time, and attention goes to nurturing a child. Nurturing involves not just providing food and a roof over the child's head, but also emotional, psychological, and spiritual sustenance. When the child is ready for separation-individuation, a normal developmental stage in adolescence, the teenager healthily begins to separate themselves from their parents; the teenager will still rely on their parents for help but begins to emerge as his or her own individual.

When a child from a home with inadequate nurturing hits adolescence, they also begin to separate but find themselves lost. This is because their parents did not bolster them with the adequate nourishment and care to know who they are as an individual apart from their caregivers. If you have ever planted a sapling or young plant in a pot in your home to make it stronger before planting it outside, the concept is the same for children. The sapling will not survive outside because it has to grow in a safe environment first to be made strong enough to withstand the harsh elements to come. Teenagers from unhealthy homes oftentimes have inadequate strength to successfully navigate stressors outside the home, making them much more prone to anxiety, depression, and unhealthy relationships.

Developing a strong sense of self and self-esteem can take a lot of work but it ultimately starts with many intentional and incremental steps in recognizing yourself as a person worthy of respect, dignity, and love. Let's take a moment to repeat that: *you* are a person worthy of respect, dignity, and love. Sometimes Muslims shy away from self-esteem work because they feel it will breed arrogance; however, healthy self-esteem is not about putting oneself on a pedestal and glorifying oneself—it's about acknowledging blessings Allah ﷻ

has given you and striving to be the best version of yourself. Start this invaluable work by doing an honest but kind inventory of your positive and negative attributes. Reflect on unique gifts, talents, and strengths that Allah ﷻ has blessed you with. If you struggle with finding good personal attributes, ask a trusted friend, teacher, or family member to assist you. Making a list of negative qualities sounds counterintuitive to working on your self-esteem, but this is only true if you have no intention of working on those qualities. Taking your negative qualities and turning them into goals for change can be a great way to improve yourself, which will not only make you a better person but increase your self-esteem in the long-term. Allah ﷻ has created you individually and put you on earth for a reason, which means you have a purpose. Take your qualities and fine-tune them to create a life both you and Allah ﷻ can be pleased with and make the world a better place.

Transforming how you relate to others

The weaker the sense of self is, the more likely an individual will cling to relationships and find little meaning outside them because the connection to others makes them feel complete and whole. It's completely healthy, natural, and necessary to our existence and wellbeing to be connected to others, but when a person can't function or find meaning in life outside of relationships this can be problematic. You can see this in people who jump from marriage to marriage because they can't tolerate the idea of being alone, a woman who completely puts her life on hold while she searches for a husband or a person who completely falls apart whenever they have a spat with friends or family members. When a person with no sense of self latches onto someone who appears to have the characteristics they lack (like bravery, intellect, spiritual devotion, etc.), that gives them a false sense of security; however, once that person leaves, the emptiness returns with a vengeance because now the hollowness is magnified by feelings of abandonment.

Unhealthy dependence for adults can also be troublesome from a spiritual standpoint as ideally complete dependence should only be on Allah ﷻ, not other human beings. When one seeks to have their needs to be met by people, they will inevitably be disappointed because human beings are fallible and can be undependable. Our purpose in life is to worship Allah ﷻ and get to *jannah*; therefore, completely falling apart and finding no meaning in life after one's children leave home, or after divorce, or in the absence of a best friend might suggest that one's overall purpose in life may need to be re-examined. Life is more joyful and comfortable with relationships, and even Prophet Muhammad ﷺ grieved after losing loved ones, but that is not to say that life is not worth living outside relationships.

Insight is the first step to understanding unhealthy views about depending on others. Reflect and analyse on how much you might rely on others:

Are you dependent on others for your happiness?

Do you rely on others to make decisions for you?

Are you dependent on others' validation to feel good about yourself?

Do you need to take care of other people's needs for your own wellbeing?

If you find in your assessment that you rely on others too much, consider going a step further and writing down all the different ways you depend on others—socially, financially, emotionally, and/or spiritually. Once you have identified the different areas that need improvement, you can begin to use cognitive restructuring (identifying irrational thoughts and replacing them with healthier thoughts) and affirmations (positive statements affirming the opposite of your negative thoughts) to correct views about your ability to do things independently.

For example, if you feel dependent on others to make decisions for you, step one would be to write out your initial unhealthy thoughts as to how this dynamic is playing out in your life. Once you have the irrational or unhealthy thought, then step two would be to write the opposite, in a way someone who cared about you would if they heard the negative thought. Lastly, take the corrected thought and turn it into an affirmation that you can repeat to yourself on a regular basis to reinforce the positive attributes you have or are trying to achieve.

Dependency thought: *I feel that others need to make decisions for me because I always make mistakes and don't know what I'm doing.*

Cognitive restructuring: *Everyone errs, not just me—and it's not like I make mistakes often. Besides, how will I learn if I don't make mistakes?*

Independence Affirmation: *I'm capable of making good decisions on my own.*

If you would like to take this process one step further, follow the affirmation with real-life evidence to support your statement. This may not be possible in all scenarios, but it is good practice when applicable.

Example: I once bought a laptop on my own that I really liked. I read reviews online, did istikhara prayer and bought it with nobody helping me—and it turned out to be a good decision.

For individuals who are highly dependent on others, psychotherapy is usually the best course of action but if you just have dependency tendencies, assessing how you rely on others too much and shifting your thoughts might be enough to empower yourself to a healthier way of thinking.

Transforming your relationship with Allah ﷻ

The long-term effects of assuming that Allah ﷻ doesn't like you can be dire. Thinking that Allah ﷻ hates you creates a barrier between having love for Him, wanting to do good deeds, seeking repentance, and having overall positive feelings about Islam. It's almost impossible for one to have feelings of love towards Allah ﷻ, His Messenger, and the religion if hate, the complete opposite emotion, is what is filling one's spiritual heart. Shaytaan loves for people to assume that Allah ﷻ hates them because this makes it easier for him to lead them astray.

If you are feeling that Allah ﷻ hates you, it's not too late to change that. Know that He has never abandoned you and has always been there, although perhaps you may have distanced yourself from Him. Begin by spending time with yourself and reflecting on how you got to this point in the first place. Thoughts often don't happen spontaneously—most of the time they are planted and become stronger over time. Go back in time and think about when you first started to feel this way:

Did someone (perhaps an adult or authority figure) say Allah ﷻ hated you?

Are you taking characteristics or assumptions about your parents as providers and unintentionally superimposing them on Allah ﷻ as your Provider?

Did someone make **du'aa** ***for Allah ﷻ to curse you, in which you assumed that all bad things happened after that was a result of the bad*** **du'aa** ***against you?***

Did something catastrophic happen that made you think Allah ﷻ hates you?

Did you feel that you are so unworthy of love that nobody, including Allah ﷻ, could love you?

Once you have identified the origin of the thought, you can begin to deconstruct the unhealthy parts of it and change it. Look objectively at your circumstances using facts. Emotions are your feelings about what happened, whereas facts simply describe what happened. This sounds very simplistic but oftentimes people don't realize they are getting the two mixed up.

If all your thoughts seem jumbled up, try writing them down. Write a narrative of what led you to feel that Allah ﷻ hates you. Highlight your feelings in red and then the facts in green. Is your narrative mostly emotion or facts? Are there parts of your story you thought were true but were based on emotion? Remember, just because you feel something doesn't make it true.

Another exercise to help identify where your feeling that Allah ﷻ hates you came from is a free association technique. Write on top of a piece of paper: "I think Allah ﷻ hates me because..." followed by all the reasons you can think of. Write as many reasons as you can. Once you have identified all the reasons you feel that Allah ﷻ hates you, begin to replace the emotional reasoning with facts. Cross out the unhealthy thoughts and replace them with healthy ones.

Example: ~~***I think Allah ﷻ hates me because my duaas are never answered.***~~

Allah ﷻ answers all du'aas but the response might not be immediate or might take a different form.

If you happen to notice any parallels between how you view Allah ﷻ and other authority figures, like your parents or teachers, be sure to deconstruct and uncouple the two in your mind. Cross out characteristics you inadvertently transferred from the authority figure to Allah ﷻ in red. Look up the 99 names of Allah ﷻ and write the opposite or a more fitting characteristic in green instead.

Example: I think Allah ﷻ hates me because everyone in my life, including my parents, hate me and think I'm useless.

Allah ﷻ is Al Latif — The Kind
Allah ﷻ is Ash Shakur — The Grateful
Allah ﷻ is Al Wadud — The Loving

Sometimes it's painful to look at past events objectively because when you realize that Allah ﷻ doesn't hate you, accountability for the traumatic incident might fall on someone else. This person could be you, a family member, or a friend. For example, you might have attributed failing out of college to Allah ﷻ hating you, when really it was because you didn't go to class or study. Or perhaps you thought Allah ﷻ didn't care about you when in fact it was your beloved parents who were feeding you misinformation about Him. The end goal of this process is not to focus on blame but to increase insight and accountability so positive changes can be made for the future.

Lastly, in addition to examining the origins of why you think Allah ﷻ hates you, it is also important to reflect on how your interpretation of your life events might be reinforcing your existing thoughts. For example, it is an Islamic concept that humans are punished for their sins in this life and the next, but this does not mean that a Muslim can attribute everything that doesn't go his or her way to punishment from Allah ﷻ or that Allah ﷻ hates them. Let's deconstruct some common beliefs about the link between "bad" things happening to a person and that Allah ﷻ hates them.

I think Allah ﷻ hates me because bad things always happen to me

Our definitions of "bad" are not always true. Just because something doesn't go as planned or makes you feel uncomfortable doesn't mean that it is bad. You not getting that job you wanted might be because Allah ﷻ has a better one in store for you. That fight you had with your spouse might be because Allah ﷻ wanted to teach you an important lesson through it. Your getting into a car accident may be because Allah ﷻ wanted to prevent you from more harm than what was waiting for you at your destination.

I think Allah ﷻ just wants bad for me through these trials

Sometimes bad things happen to us as a way of drawing our attention to the sins we have done and turning back to Allah ﷻ in repentance, but bad things can also happen to us because they are trials and Allah ﷻ wants to increase us in our rank. We know that the prophets faced huge difficulties, but we do not attribute those difficulties to their sins. If every difficulty truly translated to a punishment, why would Allah ﷻ have punished the best of humanity (the prophets) so harshly? There is no way for us to know what bad things happen to us because of our own doing, and while it's essential to contemplate about this and make *istighfar*, it's fruitless to ruminate (keep thinking about something over and over) if (i) you can't find out with any certainty why something bad happened to you; and (ii) you did sincere *tawbah* (repentance)—in which case, Allah ﷻ may have already forgiven you.

I think Allah ﷻ just wants to punish me and make me feel bad

If Allah ﷻ is punishing you for something, it doesn't mean that He hates you. One of the benefits of punishment in this *dunya* (if you are in fact being punished) is so you can feel distressed enough to change a wrong you are committing and be expiated for that sin. The end goal is not for Allah ﷻ to make you feel bad; it's for you to feel bad enough to change. This is because Allah ﷻ actually wants what is best for you. If you are engaging or persisting in sin,

Allah ﷻ may be trying to correct you to ward off future pain, as usually there is no incentive to change without distress.

> ***Anas (may Allah be pleased with him) reported that: The Messenger of Allah ﷺ said, "When Allah intends good for His slave, He punishes him in this world, but when He intends an evil for His slave, He does not hasten to take him to task but calls him to account on the Day of Resurrection."*** [6]

If you've made mistakes in assuming that Allah ﷻ hates you in the past, ask Him to forgive you and try to start over on a new page. Don't let guilt cloud the newfound hope that the Creator of the Heavens and the Earth doesn't hate you. Feel how liberating it is to understand that The One who has power over all things wants what is best for you.

Instead of focusing on weaknesses in your relationship with Allah ﷻ in the past, refocus your energy on doing things that Allah ﷻ loves in the present. How wonderful is it that Allah ﷻ tells us directly in the Qur'an how to seek closeness to Him so that He loves us even more:

> ***...Indeed, Allah loves those who are constantly repentant and loves those who purify themselves.*** [7]

> ***And spend in the way of Allah and do not throw [yourselves] with your [own] hands into destruction [by refraining]. And do good; indeed, Allah loves the doers of good.*** [8]

---

6 *Jami' al-Tirmidhi*, bk. 1, hadith 43.

7 Qur'an 2:222.

8 Qur'an 2:195.

[They are] avid listeners to falsehood, devourers of [what is] unlawful. So if they come to you, [O Muhammad], judge between them or turn away from them. And if you turn away from them—never will they harm you at all. And if you judge, judge between them with justice. Indeed, Allah loves those who act justly.[9]

So by mercy from Allah, [O Muhammad], you were lenient with them. And if you had been rude [in speech] and harsh in heart, they would have disbanded from you. So pardon them and ask forgiveness for them and consult them in the matter. And when you have decided, then rely upon Allah. Indeed, Allah loves those who rely [upon Him].[10]

Abu Hurairah (May Allah be pleased with him) reported:

The Messenger of Allah ﷺ said, "Allah the Exalted has said: 'I will declare war against him who shows hostility to a pious worshipper of Mine. And the most beloved thing with which My slave comes nearer to Me is what I have enjoined upon him; and My slave keeps on coming closer to Me through performing nawafil (prayer or doing extra deeds besides what is obligatory) till I love him. When I love him, I become his hearing with which he hears,

9 Qur'an 5:42.
10 Qur'an 3:159.

his seeing with which he sees, his hand with which he strikes, and his leg with which he walks; and if he asks (something) from Me, I give him, and if he asks My Protection (refuge), I protect him.'" [11]

Spiritual inspiration for reflection

Narrated 'Umar bin Al-Khattab:

Some sabi *(i.e., war prisoners, children and women only) were brought before the Prophet ﷺ and behold, a woman amongst them was milking her breasts to feed and whenever she found a child amongst the captives, she took it over her chest and nursed it (she had lost her child but later she found him). The Prophet said to us, "Do you think that this lady would ever throw her son in the fire?" We replied, "No, if she has the power not to throw it (in the fire)." The Prophet ﷺ then said, "Allah is more merciful to His slaves than this lady to her son."* [12]

11 *Sahih al-Bukhari*; al-Nawawi, Riyad as-salihin, no. 95.

12 *Sahih al-Bukhari*, no. 5999.

It was narrated from Abu Hurairah that:

> *The Messenger of Allah ﷺ said: "Allah says, 'I am as My slave thinks I am, and I am with him when he mentions Me. If he makes mention of Me to himself, I make mention of him to Myself; and if he makes mention of Me in an assembly, I make mention of him in an assembly better than it. And if he draws to Me a hand-span length, I draw near to him a forearm's length. And if he comes to Me walking, I go to him in a hurry.'"*[13]

Practical exercises

A. Personal inventory:

A personal inventory is a great way to start working on increasing your self-esteem and positive sense of self. Below write down as many positive traits and general strengths that you can. You can also list blessings in your life like supports and/or resources.

Positive traits, attributes, and blessings

---

13 *Sunan Ibn Majah*, no. 3822.

Everyone has desirable, positive traits unique to who they are as an individual, but also areas that need improvement as well. Can you think of specific areas in your life that need to be worked on? Instead of looking at these weaknesses as something negative, rewrite these traits or habits as positive, concrete, and achievable goals. Taking a perceived negative trait and turning it into something constructive can help improve self-esteem.

Traits to work on	Personal goals	Action item
I waste too much time.	Stay awake after *fajr* to have more productive time.	Set up automatic coffee maker for *fajr* time to increase the likelihood of staying up.
I'm overweight according to my doctor.	Obtain healthy BMI (Body Mass Index).	Substitute 2 dinner meals a week with big, healthy salads.

B. Increasing independence

To decrease dependence on others, you first have to identify ways that you might rely on others socially, spiritually, financially, or emotionally in unhealthy ways. To shift your views away from dependency (relying on others), cognitively restructure those statements and turn them into affirmations. Provide evidence from the past of times you were successful in these areas to demonstrate that you can do it again. Repeat the affirmations to yourself regularly for maximum effect.

Dependency	Cognitive restructuring	Affirmation	Evidence
I'm not going to have a fulfilling life as long as I'm not married.	Marriage is important to me, but I cannot control when I find my future spouse. On The Day of Judgement Allah ﷻ will ask me about how I spent my time. It's healthy for me to find contentment and joy in my blessings, *deen*, family and life in this moment.	*Alhamdulillah* I have everything I need. I am blessed and grateful for all the good in my life.	I once created a food pantry at my *masjid*. It made me so happy to see others benefit. Good deeds for the sake of Allah ﷻ can be a means to find fulfillment in this *dunya* and in the *akhira*.

C. Fact-checking emotional reasoning

Do you feel that your emotions cloud your judgement? Write a narrative of why you think Allah ﷻ hates you and highlight your feelings in red and then the facts in green. Is your narrative mostly emotion or facts? Are there parts of your story you thought were true but were based on emotion? Remember, just because you feel something doesn't make it true.

Take all the red statements you wrote above and next to them rewrite them as facts. If you can't turn your emotion statement into a fact statement, then just cross it out altogether.

Emotion statement	Fact
I was sexually assaulted because Allah ﷻ wanted to teach me a lesson about being out late at night.	I was sexually assaulted on my way to the car from a *halaqa* at a sister's house. I was not doing anything wrong and there is nothing in Islam that says a woman can not go out at night. I was assaulted because this man did something evil of his own volition. He is 100% to blame.
~~Perhaps Allah ﷻ was punishing me for something I did a few years ago.~~	

Emotion statement	Fact

D. Free association technique

Write on top of a piece of paper: "I think Allah ﷻ hates me because..." followed by all the reasons you can think of that He might dislike you. Write as many reasons as you can.

Once you have identified all the reasons you feel that Allah ﷻ hates you, you can begin to replace the emotional reasoning with facts. Cross out the unhealthy thoughts and replace them with healthy ones.

Allah ﷻ hates me because.... (Write emotional reasoning here)	**Re-write emotional reasoning into a fact here**
~~I repented for having a boyfriend and started praying my daily prayers again but my parents still found out about what I did which got me in a lot of trouble.~~	My parents finding out I had a boyfriend was a direct consequence of my actions. It doesn't have anything to do with Allah ﷻ hating me, my *tawbah* being accepted, or the fact that I should be praying my daily prayers anyway.

Case study revisited

During one day of feeling lonely and despondent that she would never get married, Rula decided to do the Fact-Checking Emotional Reasoning Exercise and discovered she was using emotional reasoning more than she thought. Rula realized two important things: (1) that she used emotion instead of logic in a lot of her decision-making; and (2) that she measured her self-worth by her relationships. If she had a friend or a good candidate for marriage, she put everything into that relationship, oftentimes ignoring other parts of her life and putting important matters on hold. When those relationships ended, however, Rula felt terrible. Upon reflection. Rula understood that her self-esteem was more underdeveloped than she had realized. She made a commitment to securing her wellbeing and happiness independent of the people around her. Rula did an inventory of her positive and negative traits and uncovered that she had a lot of good attributes to work with. She set aside time to enhance her positive traits and to reframe her negative traits into tangible steps she could work on.

Rula also did the Free Association Technique about why she thought Allah ﷻ hated her and quickly grasped that it wasn't that Allah ﷻ disliked her—she just felt like He hated her when things she was hoping for didn't work out as planned. Rula became more cognizant that when things went wrong, she shouldn't assume that this was because Allah ﷻ was angry with her. To counter this inclination, she made sure to always replace her unhealthy thoughts with healthy ones as soon as she realized what was happening. When Rula freed herself from the idea that Allah ﷻ hated her, she felt empowered and started taking a more proactive stance in life. She understood that the only person putting her life on hold was herself and that she could not wait around for a husband to live her life. Rula continued looking for a husband but made short-term and long-term goals related to her deen, *career, family, and well-being. These goals put Rula's life back on track, gave her hope, and made her feel like herself again.*

Chapter 6
"Everything Is Falling Apart"

Dealing with Unexpected Life Detours

Gratitude is the healthiest of all human emotions. The more you express gratitude for what you have, the more likely you will have even more to express gratitude for.

ZIG ZIGLAR

GRATITUDE JOURNEY

Case study

The day of the doctor's appointment that changed everything would remain ingrained in Salwa's mind, causing her to relive it daily. She could vividly remember the feeling of the cold chair beneath her when the doctor sat across from her and began explaining the aggressive form of cancer that would be a part of her life—or a part of her death, as Salwa constantly thought. She was alone when she got the news—she and her husband had thought it would be a routine workup. Salwa remembered feeling shaky, feeling as though she was hearing the doctor's words through a fog, and feeling overwhelmingly alone without someone to lean on as she processed this news. She began to think about her children and her husband and what this news would mean to them and the life they had built together. Salwa worried about finances and how they would pay for treatment since they didn't have insurance. How do you choose between buying your children's school supplies and paying for chemotherapy? As Salwa began chemotherapy, she tried to act as though nothing was happening. She could not quite accept the reality of the situation and tried to avoid it for as long as possible. Eventually, the pain and weakness were overwhelming. She could no longer do the things she took for granted—her husband dropped off the kids at school, a neighbour cooked meals for them, and she could no longer go *to work. Everything had changed. As a sense of hopelessness overwhelmed her, she often thought to herself, **"Everything is falling apart. There's nothing good left in my life."***

What is happening to me?

One of the most terrifying aspects of our lives is how much of it is outside of our control. On most days, we don't pay attention to the fact that if one thing was different, our lives would be completely transformed within the blink of an eye. Every day you drive to work or school, you typically arrive there unscathed. It takes a split second of someone not checking their blind spot for your life to change drastically. If we were to sit and ponder everything that could possibly go wrong, we would probably stay in bed each morning.

When we are faced with the uncertainty that comes when something major occurs, it can feel as though everything is falling apart. You no longer recognize your life; the things that were once familiar are now foreign and you yourself may have changed tremendously. When so much is changing, it is natural to feel overwhelmed and helpless. Your thoughts will reflect that as well. Some thoughts you might experience when it feels as though your life is spiralling out of control are:

I can't deal with this.

I've lost so much. What good do I have left?

There's nothing I can do to change this; it's hopeless.

When these thoughts permeate our minds and hearts, they can cause us to reduce ourselves and our capabilities to nothingness. When we view uncontrollable circumstances as an indication that nothing is within our control, we eventually succumb to feelings of helplessness and hopelessness. While this impacts our emotional, mental, and physical health, it also affects our spiritual health. In our relationship with Allah ﷻ, our thoughts may look something like this:

Allah ﷻ is sending me hardship after hardship but He promises ease too. Where is the ease?

I just don't understand why Allah ﷻ would make my life so horrible.

There is no point in going through this—nothing good can come out of it.

When so much in your life feels uncontrollable, reclaiming control over your thoughts and the impact they have on your perception of your life and your faith can be incredibly empowering. This is within your reach so let's explore how to work on it.

Understanding your thoughts and emotions

When you view your problems as larger than life, while ignoring the positive aspects, it's only natural that negative emotions will follow.

Magnification and minimization are two of the most common forms of cognitive distortions. Most of us fall prey to them occasionally—even people with relatively healthy thinking patterns. **Magnification** occurs when you look at imperfections in your life, your own errors, or the mistakes of others and exaggerate them.[1] This involves looking at mistakes or the struggles you face as huge and insurmountable. **Minimization** occurs when you look at your strengths or positive things in your life as small and inconsequential. It's like wearing glasses that strictly enhance negativity rather than accurately revealing what is really present before you.

One of the biggest issues with these cognitive distortions is that they lead to more and more self-defeating thoughts. We tend to find what we look for. When we begin to scan our environment, relationships, and ourselves for negatives, our reality will become increasingly filled with darkness because that is what we are searching for.

---

1 Burns, *Feeling Good*.

Furthermore, your relationship with Allah ﷻ will also inevitably be impacted by this. As we feel more and more overwhelmed, we can easily feel disconnected from Allah ﷻ. Your thoughts may follow a trajectory such as this:

Everywhere I look, it just seems like tragedy follows me.

There is nothing but bad in my life.

No expectations mean no disappointments. I'll just accept that Allah ﷻ has cursed me so no matter how much I try or how much I pray, only bad things will come my way.

These thoughts perpetuate a self-defeating cycle featuring painful emotions, unhealthy behaviours, and more negative thoughts. Because you are convinced that nothing you do will make a difference, you don't even try to make a change. This results in living your life passively, which affects every aspect of your day-to-day life:

It will impact your job since a lack of trying will impact future prospects in your place of employment.

Your relationships will suffer since this negativity can permeate your marriage, parenting, and friendships—magnification of the bad and minimization of the good cause you to overlook things that can bring you closer to others while emphasizing things that push you away from them.

You may refuse to reach out to friends or put effort into relationships due to fear that your efforts will only result in more negativity.

This vicious cycle will go on indefinitely unless you know how to beat it.

Take a look at this self-defeating cycle and how it can impact our faith:[2]

Self-Defeating Thought

What difference will *du'aa* make? They won't be accepted anyway since it's clear Allah's not listening to me since my life is so miserable.

Self-Defeating Behavior

You stop making *du'aa* and may stop engaging in other acts of worship as well.

Self-Defeating Emotions

Hopelessness, guilt, worthlessness, overwhelm, self-criticism, anger.

Consequences of the Cycle of Self-Defeat

You feel more and more isolated from Allah ﷻ, which solidifies the perception that Allah does not care about you. This causes you to feel stuck, alone and unable to regain control of your life, which perpetuates this cycle.

As you can see in this diagram, our thoughts, feelings, and behaviours are intertwined. When one changes, the others change as well.

2 Burns, *Feeling Good*.

We also find this concept in Islam:

Consider how Allah ﷻ comforts the Prophet Muhammad ﷺ in the Qur'an:

We know how your heart is distressed at what they say. But celebrate the praises of your Lord and be of those who prostrate themselves in adoration.[3]

Allah ﷻ prescribed *action* to alleviate the anxiety of the Prophet ﷺ and the Muslims at that time. That is why it is reported that whenever the Prophet faced a difficult time, he would rush to *salah* and say:

Give us comfort through prayer, O Bilal.[4]

This shows that a change in our behaviours can be an effective way to transform our thoughts and emotions as well.

Also, consider the saying of Ibn al-Qayyim (*rahimahullah*):

> *Ward off passing thoughts, for if you do not, they will become ideas. Ward off ideas, for if you do not, they will become desires. Fight them, for if you do not, they will become resolve and determination, and if you do not ward them off, they will become actions. If you do not resist them with their opposite, they will become habits and it will be difficult for you to get rid of them.*[5]

3 Qur'an 15:97–98.
4 *Sunan Abī Dāwūd*, no. 4986.
5 Ibn al-Qayyim al-Jawzīyah, *Kitāb al-fawāid*.

Here, again, there is an emphasis on the link between thoughts, emotions, and actions.

The Prophet Muhammad ﷺ said,

> *Allah the Most High said, "I am as my servant thinks (expects) I am. I am with him when he mentions Me. If he mentions Me to himself, I mention him to Myself; and if he mentions Me in an assembly, I mention him in an assembly greater than it. If he draws near to Me a hand's length, I draw near to him an arm's length. And if he comes to Me walking, I go to him at speed."*[6]

Here, consider one of the wisdoms of this *hadith*: Allah ﷻ is to each of us what we expect Him to be because those who think well of Allah ﷻ will mention Him, will draw closer to Him, and will walk to Him. All of these are behaviours that can change our perception of Allah ﷻ—the more we reach out to Him, the more we move toward Him, and the better our expectations of Allah ﷻ will be. It is only when we give up hope that we feel that Allah ﷻ has abandoned us.

Furthermore, we tend to find what we look for. If we seek out examples of what is missing from our lives, our positive thoughts of Allah ﷻ diminish. However, if we seek out examples of the blessings within our lives, our perception of Allah ﷻ is enhanced, which leads to further connection with Him.

---

6 *Ṣaḥīḥ Muslim*, no. 2675; *Ṣaḥīḥ al-Bukhārī*, no. 7405.

Changing your mind, body, and heart

Now that we understand the self-defeating cycle that minimization and magnification can perpetuate, let's explore different antidotes to these cognitive distortions.

Minimizing capabilities and magnifying shortcomings

Our brains tend to overestimate and amplify perceived flaws while underestimating our abilities and accomplishments. Magnification of shortcomings and minimization of our capabilities can result in the idea that whatever you do or qualities you have are not worth much. A helpful method to address this is called the "self-endorsement method."[7] This technique involves writing down the self-defeating thoughts you are struggling with and responding to them by countering them with accomplishments you have achieved (by the will and grace of Allah ﷻ) and the blessings you possess. This transforms distorted thoughts and grounds them in reality. When we discount the things we accomplish and convince ourselves that they don't matter, we begin to believe nothing we do matters. Consider this example:

7 Burns, *Feeling Good*.

Cognitive distortion:

I've accomplished nothing in life.

Antidote:

Step 1: Break down the self-defeating thoughts in order to address them one-by-one.

Step 2: Identify where you are minimizing the good and where you are maximizing the bad.

Step 3: Replace self-defeating thoughts with ones that are self-endorsing by objectively identifying accomplishments and positive qualities to counteract each of the negative thoughts.

Step 4: Turn this into gratitude to Allah ﷻ for giving you the ability to accomplish these things, no matter how trivial they may seem.

<table>
<tr><td>Self-defeating thought</td><td>I've accomplished nothing in life.</td></tr>
<tr><td>Identify minimization/ magnification</td><td>It's impossible to live a life without accomplishing <u>anything</u> at all.

Magnification: I'm focusing on the moments when things have not gone the way I hoped they would, and on all of my shortcomings.

Minimization: I am ignoring every moment when things have been okay and I've put in effort to do something positive.</td></tr>
<tr><td>Self-endorsing thought: identify accomplishments</td><td>Realistically, there wouldn't be enough space here to list all of my accomplishments since even little things count like:
• Helping my parents out by buying them groceries
• Getting the car inspected before the registration expired
• Making my spouse smile with a kind text
• Every prayer I've done throughout my life
• Working hard to provide for my family</td></tr>
<tr><td>Gratitude to Allah ﷻ</td><td>Allah ﷻ rewards me for all of my efforts and I am grateful for His guidance in granting me the physical, mental, and spiritual capabilities to achieve all of these things.</td></tr>
</table>

This antidote can also be applied to cases in which we magnify the flaws (and minimize the good) of people in our lives and can help to enrich our relationships with them. For example:

Cognitive distortion:

My husband never helps with anything at home.

Antidote:

Step 1: Break down the negative thoughts in order to address them one-by-one.

Step 2: Identify where you are minimizing the good and where you are maximizing the bad.

Step 3: Replace negative thoughts with ones that are healthier by objectively identifying the positive things this person brings into your life to counteract each of the negative thoughts.

Step 4: Turn this into gratitude to Allah ﷻ.

Relationship ruining thought	My husband never helps with anything at home.
Identify minimization/ magnification	"Never" is a very strong word. For him to never help at home would mean he refuses to lift a finger as soon as he gets home from work. I'm minimizing the things he does at home and for our family and magnifying the list of things I believe are lacking.
Relationship enriching thought: identify the positives	• He takes care of any issues I have with my car. • My husband loads the dishwasher sometimes. • He helps the kids with their homework. • He helps out with cleaning when we have guests coming over. • He works to provide the money needed to pay for home expenses.
Gratitude to Allah ﷻ	Although I take on the majority of household tasks, I am grateful for the home we have and the income Allah ﷻ has provided us with to be able to live here. I am grateful to Allah ﷻ for granting me a husband who is responsive to my need for help at home.

One common deterrent people often face when they are attempting to consider self-endorsing thoughts is the fear of this being a form of arrogance or pride. The Prophet Muhammad ﷺ said,

> *"He who has in his heart the weight of a mustard seed of pride shall not enter Paradise." A person (amongst his hearers) said: "Verily a person loves that his dress should be fine, and his shoes should be fine." He (the Holy Prophet) remarked: "Verily, Allah is Beautiful and He loves Beauty. Pride is disdaining the truth (out of self-conceit) and contempt for the people."*[8]

We should definitely be wary of arrogance; however, acknowledging our accomplishments does not need to lead us down that path. That is why a part of the antidote to self-defeating thoughts is turning our accomplishments into a form of gratitude to Allah ﷻ. Acknowledging that every capability, accomplishment, and goodness in our lives is through the Will of Allah ﷻ reinforces our understanding of His power and our dependence on Him. Rather than self-endorsing thoughts being an indication of pride, they are a testament to Allah's ﷻ blessings in our lives.

Let's consider how to further enhance a sense of gratitude by exploring another magnification/minimization issue.

8 *Ṣaḥīḥ Muslim*, no. 91.

Minimizing blessings and magnifying struggles

As human beings, we naturally tend to focus on what is lacking within our lives rather than shifting our focus to our blessings. The Prophet Muhammad ﷺ said,

> *If the son of Adam had a valley full of gold, he would want to have two valleys. Nothing fills his mouth but the dust of the grave, yet Allah will accept whoever repents to Him.*[9]

In this *hadith*, we see that even with a valley filled with gold, it is still easy to look at the valley we don't possess rather than the one we do. This is why the cognitive distortions of magnification and minimization are so common. It is easy to minimize what we have and magnify what we lack; however, living our lives in this way will yield feelings of discontentment, sadness, and frustration.

As an exercise, try to imagine yourself wearing huge glasses that amplify all of the things that are lacking in your life. What do these glasses look like? What pieces of your life do they amplify and bring to the forefront? (e.g., the mess around the house, something frustrating your spouse said, the endless work emails you can't seem to get under control, etc.). Now, picture yourself removing these glasses and replacing them with different ones that allow you to focus on the good in your life. What do these glasses look like? What's amplified when you put them on? (e.g., the sound of your children's laughter, the fridge full of food, the paycheck coming

9 *Ṣaḥīḥ al-Bukhārī*, no. 6075; *Ṣaḥīḥ Muslim*, no. 1048.

from work, etc.). Sometimes a simple visualization exercise like this can, quite literally, switch the lens through which you perceive things. By building awareness and making a conscious choice to change the aspects of your day-to-day life that you focus on, you'll find that your thoughts become much healthier.

After experiencing trauma, magnification of the bad and minimization of the good can become even more prominent. Fear can often be at the root of this. This fear could be a fear of failure, a fear of getting hurt again, a fear of rejection, or a fear of disappointment. You may struggle with allowing yourself to hope and instead focus on the difficulties in your life rather than the good to protect yourself from being surprised by setbacks that arise.

Allowing our fears to dictate how we live our lives is a recipe for sadness and a lack of fulfilment. When our decisions are based on fear, we struggle to consider things rationally because we are thinking with the part of ourselves that is afraid rather than our entire self.

A certain degree of fear is natural; however, when it becomes a barrier toward living a happy and fulfilling life, it needs to be addressed. Allah ﷻ reassures us,

> ***Indeed, those who have believed [in Prophet Muhammad] and those [before Him] who were Jews or Sabians or Christians—those [among them] who believed in Allah and the Last Day and did righteousness—no fear will there be concerning them, nor will they grieve.***[10]

---

10 Qur'an 5:69.

Part of our fears stem from doubts about ourselves but, beneath the surface, there may also be doubts about Allah ﷻ and His plans for us. Here we see that faith can be an antidote to fear. Trust in Allah ﷻ and take a leap of faith. Rather than minimizing your capabilities and the good in your life, rely on the fact that Allah ﷻ is the Most Capable and that He has given you what you need to get through this.

Shift your focus: big picture vs. pixel

One skill that can help us to cope and grow during difficult experiences is one that also overcomes the magnification/minimization thought process. Cultivating the ability to look at the whole picture through a lens of gratitude versus focusing on one pixel allows us to interpret our struggles as one facet of our lives, rather than allowing struggles to define our lives.

Imagine taking a picture of your face and then zooming in deeper and deeper. At first, you begin to see more details—every imperfection is emphasized until you can no longer see the big picture, only the flaws. As you zoom closer and closer, the picture becomes distorted and eventually, you can't recognize what the original photograph was. This is what happens when we magnify negatives and minimize positives in our lives.

Try out this activity:

Pixel	Big picture
What part of your life is your primary focus right now?	What other parts of your life can you take into consideration? What is going right?
I lost my job and now I have no idea how I will support my family.	Losing my job has been painful, but just because one thing in my life isn't going well does not mean that everything isn't going well. I have a skill set that will allow me to find a new job. I know Allah ﷻ will provide us with *rizq*. This is a way of allowing me to turn to Allah ﷻ. While I search for a job, I have the opportunity to attend prayers at the *masjid* and attend classes to learn a little more about Islam. *Alhamdulillah* my family and I are healthy, we have a roof over our heads, food in our fridge, and a means of transportation. My brother has offered to help me financially if it takes me a little longer than anticipated to find a job.

A hidden blessing: growth

Spirituality is a component that has been highly correlated with something called post-traumatic growth.[11] Post-traumatic growth is a positive change that occurs as a result of a major life crisis or traumatic event. It occurs when a person adapts to very difficult circumstances that would normally result in high levels of psychological distress.[12] Post-traumatic growth is not a direct result of trauma; rather, it comes about as a result of how a person responds to their new reality and whether they allow themselves to be positively changed by life's challenges.

Ibn al-Qayyim al-Jawziyya described post-traumatic growth when he said:

> *His Wisdom (Glorified be He) determined that happiness, pleasure, and comfort are not reached except by the bridge of difficulty and fatigue, and they are not accessed except through the gates of hardship, patience, and enduring difficulties.*
>
> *What great disparity exists between the joy of someone He relieved after affliction, and enriched after poverty, and guided after being astray, and collected his heart after its dispersal, and the joy of someone who did not taste those bitter pains.*[13]

What is this bridge of turmoil leading you toward? Your joy is on the other side, waiting for you to find it as you journey through this struggle.

---

11 O'Rourke, Tallman, and Altmaier, "Measuring Post-Traumatic Changes."

12 Tedeshi and Calhoun, "Posttraumatic Growth."

13 Ibn al-Qayyim al-Jawzīyah, *Shifā' al-'Alīl*, 448–49.

Post-traumatic growth cannot occur without pain and turmoil. It is actually *through* suffering that growth can happen. Sometimes the bad things that happen in our lives guide us toward the path of the best thing that could possibly happen to us.

Researchers have found that post-traumatic growth can be measured through positive responses in five areas:[14]

- Appreciation of life
- Relationships with others
- New possibilities in life
- Personal strength
- Spiritual change

There are so many examples of post-traumatic growth in our history. One is that of the Prophet Muhammad ﷺ. His uncle, Abu Talib, and his wife, Khadijah, died within days of one another. After this loss of his strongest supporters, circumstances became more difficult for the Muslims in Makkah, causing the Prophet Muhammad ﷺ to look for another, more welcoming community for his people. He ventured to Ta'if, hoping it would be a place where Muslims could live in peace. However, he was turned away and pelted with stones. When the Angel Jibril stated that Allah ﷻ would send the Angel of the Mountains to avenge the Prophet ﷺ, he said,

> ***No, rather I hope that Allah will bring from their descendants people who will worship Allah alone without associating partners with Him.***[15]

14 Tedeschi and Calhoun, "Posttraumatic Growth Inventory."

15 *Ṣaḥīḥ al-Bukhārī*, no. 3059; *Ṣaḥīḥ Muslim*, no. 1759.

Consider how the Prophet Muhammad ﷺ responded to loss and devastation. With the option to avenge what had been done to him, he instead used this opportunity to hope for better possibilities for himself as well as for the people who had hurt him. This illustration of post-traumatic growth shows us the possibility of gaining greater emotional and mental strength as well as closeness to Allah ﷻ through our struggles.

Post-traumatic growth occurs when we make our struggles a part of our life story without them controlling us or defining us. We cannot control what befalls us, but how we deal with our struggles can make the difference between growth and decline. Here are some ways to encourage growth as we face difficult experiences:

- **Trust:** Trust in Allah that He is truly the Best of Planners.
- **Courage:** Have the courage to put forth effort to change things within your control.
- **Confidence:** Use strength-based words to describe yourself and your capabilities and understand that you are capable of handling whatever comes your way.
- **Identity:** Understand that you are defined by much more than your struggles.
- **Process:** Accept emotions and allow yourself to feel them rather than avoid them.
- **Acceptance:** Accept the situation and realize that despite being unable to control circumstances, you can control how you choose to respond to them.

The incredible thing about post-traumatic growth is the fact that, without an intensely difficult experience, you may never have had the opportunity to become your best self. Sometimes tragedy is what propels a person to live their best life and to bring out their best qualities.

It may be strange to think that something so painful is what you needed in order to become your best self but Allah ﷻ sends us what we need, despite it being packaged in a form we don't want. As Asmaa Hussein says in her powerful book, *A Temporary Gift: Reflections on Love, Loss, and Healing*:

> *The beauty of a gift has less to do with what's actually given, and more to do with the relationship between the gifter and the receiver.*
>
> *Prophet Muhammad ﷺ said, "Give gifts to one another and you will love each other." So it's not about gifts, really. It's about love. When you love someone, you want to show it—and one way to do that is through gifts.*
>
> *Sometimes I think about the endless gifts that Allah ﷻ gives us. We tend to think of the beautiful, happy things in our lives as 'gifts,' and the difficult, painful things as 'tests.'*
>
> *And so they may be! But what if we recalibrated our hearts a little and convinced them to believe that everything is a gift. Everything. The terribly painful to the unbelievably blissful.*

I know it's hard, but gifting is about fostering love, right? It's about strengthening bonds and bringing hearts together.

Every happy thing you're given is a chance to be grateful to Allah. Every difficulty you're given is a chance to be patient and seek help and comfort from Him.

Everything you're given is either about fostering gratitude or patience—both of which are things that Allah loves and both of which strengthen your connection with Him.

So yes, everything from Allah must be a gift because it's an opportunity to do better and be better.

Our entire existence is about worshiping Allah. All that comes our way is calling us to this one, true purpose.

He is Allah, Al-Wahhab. The Giver of gifts.[16]

Spiritual inspiration for reflection

Ash-Sha'bi reported: Shuraih (*radi Allahu anhu*) said:

> *Verily, if I am afflicted with a calamity, then I praise Allah four times. I praise Him that it was not worse than it was. I praise Him when He provides me patience to bear it. I praise Him when He guides me to supplicate appropriately and hoping for reward, and I praise Him for not making it a calamity in my religion.*[17]

---

16 Hussein, *Temporary Gift*.

17 *Siyar A'lām al-nubalā*, 4/105.

Ibn Mas'ud (*radi Allahu anhu*) said:

> *A person may hope for some matter of trade or position of authority, until he is close to attaining it. Thereupon Allah looks at him from above the seven heavens and says to His angels: "Divert it from him, for if he attains it, he will enter into the Hellfire." Thus, Allah diverts it from him and the slave of Allah remains pessimistic, saying "So-and-so preceded me to it, So-and-so outwitted me," when in fact it is a favour from Allah.*[18]

Practical exercises

A. Conquering self-defeating thoughts with self-endorsing thoughts

Step 1: Break down the self-defeating thoughts in order to address them one by one.

Step 2: Identify where you are minimizing the good and where you are maximizing the bad.

Step 3: Replace self-defeating thoughts with ones that are self-endorsing by objectively identifying accomplishments and positive qualities to counteract each of the negative thoughts.

Step 4: Turn this into gratitude to Allah ﷻ for giving you the ability to accomplish these things, no matter how trivial they may seem.

18 Ibn Rajab, *Jāmi 'al-' Ulūm wa al-Ḥikam*.

Self-defeating thought	
Identify minimization/ magnification	
Self-endorsing thought: identify accomplishments	
Gratitude to Allah جل جلاله	

Conquering relationship-ruining thoughts with relationship-enriching thoughts

Step 1: Break down the negative thoughts in order to address them one by one.

Step 2: Identify where you are minimizing the good and where you are maximizing the bad.

Step 3: Replace negative thoughts with ones that are healthier by objectively identifying the positive things this person brings into your life to counteract each of the negative thoughts.

Step 4: Turn this into gratitude to Allah ﷻ, no matter how trivial the positives may seem.

Relationship ruining thought	
Identify minimization/ magnification	
Relationship enriching thought: identify the positives	
Gratitude to Allah ﷻ	

B. Cultivating post-traumatic growth

Trust: Trust in Allah ﷻ that He is truly the Best of Planners.

Has anything happened in the past that you imagined was detrimental to your life but ended up turning out for the best? When has Allah ﷻ shown you that His plan for you is better than the plan you imagined for yourself?

Courage: Having the courage to put forth effort to change things within your control.

What is within your control at this moment? What can you do to address the factors in your control in the best way possible?

Confidence: Use strength-based words to describe yourself and your capabilities and understand that you are capable of handling whatever comes your way.

What qualities do you possess that will help you through this struggle?

Identity: Understanding that you are defined by much more than your struggles.

Who are you as a person? What is at the core of your identity? What are the different facets that make you who you are?

Process: Accepting emotions and allowing yourself to feel them rather than avoid them.

How are you feeling right at this moment? Write it all out and allow them to come to the surface rather than keeping them at bay.

Acceptance: Accept the situation. What do you need to accept about your life at this moment in order to move forward?

C. Identifying signs of post-traumatic growth

Appreciation of life: Is there anything in your life that you appreciate more now than before the trauma you experienced?

Relationships with others: Have any of your relationships improved or have you made new relationships since your trauma?

New possibilities in life: Do you see opportunities and possibilities in your life differently than you did before?

Personal strength: Do you feel more capable of handling situations that come your way? Do you find that life's small annoyances do not seem as big after your trauma? Do you feel mentally and emotionally stronger?

Spiritual change: Do you feel a deeper connection with Allah ﷻ since your trauma?

D. Cultivating gratitude: pixel vs. big-picture activity

Think about the thing you are struggling with most right now. Now click the "zoom-out" button in your mind and gradually start to see the other facets of the big picture of your life.

Pixel	Big picture
What part of your life is your primary focus right now?	What other parts of your life can you take into consideration? What is going right?

Case study revisited

Salwa was dealing with a lot after her cancer diagnosis. It was hard to accept the fact that this was her new reality, and this became even more difficult once treatment began. As she continued reliving the day she received the news, she realized that she viewed her cancer as the end of her life and responded accordingly. Her self-defeating thoughts took over and she found herself saying:

I can't do anything with my life anymore.

Nothing will ever be the same.

Everything is falling apart.

There's nothing good in my life.

When Salwa realized that she could no longer get out of bed in the morning even on days when she didn't feel nauseous or weak from the chemotherapy, she talked to a friend who pointed out that she seemed to be afraid to participate in life again. Salwa realized the truth in this and realized how afraid she was to allow herself to see the joy in life when she remembered how suddenly her life was transformed with her cancer diagnosis.

Salwa realized that she had been magnifying all of the intense hardships in her life and minimizing her capabilities and the good she still had that cancer had no power to take away. She began working to conquer her self-defeating thoughts and replacing them with self-endorsing ones and noticed that her emotions and behaviours also began to change.

When she woke up without nausea, she was able to get out of bed and start her day with a smile. Instead of thinking, "Nothing will ever be the same," Salwa began to tell herself, "There are some things in my life that have changed and that's hard but, in this moment, it feels really good to wake up without feeling nauseous. There are many things in my life that are still here—my kids, my husband, my home. I'm grateful for them."

As she worked on her self-defeating thoughts, Salwa learned about posttraumatic growth and strove to:

- *Accept that cancer was now a part of her reality.*
- *Trust that her cancer was part of Allah's ﷻ plan to elevate her status with Him and emphasize her inner strength.*
- *Have the courage to strengthen her bond with her children since she now realized the finality and unpredictability of life.*
- *Let small annoyances slide since they didn't seem to matter as much in the big picture anymore.*
- *Have confidence in her ability to push through any challenges that came her way.*

- *Identify herself through all of the facets of her identity as a Muslim, mother, wife, employee, and survivor.*

- *Allowing herself to process her experience by feeling the waves of emotions that would come and go throughout her battle with cancer.*

Salwa also worked on the "Cultivating Gratitude: Pixel vs. Big Picture" activity and realized how much she had magnified the role cancer played in her life while minimizing all of the other blessings she experienced. When looking at the big picture, she discovered that on most days, she could find more blessings in her life than hardships and that some of these blessings actually developed from her cancer. She made new friends who were cancer survivors, and these became lasting relationships despite having always thought she was "too old" to make any new, strong friendships. Salwa and her family developed family traditions to ensure they made more time for one another, which allowed them to feel closer. Salwa rediscovered her love of listening to the Qur'an, particularly when she was at the hospital for chemo treatments. Friends came by with food often and the local masjid created a GoFundMe account to raise money to make up for Salwa's inability to work during her recovery. As she listed all of these blessings, Salwa realized that magnifying the hardships in her life had prevented her from seeing all of the good in it.

Chapter 7
"It's All My Fault"
Quieting and Healing Your Inner Critic

Out of suffering have emerged the strongest souls; the most massive characters are seared with scars.

EDWIN HUBBELL CHAPIN

GILBERT, *DICTIONARY OF BURNING WORDS*

Case study

Halima was ecstatic when she found out she was pregnant with her first child. She had wanted a baby as long as she could remember and couldn't wait to meet her unborn son. She would daydream about him being a leader of the believers and wondered if he would memorize the Qur'an or help the ummah *in amazing ways. Immediately after she gave birth, her baby unexpectedly had to be rushed for emergency heart surgery. While still recovering at the hospital NICU, a doctor came by to tell Halima that all the test results had come back and showed that her son had a rare genetic disorder. The syndrome was not curable and although doctors didn't know her baby's prognosis yet, it was likely that her child would have severe physical, mental, and psychiatric issues for the rest of his life. Her son was going to have special needs, would very likely have to go to a special school, and would probably need extra care even as an adult. Halima was completely devastated. This is not what she imagined for her child at all. How could this have happened? There were no genetic disorders in her or her husband's family, and her pregnancy had been uneventful.*

Halima kept asking herself if this was her fault until she started to believe it. She began to think she must have done something wrong during her pregnancy. Perhaps it was something she ate or medicine she might have taken.

As the weeks passed by and her baby grew, she also started to blame herself if anything didn't go as planned with him. If he didn't eat enough, had the sniffles, or was crying more than usual, she would blame herself for not being a good mother. She agonized over her child's health and wondered if on the Day of Judgement she might be held accountable for causing her child unnecessary pain. Halima fell into a depression making it very hard for her to take care of her baby. Every morning Halima would wake up with a massive invisible weight on her chest and think, ***"Everything is my fault."***

What is happening to me?

Unexpected events can knock the wind out of us. When we build up expectations of ourselves, people around us, or things to come, a part of us begins to live in our future dreams. Yearning for what is coming and fantasizing about what lies ahead helps us get through our mundane lives. These dreams inspire us and motivate us to be better versions of ourselves, with our families, and even with the world. When our expectations don't develop or materialize, all those intense feelings of hope and longing feel like they are crashing down all around us. Hope is one of the most powerful emotions a human being can have and when snatched away, its loss can be a very painful and traumatic experience. For the person already living with a particular fantasy in their mind, the jolt back to reality can feel like a part of their world has been ripped away from them

Dreams that don't turn out as expected might include:

A job you worked very hard to get, maybe even took years and years to get promoted to, doesn't pan out.

A marriage you had very high hopes for, and perhaps waited for all your childhood and young adult life, ends in divorce.

A baby or child who you envisioned would mature a certain way develops an illness or condition that changes the trajectory of your family's life.

Understanding your thoughts and emotions

When something major happens that impacts our lives in unexpected ways, one of the first things our brain does is ask two questions:

1. ***What just happened?***

2. ***Why did this happen?***

We are wired for survival purposes to ask "why" when something bad happens. This protects us from making the same mistake twice. It's also our brain's way of making sense of unexpected events. If unexpected things happened to us all the time, we would not be able to cope with day-to-day life. For example, if you thought you could get into a car accident randomly at any given time, you would probably not drive. However, if you attribute car accidents to faulty car parts or bad driving, you are more likely to continue driving because you know that if you monitor these causes, your risk of an accident will decrease dramatically. This is why when we are ill and go to the doctor the first thing we want to know is, "Why is this happening to me?" And this is why when something bad happens, our first instinct is to ask, "Who or what caused this?"

When unexpected events occur, we go through an appraisal process in which we review all variables that led to what happened, including our own actions.

Could this have been prevented?

Maybe I caused my cancer with unhealthy eating habits.

Was this my fault?

Perhaps my child has autism because I painted her nursery while pregnant.

Was I negligent?

Maybe if I had double-checked everyone's seat belt, then my nephew would have survived the car crash.

Taking responsibility for one's actions (accountability) is one of the most important attributes a person can have. It's integral to understanding the law of cause-and-effect, being able to reflect on one's mistakes, and accepting responsibility when things go wrong. A healthy individual will engage in this skill to maintain wellness, redress wrongs, and prevent undesirable things happening in the future. Holding oneself accountable is a healthy way of thinking and is different from **self-blame.** Self-blame and self-criticism involve accepting fault with the main purpose of making oneself feel bad or punishing oneself.[1]

---

1 Burns, *Feeling Good*.

Accountability	Self-blame
Acknowledges mistakes to fix them.	Acknowledges mistakes to pin the blame on oneself.
Sees oneself as resilient and able to bounce back from adversity.	Sees oneself as having caused irreparable damage.
Uses difficulty or trial to make oneself and surroundings better.	Uses difficulty or trial to punish oneself or validate bad qualities about oneself.

Where does self-blame come from?

Early in childhood, children are very egocentric which means they feel everything revolves around themselves, and it's difficult for them to see perspectives different from their own. Egocentrism never goes away completely but is more common during some parts of the lifespan than others.[2] As children mature, they begin to understand that not everything that happens is for them, because of them, or about them. It is not unusual for a 5-year-old whose parents are experiencing a separation to think that his parents are getting a divorce because of him, whereas a 15-year-old can understand that his parents are getting a divorce for many reasons that have nothing to do with him.

Egocentrism can be affected by many things including parental affection and rejection.[3] If a child does not successfully navigate through egocentrism because of environmental factors (bad parenting, bullying, trauma, etc.), he or she may have more difficulty with unsubstantiated guilt or self-blame than the average person when he or she gets older. Lack of development in this area may lead a person to feel guilty for things not within their power, take blame for things that are not their fault, and even take blame for other people's mistakes.

Children who come from families with high conflict and trauma often feel responsible for circumstances that have nothing to do with them. Lack of appropriate boundaries in families can also lead to unnecessary feelings of guilt. In a healthy family, members

---

2 Riva et al., "Emotional Egocentricity Bias."

3 Riley, Adams, and Nielsen, "Adolescent Egocentrism."

are interdependent, meaning they have autonomous identities, but they rely on each other and function better when connected with each other. If family members are enmeshed (overly reliant on each other) or have weak boundaries between them, there can be high risk for emotional dependency and confusion about accountability. Some examples may include:

The oldest sibling gets punished for something their younger sibling did just because they are the older sibling.

A young child gets blamed for causing a fight between her parents when the parents should have enough insight, discipline, and self-control to work through their conflict.

A young girl tells her mother she was molested by a family member and, instead of taking action against the perpetrator, the mother blames her daughter.

Many people who suffer from self-blame can trace that critical voice in their head back to a particular parent or authority figure (like a teacher or caregiver) who may have meant well in teaching the concept of accountability but did it in the wrong way. For example, if you did poorly on an exam, they might have said to you:

"You didn't do well because you are lazy and didn't study," instead of ***"Why do you think you got a poor grade? Let's look into what you can do differently next time."***

Another example might be:

"Nobody likes you because you cry all the time," instead of ***"Sometimes it looks like you might have a hard time managing your emotions; maybe we can work on that together."***

Or lastly:

"Stop eating so much junk, if you are fat now it's going to be even harder to change when you are older," instead of, ***"I think we need to replace all the junk food in the house with delicious fruits and vegetables so we can all be healthy together."***

In all the examples above, the first statements are designed to make a person feel bad in order to motivate them to change, whereas the second statements offer feedback for the purpose of growth. Both statements aim at changing behaviour, but the first uses emotional pain as a motivator instead of fostering intrinsic motivation (wanting to do something because you actually want to do it vs. avoiding some kind of punishment). When children, who are very impressionable, hear negative statements like the ones above repeatedly, they can begin to internalize their parent's critical voice. This critical voice can become part of their internal script for how they tend to talk to themselves when they grow older.

Changing your mind, body, and heart

If self-blame appears to be a recurring theme in your life, or perhaps emerged after a recent major change, consider reflecting back on your childhood to see where this thought process might have developed. Take time to contemplate:

> ***When you made mistakes as a child (which we all do), how did family members treat you? Were authority figures supportive or did they reprimand you?***
>
> ***Did anyone call you names or put you down?***
>
> ***If something bad happened in your family, to whom or what did family members attribute the cause?***
>
> ***When your parents did something wrong, did they beat themselves up over it? Did they blame each other? Did they blame you?***

While negative self-talk often develops in response to early experiences, it is also a common technique of Shaytaan. Shaytaan uses self-blame to demoralize people and push them to the brink of questioning the *qadar* of Allah ﷻ. While it's very normal to ask why certain things happened, Shaytaan sometimes leads us to forget that some things in life are destined to happen and that no amount of preparation can deter the inevitable. Some events happen because of things we did, and sometimes things happen because they are part of a bigger picture that we may not fully understand.

An excellent way of internalizing the concept that hardships can be a part of the bigger picture is reflecting on the prophets (peace be on them all), who are the best of mankind, and their ongoing struggles with poverty, death, assault, imprisonment, rejection, etc. Prophet Muhammad ﷺ faced many difficulties including being orphaned, war, extreme hunger, physical violence, emotional abuse, and persecution. Prophet Yusuf was thrown by his brothers into a well to die, became a slave, and went to prison. Yet we never blame them or attribute these misfortunes to their sins. These were all events that had a purpose in the lives of the prophets as well as the Muslims who came after them.

Your answers to the questions above might help you discover where some of your unhealthy thought patterns might have come from. Once you have identified where they originated, you can begin to gently repair that way of thinking by inserting healthier messages about yourself.

It might feel unnatural at first, but over time you can re-write the negative script in your head with a more positive one. Every time you think in your mind or feel in your body that you are responsible for something that you are not, try the following:

Sit down in a quiet and comfortable space alone. Keep your eyes closed.

Identify where in your body you feel tension when you are engaging in self-blame.

Begin deep breathing (breathe in for 3 seconds, hold it for 2 seconds, and then exhale for 6 seconds).

Gently visualize coming face-to-face with one self-blaming thought. Let the thought come to you in the form of a picture or words. Take a moment to sit with that thought.

As you look at the thought try to examine it more closely. When did this thought first root itself in your mind? Where did the thought originate from?

Begin to challenge the thought with an opposite statement (***Examples:*** "This is not my fault," "There is a silver lining to every cloud," "If I could go back in time and change things, the outcome would still have been the same," "There is good in every decree of Allah even if I'm struggling to see it right now," etc.).

Imagine the thought's strength dissipating with your counterthoughts. Breathe. As you assert yourself, visualize the words or image fading until invisible. Take as much time as you need.

As you address the negative thought, allow the tension in your body to release as you exhale. For example, if you feel tightness in your neck, imagine your negative thought and the tension dissolve as you exhale the air out.

Another technique you can use if you have an internalized voice from someone in your past is to visualize the person and remember how those negative thoughts are from them and not you. In your mind, imagine your negative thoughts as real words you can hold in your hands. Take all those negative thoughts and put them in as a big a basket as you need. Visualize handing that basket of words back to that person and telling them you will not hold on to them anymore. Then create distance in your mind from that person by walking away. If you catch yourself in the future using those negative words, repeat the exercise.

To help reinforce these concepts on paper, you can write down your thoughts in an Unhealthy Thought Dump and Repair Activity. Fold a piece of paper in half vertically. At the end of the day reflect and write down all the unhealthy negative thoughts that passed through your mind on the left-hand side. On the righthand side, directly next to the unhealthy thoughts, write down healthier versions of those same thoughts.

Self-blame thought	Reframed thought
I'm always late.	I need to work on leaving the house 15 minutes earlier in order to get to things on time.
I'm such a jerk to my family.	When I'm stressed I can be snappy. I would like to read up on stress management to help me with my agitation.
My marriage is in shambles because I do everything wrong.	My wife and I need to work on our marriage. We both need to work on communication and being good to one another.

Research indicates that expressive therapies, including art therapy, can be very healing for those who have experienced certain types of trauma.[4] If you are artistically inclined, consider using art as a medium to express your hurt, sadness, anger, and frustration in healthy ways. Transformative art, or artistic activity aimed at productively reconstructing thoughts and feelings, can be especially therapeutic.[5]

Get a large piece of paper and a crayon, marker, or paint colour that accurately expresses how you feel. The colour red is commonly associated with trauma, but you can use whatever colour you feel best captures what you are feeling.

Write down all your self-blaming thoughts. Write as messily, creatively, or neatly as you would like—there is no wrong way to do this.

Then pick another colour that you associate with healing- perhaps a colour that might represent restoration or transformation. Scribble, colour, or paint over those negative feelings.

Address your frustration and pain by visually and artistically obliterating all your negative thoughts with this second colour. Let this new colour take over the images and feelings of pain from before. Add positive thoughts or images if you would like.

Transform your art into something that feels beautiful to you. Add additional colours or images to convert what was once a paper with difficult feelings to something that feels soothing or invigorating.

Decide what you want to do with the art. You can keep it somewhere safe or discard it if that feels more cathartic for you.

---

4 Li, "Treating Complex Trauma with Art Therapy."

5 Preminger, "Transformative Art."

Unique circumstances of complex trauma

Self-blame can happen with everyday stressors and minor traumas, but self-blame associated with complex trauma (long-term and/or ongoing trauma) warrants special attention. One of these circumstances, as illustrated in the case study, is the birth of a child with lifelong disabilities. Parents of children who have special needs can face a unique type of trauma. Many of these parents feel, although they know it is not logical, that they could have prevented what happened or that they are somehow to blame for their child's hardships. Some also feel a great sense of loss. We now turn to how overcoming trauma and grief may be slightly different for this population.

Stages of grief

When someone experiences a loss, they are typically expected to go through the stages of grief, which are: denial, anger, bargaining, depression, and acceptance.[6] These stages are not always linear but typically involve the following reactions.

Denial: "This is a mistake. This can't be happening." In this stage, the person may be in shock or feel numb. The loss or trauma may feel like it hasn't quite registered yet.

Anger: "Why did this happen to me?" "Whoever did this will pay." Anger can be projected at oneself, others, or sometimes even Allah ﷻ.

6 Kübler-Ross and Kessler, *Life Lessons*.

For parents of children who have special needs, many times this anger is pushed inward at oneself and turns into self-blame.

Bargaining: "Allah, if you fix this situation, I will fast Mondays and Thursdays for the rest of my life." "If I do such-and-such, maybe this can be reversed." This can be a person's last-ditch effort to try and fix things before starting to accept what happened.

Depression: "This is all my fault," "I'm never going to get over this." Before coming to full acceptance, it's not unusual to fall into a phase of depression. In this phase, there is a lot of sadness about the loss. For the parent of a child with special needs, this can be the loss of what is considered a "normal" lifestyle or the loss of what they envisioned for their child's future. It can also feel like a loss of independence as the child will grow into an adult who may need them indefinitely or a loss of time in that the parent will have to put more effort into taking care of the child than would be expected of other children.

Acceptance: "I'm still sad, but I've come to terms with what has happened." This doesn't mean that the person is okay with the loss but has accepted the reality of the situation. For the parent of a child with special needs, this involves looking beyond the diagnosis to really see one's child; it involves appreciating their child's differences and loving them for being exactly who they are and were meant to be.

Moving back and forth through the stages of grief is expected with regular trauma, but the whole process is generally viewed as one journey. The stages of grief related to having a child with special needs, however, often look cyclical because the trauma unfolds over a long period of time and is ongoing. The acceptance phase can be short-lived; every time a parent goes to the doctor and gets new information about how his or her child needs extra care may lead them back to earlier stages. For example, a child might be born with a genetic syndrome, then at age 3 is diagnosed with autism, and then at age 13 develops further complications. The new information doesn't necessarily trigger the original trauma—it can initiate a new trauma. Additionally, every time there is an important life event that is expected to happen and doesn't, the parent might find themselves going through the stages of grief from the beginning again.

Parents experiencing these struggles may simultaneously face both solace and difficulty in realizing that this cycle of grief might not end. It's difficult to accept that the struggles are long-term but knowing that the struggles are long-term also takes away from the jolting reality each time something new hits. When a parent expects to go through the cycle of grief only once, they may feel ashamed, guilty, or weak for "not getting over it." Fostering self-compassion and knowing that these feelings are expected to be ongoing can be a relief for some.

Coping with complex trauma and bereavement

Ongoing trauma is like being a traveller on a journey to a faraway destination. The trip is fatiguing and long; however, putting down one's luggage and resting is imperative to keep moving forward. The journey ahead will still be there tomorrow, and self-care is the only way to find the strength to keep going forward. Continuously walking on the journey with no rest will only lead to excruciating pain and exhaustion. Self-care doesn't consist of extravagant or expensive things, but simple activities to keep oneself physically and mentally healthy. If you feel that this analogy accurately captures your experience, consider making your own go-to list of self-care activities, like the one at the end of this chapter, to help maintain wellness long-term. It is recommended that we have self-care activities in four different spheres of our lives: intellectual, spiritual, emotional, and physical.[7]

Mindfulness is one self-care practice that can be useful in working with complex trauma. When there is pressure to figure out and cope with everything at once, slowing down and taking things as they come can reduce anxiety. You don't need to figure out what life will be like ten, five, or even one year from now. All that you need to know now is that you are trying the best you can today. When you do your best, Allah ﷻ will take care of everything else—there is no purpose or benefit to agonizing over a future you can neither predict nor control.

The practice of mindfulness involves learning to be fully present in day-to-day life through one's senses. You can be present by focusing on what's going on right now at this very moment. What do you see? What sounds do you hear? What do you feel with your skin? Perhaps your clothing or what you are resting on with your body. What does the temperature of the room feel like? You only have to figure out one thing at a time, so shift your attention to what's in front of you.

---

7 Covey, *7 Habits of Highly Effective People*.

Orienting yourself to the present can decrease anxiety, which focuses on the future, and depression, which usually focuses on the past.

In day-to-day life, mindfulness involves paying attention to the small things. It may be smelling your child's hair when you cuddle with them or savouring your food at dinner time. Mindfulness might involve enjoying nature as you walk around your neighbourhood or snuggling up with a warm blanket. Mindfulness can also be a way of connecting to Allah ﷻ by appreciating the faculties He has given you to experience His Creation. Bearing witness to the beauty of His Creation and the blessings around you can increase gratefulness.

Although being a parent of someone with special needs can be difficult, it is also tremendously rewarding. Some of the lows in the journey can be met with extreme highs of happiness, gratitude, and love for one's child. Many parents feel that it's an honour and privilege because Allah ﷻ directly chose them for the task, and this honour is not for the weak but the strong. Keeping perspective can help a tremendous amount, and one way of doing that involves connecting with other parents who have similar challenges. These days there are many support groups available, in one's local community as well as online.

Spiritual inspiration for reflection

It was narrated that Abu Hurairah said: The Messenger of Allah ﷺ said:

> *"The strong believer is better and more beloved to Allah than the weak believer, although both are good. Strive for that which will benefit you, seek the help of Allah, and do not feel helpless. If anything befalls you, do not say, 'If only I had done such and such;' rather say, '*Qaddara Allahu wa ma sha'a fa'ala *(Allah has decreed and whatever he wills, He does).' For (saying) 'If' opens (the door) to the deeds of Satan."* [8]

> *"No disaster strikes upon the earth or among yourselves except that it is in a register before We bring it into being—indeed that, for Allah, is easy."* [9]

Ubadah b. al Samit said to his son:

> *"Son! You will not taste the reality of faith until you know that what has come to you could not miss you and that what has missed you could not come to you. I heard the Messenger of Allah ﷺ say: 'The first thing Allah created was the pen.' He said to it: 'Write.' It asked: 'What should I write, my Lord?' He said: 'Write what was decreed about everything till the Last Hour comes.' Son! I heard*

---

8 *Sunan Ibn Mājah*, vol. 1, bk. 1, hadith 79.

9 Qur'an 57:22.

the Messenger of Allah ﷺ say: 'He who dies on something other than this does not belong to me.'" [10]

On the authority of Abu Abbas Abdullah bin Abbas (may Allah be pleased with him) who said:

> *One day I was behind the Prophet [riding on the same mount] and he said, "O young man, I shall teach you some words [of advice]: Be mindful of Allah and Allah will protect you. Be mindful of Allah and you will find Him in front of you. If you ask, then ask Allah [alone]; and if you seek help, then seek help from Allah [alone]. And know that if the nation were to gather together to benefit you with anything, they would not benefit you except with what Allah had already prescribed for you. And if they were to gather together to harm you with anything, they would not harm you except with what Allah had already prescribed against you. The pens have been lifted and the pages have dried."* [11]

---

10 *Sunan Abī Dāwūd,* no. 4700.

11 Al-Nawawī, *40 Hadith, ḥadīth* no. 19.

Practical exercises

A. Unhealthy thought dump and repair activity

Fold a piece of paper in half vertically. At the end of the day, reflect and write down all the unhealthy negative thoughts that passed through your mind on the left-hand side. On the right-hand side, directly next to the unhealthy thoughts, write down healthier versions of those same thoughts.

Self-blame thought	Reframed thought
I'm such a slob.	I'm very busy and would benefit from implementing organizational techniques. I will set aside 5 minutes in the morning, afternoon, and evening to plan, organize and stay on top of things.

B. The un-blame game

The absence of a clear cause for your trauma doesn't mean you are to blame. Write down all the reasons you assumed you were at fault or felt guilty about a recent difficulty in your life. The more reasons you can think of the better, even if the reasons sound silly.

1. Example: My son has autism because one day in my first trimester I had a migraine and took a Tylenol.

2. ______________________________

3. ______________________________

After writing the reasons why you feel bad, do a truth check and examine the accuracy of the above statements. Write down below, matching the number above, a fact that counters your irrational thought.

1. Example: The cause of autism is unknown at this time, but researchers believe it's a combination of genetic and environmental factors. Many women take Tylenol during pregnancy. Taking a pain reliever was not the cause of my son's autism.

2. ______________________________

3. ______________________________

If these truths or counter thoughts don't feel genuine initially, that is okay. Turn them into affirmations and repeat them daily until they become internalized.

C. Self-care

Self-care is important for everyone, but it is especially important for those who have experienced trauma, loss, or ongoing hardship. Many people assume that self-care is something that is indulgent, but this is a myth. Self-care activities are things you can do once a day or throughout the week that are healthy and help sustain or nourish you. While going to the spa and your favourite restaurant can be nice self-care activities every once in a while, they are not sustainable daily. Reasonable daily self-care activities can include a 10-minute walk outside, savouring a nice piece of fruit, reading, speaking with a trusted friend, or making *duaa* after *salah*. Self-care is ongoing and should nurture different aspects of your life. Below, write regular self-care activities that can keep you strong in the face of adversity.

Self-care for your body (physiological):

1. ______________________________

____

2. ______________________________

____

3. ______________________________

____

Self-care for your spirit or deen (spiritual):

1. ______________________________

____

2. ______________________________

____

3. ______________________________

____

Self-care for your mind (intellectual):

1. ______________________________

____

2. ______________________________

____

3. ______________________________

____

Self-care for your soul (emotional):

1. ______________________________

____

2. ______________________________

____

3. ______________________________

____

D. Master list of coping skills

Coping skills are activities that we can practice during times of stress. They help distract and can give temporary relief when feeling a lot of pressure. Although it's okay to have one or two favourite coping skills, it's better to have several. Below is a list of coping skills you can use when experiencing difficult feelings. Circle the ones that work for you and add as many more as you can.

Exercise

Talk to Allah about our frustrations

Bake

Play with silly putty or play-doh

Visit someone sick

Make a craft

Meet up with friends to play basketball or soccer

Write in your journal

Write a poem

Sing

Draw an abstract picture of your feelings

Listen to nature sounds

Practice deep breathing

Practice your affirmations

Do a random act of kindness

Hug a family member

Squeeze a stress ball

Take a short drive with the windows down

Read Qur'an

Pray a *sunnah* or *nawafil* prayer

Count to 100

Clean your room

Read positive quotes online

Eat a small, healthy snack

Do a puzzle

Take a 15-minute nap

Learn a new skill

Plank

Do jumping jacks

Try progressive muscle relaxation *(look up "progressive muscle*

Case study revisited

Halima got a routine call one day from her son's social worker. After holding so much sadness inside, she broke down on the phone and told her how she had been feeling. The social worker suggested that Halima finding out about her son's diagnosis may have been a traumatic experience for her. Halima had no idea that the feelings she was experiencing were "normal" for someone who was experiencing traumatic grief.

Halima realized that a lot of her grief came from unhealthy guilt about her son's condition. Halima's parents were very critical of her as a child and made her feel bad any time something didn't go as expected or planned. Over time, she became accustomed to thinking everything was her fault and when her son was born, it was easy for her to fall into that same thought pattern. To help break this cycle, Halima made sure to take 10 minutes every day to journal and do the Thought Dump and Repair Activity that her social worker recommended. Halima felt like writing was similar to combing her hair; if she went a day without brushing her hair, it would get knotted just the way consistently journaling helped detangle her thoughts.

Halima knew that the journey with her son was going to be long and decided that the best thing she could do was take life one day at a time. She became determined that she and her son were not going to be defined by his diagnosis. To help manage the ups and downs of their day-to-day life she joined online support groups for mothers who have children with special needs. She also made sure to create a self-care list which included reading, yoga at home, crocheting, and doing tahajjud *once a week. Halima's life was mostly dedicated to taking care of her child but setting time aside for mindfulness and self-care on a consistent basis made her feel like her life was still her own. Halima believed that by taking care of herself she could better take care of her son long-term.*

Chapter 8

"How Can I Ever Get Past This?"

Reclaiming Your Future After the Abuse Has Ended

You look at me and cry, everything hurts. I hold you and whisper, but everything can heal.

RUPI KAUR

MILK AND HONEY

Case study

TRIGGER WARNING

This section contains information about sexual assault, which may be triggering to survivors.

Muna came from a religious, traditional family. She grew up with a solid foundation of Islamic learning and practise. When Muna was 12 years old, her uncle came to live with the family from overseas. The touches started off subtly. At first, she wasn't sure if she was imagining things, so she didn't say anything. She tried to avoid her uncle as much as possible as she began to feel more and more uncomfortable. One day Muna got home and neither of her parents was there. She felt trapped and unable to do anything when her uncle touched her more than he ever had. When she tearfully told her mother what happened, her mother was in disbelief and said, "He couldn't have done that! He's a good man! How were you acting? Don't tell your father about this—he couldn't bear it." Muna was devastated and felt even more hurt after her mother's response. She thought, "I'm a dirty and worthless person. I'm a bad Muslim now. How can I ever get past this?"

What is happening to me?

After experiencing something traumatic, particularly traumas like abuse, sexual assault, physical violence, or even the threat of harm, it's hard to know how to react. You may be physically hurt, emotionally drained, and unsure of what to do next. After a boundary has been violated, you may feel helpless, particularly since so much feels outside of your control, including your physical safety.

The mix of emotions you may be experiencing after something so traumatic can make everything seem incredibly confusing. You may be scared, angry, and shocked. You may also find yourself feeling guilty despite this experience not being your fault. It is never okay for someone to hurt you, take advantage of you, or do anything that makes you feel uncomfortable or scared.

When we go through a traumatic experience, we may experience self-doubt and we may inadvertently start to identify ourselves and the rest of our lives through the lens of what we've endured. You may find yourself thinking:

> ***I've always been a loser, so it's no wonder I haven't been able to keep any friends.***
>
> ***I got laid off from my job; well, there's another example of how inadequate I am.***

My parents always told me no one would want to marry me; that explains why my marriage failed—because I've always been worthless and ugly.

If we imagine we deserve the pain we're enduring, it might hurt more but at least it makes the world predictable. Sometimes it can be scarier to deal with unpredictability, so we begin to base our identities on the negative events that have happened in our lives. We scan our lives and ourselves for evidence that we are failures, sinners, victims, worthless, or inadequate in some way. When you think negatively about yourself, your mind will inevitably find evidence to support your thoughts.

This negative self-perception can lead every day to begin with a cloud of distress over our heads as we live our lives based on the incorrect assumption that we are not good enough.

Understanding your thoughts and emotions

What is Labelling?

This negative thought pattern of basing our self-image on a negative trait or incident in our lives is called labelling. Labelling is a cognitive distortion in which we overgeneralize by taking one incident or characteristic of a person and applying it to the whole person. For example:

I can't believe I lost my car keys again. I'm such an idiot.

Why has my wife been so distant lately? I'm unlovable.

My husband is late again. He's such a jerk.

My son failed his math test. I don't spend enough time going over his homework. I'm a bad parent.

I was sexually assaulted. Now I'm permanently disgraced.

Rather than considering the situation or behaviour objectively, when we engage in labelling, we globally describe the whole person. This results in viewing ourselves, and others, through a label that is inaccurate, causing us to ignore any evidence that doesn't fit under the umbrella of the picture we've painted.

For example: If you have been passed over for a promotion, rather than focusing on the positive feedback your supervisor gave you last month, you label yourself a failure and an inadequate worker. By viewing yourself in this way, you lose motivation at work, which perpetuates these negative emotions and patterns and can become a self-fulfilling prophecy.

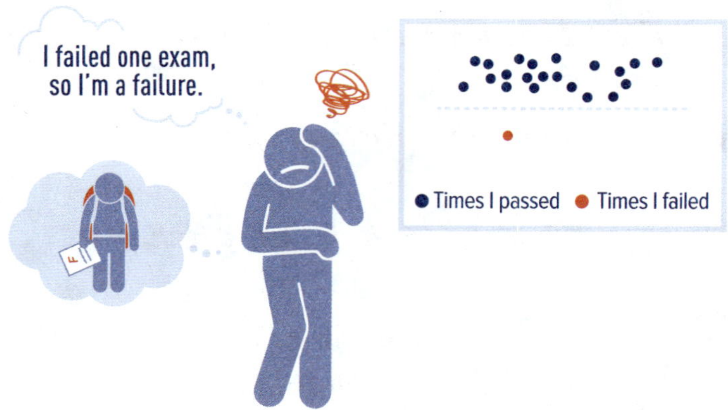

Making an overgeneralization about yourself or someone else based on one isolated data point, or just a few data points, is inherently problematic. Learning that you did not get a promotion would likely lead to feeling some disappointment, whereas labelling yourself a complete failure results in the disempowering feelings of despair and hopelessness. Thus, labelling yourself negatively will prevent you from working towards solutions to the problem since it fuels a belief that the problem is, fundamentally, you.

How are our identities impacted by labels?

The narrative and labels that run through our heads screaming that we are inadequate or that we are defined by our struggles can further advance a negative self-fulfilling prophecy. The "I ams" that we say to ourselves are an incredibly important factor in terms of how resilient we are during times of stress. This can be seen through labelling theory. Labelling theory is the theory of how our identities and behaviours are influenced by the way we describe ourselves.

Researchers Wright, Gronfein and Owens[1] found that stigmatization of mental illness labels resulted in social isolation and negative self-concepts in patients who had been discharged from a psychiatric hospital. The way these individuals labelled themselves resulted in them isolating themselves socially, which perpetuated a cycle of low self-esteem and feelings of rejection by others.

For example, someone who is suffering from depression may label themselves as a depressed person. When you begin each day with the perception that being depressed is the core of who you are, it will be difficult to engage in activities that are not in line with depression. Therefore, as a depressed person, you may stay in bed rather than go to work and ruminate on negative thoughts about yourself rather than focusing on your positive traits. The way we define ourselves can be incredibly powerful.

The impact of labelling on spirituality

The labels we create for ourselves can also impact us spiritually. We have all sinned, but should we constantly label ourselves as sinners? If you define yourself as a sinner, you lose hope in the mercy of Allah ﷻ, and this can lead you to further sins. If you label yourself a failure, when something goes wrong you think, "Of course Allah is sending me hardships as a punishment because I'm a sinner and beyond hope no matter how hard I try."

Instead, imagine thinking of yourself as a repenter because you sin but turn back to Allah ﷻ. With this label, you may think to yourself,

---

1 Wright, Gronfein, and Owens, "Deinstitutionalization, Social Rejection, and the Self-Esteem of Former Mental Patients."

"Allah is testing me with this trial as an opportunity to get closer to Him and as an indication of how strong I am to be able to handle this."

That shift in how you define yourself makes all the difference.

Happiness starts from the inside out, not the outside in. If, at the core, you believe yourself to be worthless, hopeless, inadequate, or a bad Muslim, external factors will be unable to change that. A person complimenting you for a job well done will not make you feel accomplished if you label yourself a failure. No matter how many pages of Qur'an you recite, you will never feel closer to Allah ﷻ if you label yourself a bad Muslim. No matter how happy your children are, you will never feel a sense of fulfilment in motherhood if you label yourself an inadequate mother. Even if you are loved deeply, you will be unable to accept it if you believe yourself to be undeserving of love—including the love of Allah ﷻ.

Learned helplessness after victimization

***Note**: In the following sections, steps to begin the recovery process after victimization are discussed. While the idea of re-labelling oneself as a survivor rather than a victim is mentioned below, it is important to note that not every victim of abuse survives. And those who do live through their trauma are faced with the arduous task of moving forward after the loss of a piece of themselves and the life for which they had hoped. When exploring the idea of shedding the victim label, it is important to remember that it was not your choice to become a victim. This was something forced upon you. Rather, it is intended as a step forward in reclaiming your power and redefining your life on your own terms. May Allah ﷻ grant you healing and peace on this journey. Your strength is immeasurable and something unfathomable to most.

After experiencing a traumatic incident, particularly at the hands of another person, feelings of helplessness and victimization can arise. After a boundary has been violated, knowing that you were helpless to stop this from occurring is a disturbing realization. It shakes your view of everything—including yourself. Even when you are no longer powerless, you may find yourself unable to let go of this feeling.

Furthermore, this feeling may lead you to label yourself as a victim and live your life through this lens. This is called learned helplessness. Learned helplessness is a concept that was developed by Martin Seligman and first seen in animals;[2] however, the same phenomenon occurs in people as well. Researchers discovered that when animals were repeatedly exposed to painful shocks that they could not avoid, they would eventually stop trying to escape. Even when the situation was changed and the animals were able to escape the shocks, they lacked the motivation to try and instead continued to passively accept the pain.

2 Maier and Seligman, "Learned Helplessness."

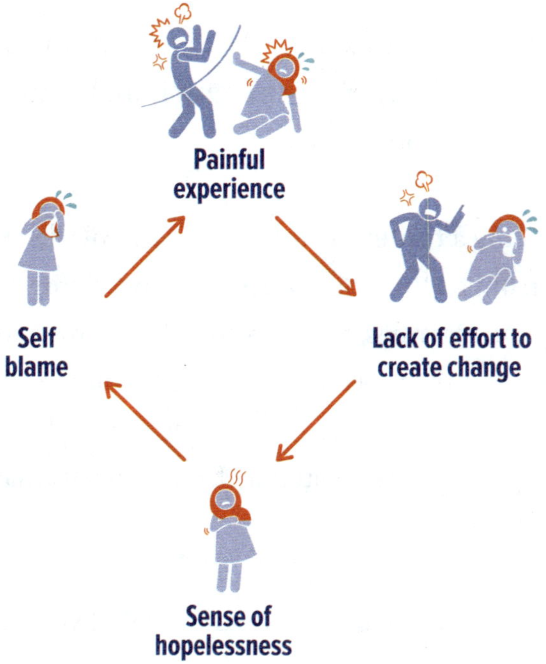

We find the same pattern in our own lives: we eventually stop trying to change things when we feel that control over a situation has been lost, even when the situation changes so that control might be taken back. There may have been circumstances in your life in which you felt completely powerless, and this may have contributed to the development of negative beliefs about your abilities, a tendency to take on blame when things go wrong, and/or a sense of hopelessness regarding the possibility of change.

If abuse, bullying, or any type of violation occurs repeatedly, you may begin to believe that there is no way out and that you are someone who is doomed to be a victim. The feeling of powerlessness to change your life is attached to the victim label. Reclaiming control of your life and its different facets is a hard journey but one that is possible. Just as we can "learn" helplessness, we can "unlearn" it as well. The road to agency and self-empowerment is there if you're willing to walk it.

Changing your mind, body, and heart

Unweaving the tapestry of our minds

Labelling can be deeply ingrained within us so it can take some effort to begin to release the grip of this cognitive distortion. The neurological network within our brain is like a blanket we have woven with multiple spools of wool.

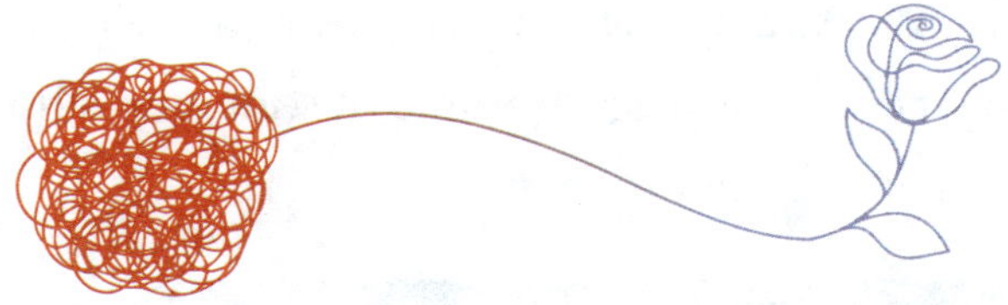

Imagine you've chosen to weave a tapestry—a picture of your life. Now imagine being asked to take the tapestry apart, thread by thread, in order to weave a new picture of your life. That is no easy feat! In the same way, retraining our brains to view our lives without the negative labels we have created can be a strenuous process, but it is definitely possible—and definitely worth the hard work.

If the thought, "This is just who I am. I've been through so much pain so how can I ever get past this?" comes to mind, consider this: Our brains are plastic, which means they can change throughout our lives.[3] It was once believed that the connections in our brains are fixed and unchangeable, making the idea of brain growth in adulthood an impossibility. However, research within the past 50 years has shown that substantial brain changes occur throughout our lives. Whenever something new is learned, our brain changes.[4] Therefore, no matter how ingrained our negative thoughts become—even the ways we view ourselves and our identities—we are capable of change.

Sense of inadequacy

Why is labelling so hard to "unweave" from our minds? Labelling creates and solidifies a sense of inadequacy. The fear at the surface may actually indicate a deeper sense of inadequacy if we explore it. Let's consider a commonplace example of someone who feels put down and criticized by her in-laws.

Suppose your mother-in-law is critical of something you do. Why would that be particularly upsetting to you?
Therapist

Because it means she does not think I'm good enough for her son.
Client

What would happen if she did not believe you are good enough for her son?
Therapist

3 Bennett et al., "Chemical and Anatomical Plasticity of Brain."
4 Rakic, "Neurogenesis in Adult Primate Neocortex."

I would be ashamed. It would mean that I am failing at the one thing I should be good at. I am failing at the one thing I have looked forward to being for so long: a wife.
Client

We know that your mother-in-law's opinion is not fact. But, to delve in a bit deeper: What would happen if you failed at being a good wife? What would that mean?
Therapist

My husband would divorce me, and it would mean I'm worthless.
Client

Here, we see that this individual ties people's opinions of her to whether she is a "good" or "bad" wife and that she ties her self-worth to the success of her marriage. She believes that something that is outside of her control (i.e., her mother-in-law's criticism), would mean she is a failure as a wife. She struggles to extricate her sense of self-worth from the approval of others and labels herself based on a measurement of the way others perceive her and on standards and expectations that are outside of her control.

While this might be self-defeating and unhealthy, it's important to realize that it feels real and logical to someone in these shoes. No matter how these labels are defined, they will never be realistic.

Labelling ourselves results in an inability to change because we imagine that we are beyond solutions.

In order to overcome labelling, we have to come to the conclusion that our lives are complex and constantly changing so our sense of self cannot be equated with any one thing we do or any one situation. Labelling a human being is overly simplistic. David Burns explains this by asking, "Would you think of yourself exclusively as an 'eater' just because you eat, or a 'breather' just because you breathe?[5] This is nonsense, but such nonsense becomes painful when you label yourself out of a sense of your own inadequacies."

Relinquishing the victim mindset: from victim to survivor

Why do I still feel like a victim?

Feelings of helplessness and powerlessness do not develop in a vacuum. Your experiences of feeling incapable in difficult circumstances can be factors that lead to labelling yourself as a victim. You can continue to struggle to let go of this label even when you are no longer being victimized. Although you may currently be safe, your brain and your body may struggle to realize this.

A traumatized brain maintains a mindset of impending harm. There is always a fear that something bad will happen again. These feelings of fear maintain the victim label and the threat patterns in our minds.

It is not your fault that this happened to you. And it is not your fault that these patterns have developed in your mind and that you're struggling to undo them. If you have been abused in any way, your human rights

5 Burns, Feeling Good.

have been violated. It is your right not to be hurt or harmed and that right was taken away from you. The Prophet Muhammad ﷺ said,

> ***Shall I not tell you what distinguishes the best of you from the worst of you? The best of you are those from whom goodness is expected and people are safe from their evil. The worst of you are those from whom goodness is not expected and people are not safe from their evil.***[6]

What can I do to see myself as a survivor rather than a victim?

Build awareness: What happened to you is not okay. Your mind continues to hold on to familiar patterns of fear even after the threat has passed; it is a compilation of your experiences and the ways these experiences have affected you.

There are so many aspects of your life that you did not choose—from your eye colour to your parents to the traumas you have experienced. Your job is not to blame yourself for what happened to you or what you are mentally, physically, spiritually, and emotionally struggling with right now. Your responsibility is to get to know the programs that are running in your brain that were developed because your past environment was threatening.

Building awareness is the first step in regaining control of your choices, actions, and responses to situations.

---

6 Jamiʿ al-Tirmidhi, no. 2263.

Acknowledge the struggle with compassion: There is often shame, anger, fear, disgust, and self-doubt associated with experiences of abuse. Acknowledge all of the different thoughts and emotions you are experiencing without judgement. There is nothing wrong with anything you may be feeling. "Naming" the emotion you are feeling helps to tame it; it reduces the hold it has on you and normalizes it.

Criticizing yourself for struggling or being hard on yourself because you expected yourself to have "gotten over it by now," will only hurt you more. Remind yourself that what happened to you was not okay, that pain is a normal human experience, and verbalize the intention: "I want to be helpful, not harmful to myself."

Focus on what you can control: Making a conscious choice to no longer give your struggles the power to define you is an empowering step forward. When it comes to shedding the victim label and viewing yourself as a survivor, focusing on the things you can control in different situations—even minuscule details—is key.

Begin by focusing on small steps you can take toward accomplishing something. This can be as simple as acknowledging the choices you make in preparing something to eat when you feel hungry.

When you feel stuck and as though you are unable to control any aspect of your life, ask yourself what you would tell a friend in your situation: What small aspect of your friend's situation can they change at this very moment? You likely wouldn't tell them to give up; you'd likely help them to walk through all of the different choices they have at their disposal. Treat yourself as you would treat this friend.

Regain control of your body: Survivors of abuse, particularly physical violations, struggle with an additional feeling of powerlessness—an encroachment on the sanctity of their own body. Reclaimed ownership of your body is an empowering step. It can be beneficial to engage in forms of physical activity that lead to a sense of regained body control. Exercise, including martial arts, running, and yoga can help you reconnect with your body in a powerful way to relieve feelings of helplessness as a sense of control over the body returns. Furthermore, recognizing the capabilities of your body, the way it functions, and what it gives you shifts your focus to your strengths, power, and sense of agency.

Remember the ultimate justice: Allah ﷻ says,

> *That is a nation which has passed on. It will have [the consequence of] what it earned, and you will have what you have earned. And you will not be asked about what they used to do.*[7]

You may be bearing the burden of your abuser's choices; however always remember that they will be asked by Allah ﷻ about every single choice, every single consequence of that choice, and every single ounce of pain you are currently experiencing. *"They will have what they earned."* On the Day of Judgement, you will not be asked about the faults and abuses of others. Focus on what is in your control today and know that the accountability of the soon-to-come tomorrow will be weighed by Allah ﷻ who has seen all you have suffered.

---

7 Qur'an 2:141.

Dismantling negative labels

Challenging the labels, you have developed over the years and through traumatic experiences can yield a huge change in the way you see yourself and interact with Allah ﷻ and others in your life. Here are some steps to consider when dismantling the negative labels, we assign to ourselves:

> ***What label do you use to describe yourself? (e.g., bad Muslim, loser, failure, etc.)***

Example: I really believe I'm a bad Muslim because of everything that's happened.

> ***What is your evidence that this label is accurate?***

Example: I know I'm a bad Muslim because I couldn't stop my uncle from touching me. Now I feel so dirty that I can't bring myself to pray, which proves I'm a bad Muslim.

> ***If someone asked you to describe the opposite label (e.g., "a good Muslim," "an intelligent person," "a winner," etc.), what would you say?***

Example: A good Muslim is someone who follows the rules of Islam all the time. It's someone who was never abused because a good Muslim wouldn't be punished that way.

Look back at your description and see if it includes words like always, never, should, or shouldn't. Is your definition attainable and realistic?

Example: My definition of a good Muslim necessitates perfection. I know that Allah ﷻ didn't create human beings to be perfect and that it's impossible for a person not to make a mistake. We are also not responsible for what others do. So, I cannot be responsible for someone else abusing me. Even the prophets experienced emotional, verbal, and physical abuse and they were the best Muslims.

Labels often hurt us and hold us back from growth rather than helping us to cope with pain. When you hear the label, you use to describe yourself, how do you feel?

Example: When I think of myself as a bad Muslim because of what happened to me, I hate myself.

How do you want to feel when you think back to that experience?

Example: I want to feel safe and reassured that it's not my fault and that I'm not dirty. I want to feel loved by Allah ﷻ and to feel sure that I didn't do anything wrong.

What needs to happen for you to feel like that?

Example: I need to feel safe, cared for, and loved. I need to focus on the feelings of warmth, care, and compassion I have for myself and on the feeling of knowing that I am honoured and loved by Allah ﷻ. I need to let myself feel sad and hurt about what happened to me and to understand how hard this was for me.

Can you hold those feelings in your mind, body, and heart? Experience it for a moment. How do you feel?

Example: I feel stronger. I know I'm safe and I know Allah ﷻ is always there to care for me. I feel soothed knowing that He ﷻ has given me the strength to survive this.

Self-compassion, warmth, and safety

When our minds are in "anxious mode," our thoughts and our physical sensations can create a loop that causes us to perpetually remember the worst times in our lives. At random times throughout your day, your thoughts may naturally seem to drift back to the pain you've experienced, plunging you back into feelings of fear, despair, self-criticism, and loneliness. When these thoughts make you think horrible things about yourself, it can be helpful to remember times when you felt the opposite.[8] Were there times in your life when you experienced a sense of safety? Times when you felt happy? Can you recall times when you experienced compassion and warmth from yourself or someone else?

---

8 Matos, Duarte, and Pinto-Gouveia, "Constructing a Self Protected against Shame."

To change the direction that your thoughts take when they lead you down the path of reliving the trauma you've experienced, try this exercise to change the ending of your story. This exercise includes components that have been shown to lead to reductions in depressive symptoms and self-criticism as well as to an increase in self-compassion.[9]

Change the ending of your story

Imagine seeing a child in front of you who is sitting all alone, crying into her arms. You can tell she's feeling lonely and hopeless. She's not sure what to do and feeling scared about whether she can get past these huge, difficult feelings. You feel the urge to comfort her. What do you say? What do you do? You may say something like, "I know you feel broken now, but it won't be like this forever." Or "You are a wonderful person and what happened to you was not okay." You may choose to take her by the hand and walk somewhere peaceful and beautiful together. You may choose to sit down next to her and wrap your arms around her.

Now, remember something that happened to you that you are struggling to get past. Can you give yourself or tell yourself what you needed at that moment? Just as you were able to show compassion for this child, can you say to yourself exactly what you said to her? Can you imagine the feeling of holding a hand, receiving a hug, or hearing words of reassurance? Picture what you need and allow yourself to imagine receiving that. Pay attention to how you feel emotionally and physically as you visualize this.

9 Falconer et al., "Embodying Self-Compassion."

Imagine your best possible future self

The "Imagined Self" technique is an exercise that can get us to start moving toward the life we want to live rather than remaining stuck in our current negative labels.[10] When you can picture the best possible version of yourself, it paves the way for negative labels to be replaced with positive ones. It is an opportunity to learn about yourself, restructure your priorities, and increase insight into the obstacles that may be preventing you from regaining control of your life. Research has also found that writing a description of your best possible future self for a few minutes each day for a few days in a row was associated with a significant immediate increase in positive mood and increased sense of well-being for 3 weeks after engaging in this exercise.[11]

Try it out for yourself by following the instructions in the following section.

The imagined self technique[12]

Imagine yourself in the future, after everything has gone as well as it possibly could have. You have worked hard and succeeded in accomplishing all of your life goals. Think of this as the realization of your life dreams and of your full potential. In all of these cases, you are identifying the best possible way that things might turn out in your life in order to help guide your decisions now. You may never have thought about yourself in this way before so it might feel strange but allow yourself a few moments to visualize this.

---

10 Sheldon and Lyubomirsky, "How to Increase and Sustain Positive Emotion."
11 King, "Health Benefits of Writing about Life Goals."
12 Sheldon and Lyubomirsky, "How to Increase and Sustain Positive Emotion."

As you do this, think about the small details that make your future self and your future life wonderful. Who is there with you? What are you struggling with now that you have achieved in the future? How did you get to this point—what did you need to do to achieve all of this? Immerse yourself in your future self. What feelings do you experience as you imagine this?

Spiritual inspiration for reflection

Consider the following *ayah* and when you label yourself negatively, think about how Allah ﷻ describes the honour of human beings:

> ***O you who have believed, let not a people ridicule [another] people; perhaps they may be better than them; nor let women ridicule [other] women; perhaps they may be better than them. And do not insult one another and do not call each other by [offensive] nicknames. Wretched is the name of disobedience after [one's] faith. And whoever does not repent—then it is those who are the wrongdoers.***[13]

This verse prohibits us from using negative labels in referring to others so we should also avoid labelling ourselves in disrespectful ways. Through this command, we see how Allah ﷻ honours us through ensuring that the words we use with ourselves and others build us up rather than tear us down.

13 Qur'an 49:11.

And We have certainly honoured the children of Adam and carried them on the land and sea and provided for them good things and preferred them over much of what We have created, with [definite] preference.[14]

Do you not see that Allah has made subject to you whatever is in the heavens and whatever is in the earth and amply bestowed upon you His favours, [both] apparent and unapparent? But of the people is he who disputes about Allah without knowledge or guidance or an enlightening Book [from Him].[15]

In these verses, Allah ﷻ tells us that He prefers us above so many other creations and He treats us accordingly.[16] He also reminds us of the blessings He bestows upon us. The amazing sky you see above you has been subjugated to give us light during the night and day and clouds to bring us water. The earth grants us sustenance through its rivers, trees, crops, and animals. When you label yourself negatively—as a "failure," as "worthless," or as "nothing," remember that Allah ﷻ is talking about you in these verses. Think about how He ﷻ sees you, rather than your negative view of yourself.

Abdullah ibn Umar reported: I saw the Messenger of Allah ﷺ circling the *Ka'bah* and saying,

How pure you are and how pure is your fragrance! How great you are and how great is your sanctity!

14 Qur'an 17:70.
15 Qur'an 31:20.
16 Ibn Kathīr, Tafsīr Ibn Kathīr.

By the One in whose hand is the soul of Muhammad, the sanctity of the believer is greater to Allah than your sanctity, in his wealth, his life, and to assume nothing of him but good.[17]

In this hadith, the Prophet ﷺ tells you that you are even more honourable to Allah ﷻ than the *Ka'bah*. You don't deserve the harsh words you call yourself. You deserve to be honoured.

And [mention] when We said to the angels, "Prostrate before Adam"; so, they prostrated, except for Iblees. *He refused and was arrogant and became of the disbelievers.*[18]

The Prophet ﷺ said:

Allah created Adam in His image, and he was sixty cubits tall. When He created him, He said, 'Go and greet that group of angels who are sitting and listen to how they greet you, for that will be your greeting and the greeting of your descendants.' So, he said, 'Al-salāmu 'alaykum *(peace be upon you),' and they said,* 'Al-salāmu 'alayka wa raḥmat Allah *(Peace be upon you and the mercy of Allah).' So, they added (the words)* 'wa rahmat *Allah.' Everyone who enters Paradise will be in the form of Adam, but mankind continued to grow shorter until now.*[19]

17 Sunan Ibn Mājah, no. 3932

18 Qur'an 2:34.

19 Sahih al-Bukhari, no. 6227; Saḥih Muslim, no. 2841.

When you read this *ayah* and *hadith*, remember that you are a descendant of Adam and that you, too, were created in the image of the Almighty Allah ﷻ. What greater honour could there be than to be from amongst creation who Allah ﷻ created in His image and to whom Allah ﷻ commanded the angels to prostrate? When you find yourself doubting your worth or allowing the inner critic to take over, remind yourself of the honour Allah ﷻ has bestowed upon you. If He deemed you worthy of such an honour, doesn't that say something pretty incredible about you?

Practical exercises

A. Dismantling negative labels

What label do you use to describe yourself?

Example: bad Muslim, loser, failure, etc.

____

____

____

What is your evidence that this label is accurate?

1. ______________________________

____

2. ______________________________

____

3. ______________________________

____

If someone asked you to describe the opposite label, what would you say?

Example: a good Muslim, an intelligent person, a winner, etc.

Look back at your description and see if it includes words like *always*, *never*, *should*, or *shouldn't*. Is your description attainable and realistic?

Labels often hurt us and hold us back from growth rather than helping us to cope with pain. As you hear the label you use to describe yourself when you think about a difficult past experience, how do you feel?

How do you want to feel when you think back to that experience?

What needs to happen for you to feel like that?

Can you hold those feelings in your mind, body, and heart? Experience it for a moment. How do you feel?

B. Memories of safety, warmth, and compassion

Our negative memories often stand out, leading us to relive them repeatedly.

Instead of fear, describe a time in your life when you experienced a sense of safety.

Instead of despair, describe a time when you felt happy.

Instead of criticism, describe a time when you experienced compassion from yourself or someone else.

Instead of loneliness, describe a time when you felt warmth from others.

C. Change the ending of your story

When a difficult memory comes up in which you remember feeling scared, hurt, or helpless, ask yourself: What did I need at that moment?

Example: This can be someone to protect you, words of reassurance and compassion, a hand to hold, etc.

Can you imagine giving this to yourself at that moment? Picture what you need and allow yourself to imagine receiving that. What would that have been like and how do you feel as you picture this?

D. Imagine your best possible future self

Imagine yourself in the future, after everything has gone as well as it possibly could have. You have worked hard and succeeded in accomplishing all of your life goals. Think of this as the realization of your life dreams and of your full potential. In all of these cases, you are identifying the best possible way that things might turn out in your life in order to help guide your decisions now. You may not have thought about yourself in this way before so it might feel strange but allow yourself a few moments to visualize this.

As you do this, think about the small details that make your future self and your future life wonderful.

Who is there with you?

What are you struggling with now that you are no longer struggling with in the future?

How did you get to this point—what did you need to do to achieve all of this?

Immerse yourself in your future self.

What feelings do you experience as you imagine this?

Case study revisited

Muna had endured a severely traumatic event involving inappropriate touch by a trusted family member. Her view of the incident and her perception of herself was further confused by her mother's negative and shaming reaction in response to what happened. Muna was devastated and began to wonder if there was something fundamentally wrong with her and how it would be possible to get past this.

Muna realized that she could do nothing to change what had happened and knew she would struggle with the aftermath of it for a long time. Although she did not have control over her uncle's choices or her mother's reaction, Muna realized that she could control the way she labelled herself.

Muna realized she had been labelling herself as a "bad Muslim," "worthless," and "dirty." She realized that the way she viewed herself was intensifying her negative emotions. She realized that, because of these labels, she considered the abuse she endured to be further evidence supporting the way she viewed herself. By working to develop a more compassionate and realistic image of herself and working toward differentiating who she was as a whole person from the experiences she endured, Muna's self-confidence increased, and she was able to take greater control of her life and her identity.

Muna did the "Dismantling Negative Labels" exercise and realized that she had been viewing herself strictly through a lens based on her struggles, rather than her strengths. She discovered that, due to labelling herself a "bad Muslim," she wondered if Allah ﷻ had sent her uncle as a punishment for something. Muna realized that her definition of a "good Muslim" was someone who doesn't go through any hardships since she thought struggles were a punishment from Allah ﷻ. When she was able to work on redefining this to understand that even the best of people (prophets) went through hardships and pain, she realized that what happened to her didn't mean that she was a bad Muslim. She realized that she didn't need to identify herself based on her traumatic experience and that labelling herself as "dirty" because of abuse perpetrated against her gave her uncle the power to define her life, which she definitely did not want. By separating the trauma from her perception of herself a person, Muna felt empowered and was able to begin the healing process.

As Muna developed a new vision of her identity, her mood improved, and she was able to speak with a therapist about the incident. Through therapy, she was able to process her trauma, talk to other family members about what had happened, and eventually reported her uncle for his crime.

Chapter 9

"Why is Everyone's Life Better Than Mine?"

Protecting Yourself from the Dangers of Comparison

Everyone has his own specific vocation or mission in life; everyone must carry out a concrete assignment that demands fulfilment. Therein he cannot be replaced, nor can his life be repeated. Thus, everyone's task is unique as is his specific opportunity to implement it.

VIKTOR E. FRANKL

MAN'S SEARCH FOR MEANING

Case study

Whenever Yaser went on Facebook his heart would sink. His newsfeed was filled with friends' achievements, pictures of beautiful homes and details of exotic trips abroad. Yaser, on the other hand, was just let go from a place he had been working at for eight years and lived at home with his mother who was very ill. As the breadwinner and only child left in his childhood home, this was a devastating situation to be in. For the first time in his life, he had to go to social services to apply for financial assistance as his mother's professional nursing care was very expensive. Everyone's life looked so easy on social media, and he wondered if he was doing such an honourable thing, then why were his circumstances so difficult? It pained him seeing wedding and baby pictures on social media. Yaser wanted to start a family of his own, but it seemed that women were not interested in marrying him when they found out he had to take care of his mother. Yaser was not doing anything exciting like his peers and often wondered if others thought he was a loser—because that is exactly how he felt. Yaser would get so anxious and depressed looking at pictures and videos online, but it was so hard to stop. He found himself experiencing tremendous jealousy and wondered why his life turned out the way it did. Yaser wanted to know, "Why is everyone's life better than mine?"

What is happening to me?

Jealousy is painful and demoralizing. It can feel like a raging fire lodged in your soul that's beyond your reach to extinguish. It's often compounded by feelings of sadness, anxiousness, and dread. Nobody wants to feel jealous and be consumed by desiring what others have. Nobody. Yet it's so hard to stop.

Jealousy at times can also feel ungrateful and petty, which exacerbates layers of guilt deep within. In our pain, feelings of entitlement can surface making it more challenging to work through emotions. On the outside you might wonder if others can see the burden you are carrying. While jealousy is invisible, the impact on the one experiencing it can be so apparent.

For many people, jealousy stems from the cognitive distortion of **disqualifying positives**. This is when a person minimizes the good in their life by thinking less of themselves, their actions, or what has been given to them.[1] The comparison might be something very specific (e.g., we both got an A on the test, but I had to study much harder) or it could be a more general global comparison (e.g., everyone likes her more than they like me).

---

1 Burns, *Feeling Good*.

The dark path of comparing oneself to others and falling into jealousy has been present since the beginning of human existence. In Islamic (and Judeo-Christian) tradition, we know the story of Qabil (Cain) and Habil (Abel) in which both of Adam's sons offered a sacrifice to Allah ﷻ, but only one was accepted. As a result of envy, Qabil killed his brother Habil and became overwhelmed with regret. Qabil suffered in a few ways: (1) immediately from the pain of his jealousy; (2) long-term by incurring the sin of being the first to commit murder, and (3) inadvertently elevating the status of his brother by making him the first martyr. Jealousy and envy are some of the most destructive forces in life, causing internal upheaval and irreparable damage to relationships. Sometimes jealousy does not make much sense and may seem unwarranted, while at other times it feels justified because of our difficult circumstances.

During great hardship, jealousy can sometimes be associated with incredible feelings of resentment and bitterness. That trauma adds another layer of pain and can be a barrier to healing.

Why does his family look so "normal"? I wish my parents were that loving and supportive. My parents just criticize and beat me for the littlest thing.

It's not fair that I have cancer. How many 20-year-olds do you know that pause going to school because they have to get chemo and radiation?

Why does she have such as easy life staying at home with her children while I have to work two jobs to make ends meet after my awful divorce?

A person who has experienced trauma does not necessarily wish harm on others but might wonder why they have to go through excruciating difficulties and others do not.

Understanding your thoughts and emotions

While the example of Habil and Qabil is extreme, comparing ourselves to others is now arguably worse than it has ever been, especially with the advent of social media. In the past, accomplishments and blessings were typically shared with immediate family, friends, and relatives, whereas now every life detail is openly shared with the public in real-time. Modesty is an elusive concept and oversharing has opened up everyone's once private life to the world. Much is laid bare for others to comment on, including one's deep thoughts, day-to-day activities, meals eaten, items purchased, report cards, awards from work, engagements, and pregnancies. It's almost like TV, but even better because it's people you know. Social media can be very beneficial but can also be extremely toxic if one is not careful. You don't have to be online to participate in the comparison game as people create public personas in real day-to-day life as well. Many individuals and families act differently in public than they do at home, and brand themselves to appear different from who they truly are. Mirages are created about homes, children's behaviour, possessions, and marriages. At a *halaqah*, a father might brag about his son getting a scholarship to an Ivy League school but would never disclose that his son has a drug problem. During a playdate, a woman might talk about all the jewellery her husband buys her but would never talk about his infidelity. At an extravagant party, the host might appear very generous and have the best of everything, but nobody would ever know that the family is swimming in debt. These innocent deceptions breed jealousy as friends and family compare themselves to false standards. If one also has low self-esteem by continuously disqualifying positives, then the feelings of self-loathing and pain are even greater.

In most societies and cultures around the world, the average person does not discuss failures and tragedies except with a few people. When was the last time you heard a coworker or acquaintance say: "I'm lonely," "I think my spouse doesn't love me anymore," or "I'm not as a good father as I should be"? The answer is likely "never" because although it might be very authentic, it would not be socially appropriate. One might be labelled as negative, needy, or trying to attract unnecessary attention, although everyone experiences these types of emotions. If someone appears positive, attractive, witty, intelligent, and well-rounded, however, they tend to get that acceptance and recognition that all human beings crave. As a result of invisible social rules, a lot of effort is expended to create public personas that just reflect the best parts of ourselves, creating illusions of how we truly live life. While the average person understands all of this, there is still competition, jealousy, and deep resentment when other people's lives appear better than our own.

Changing your mind, body, and heart

What is the cure for comparing yourself to others and disqualifying your positive attributes? There is no easy fix, but it starts with internalizing key concepts about how you view yourself and look at the world. You cannot change your feelings or behaviours until you home in on the thoughts that are contributing to them.

To help break out of the cycle of thinking that everyone's life is better than yours, remember that you are special, and nobody can fulfill the calling and purpose Allah ﷻ has planned for you. You have the same power as anyone else to create the life you want and envision. Your life may not look like the life of your friends or people you see on social media, but then again why would you want it to? If you firmly believe that you are a person of irreplaceable value and can bring meaning to the world that nobody else can, you will not want to be anyone else.

When you feel like you are getting pulled into thinking that everyone's life is better than yours, start by paying attention to thoughts about your self-worth and reflect on the script or recurrent messages playing in your head. Many times, those unhealthy thoughts are related to (1) low self-esteem; (2) misunderstanding Allah's ﷻ bounties; and/or (3) unrealistic or false expectations of how the world works.

Low self-esteem

I'm not as popular and respected as my friends.

I will never be as accomplished as my brother.

My friend's children are so much smarter than mine.

Low self-esteem causes feelings of self-doubt and never feeling good enough. It leads to minimizing good qualities and focusing on negative qualities (which we all have). How can a person with low self-esteem objectively judge if their life is better or worse than others if their assessment is clouded by negative feelings about themselves? If you think negatively of yourself, everyone else will appear better by default. When you begin to have healthier self-esteem, however, your perspective will not be as skewed.

Where does low self-esteem come from? The biggest predictors of low self-esteem are early childhood emotional neglect, physical, and emotional abuse.[2] Parenting style, perceptions of successes and failures (especially in the domain of academics), and genetics also play a big role in self-esteem.[3] These childhood factors have profound emotional and physical effects on individuals into adulthood.[4] Understanding the impact of emotional neglect is imperative, as it's widely acknowledged that physical abuse is a type of trauma whereas emotional abuse is often overlooked or minimized. Many people who grow up with low self-esteem due to emotional neglect do not know that they may also be victims of trauma.

---

2 Sajjadi et al., "Predictive Role of Early Trauma Dimensions"; Spertus et al., "Childhood Emotional Abuse."

3 Joseph Rowntree Foundation, *Costs and Causes of Low Self-Esteem.*

4 Joseph Rowntree Foundation, *Costs and Causes of Low Self-Esteem.*

Another contributor to low self-esteem can be the occurrence of a negative experience, like failure or rejection.[5] The negative experience can be any event that was emotionally painful and decreased the individual's perception of self-worth and core values about themselves. Every individual has core values about who they are; a negative experience may be perceived as an anomaly, or it may open up a new door on how they view themselves. For example, a person who is verbally attacked with xenophobic slurs may look at the experience as a happenstance whereas another person might internalize the experience to the point that they change how they view themselves. Core values like "I belong," "I'm worthy of being safe," and "I'm a good person" can change to "I will never be accepted for who I am," "I'm not safe," and "There is something wrong with me."

Self-esteem work in adulthood is not easy but can be accomplished by focusing on positive traits and building mastery in those areas. To begin to counter low self-esteem, make a conscientious effort to shift your attention to your good qualities. This might feel unnatural and uncomfortable, but you will never be able to foster positive regard in a long-lasting and meaningful way if it doesn't come authentically from yourself.

Take a moment and reflect on your good qualities and positive attributes. Your strengths are not necessarily going to be the same as those of your friends or the person who is the subject of your jealousy. If it's difficult to think of anything, know that that is not

---

5 Emler, "Self Esteem."

a reflection of a lack of positive characteristics but how long it has been since you saw yourself in a positive light.

Reflect specifically on your unique qualities and how you can nurture and strengthen them. For example, if you are not very academically inclined, but are good at making things with your hands, then focus your efforts on improving those skills. If you are not great at making friends, but excel at writing, then work on your writing skills to uplift you and make the world a better place. Also keep in mind that just because someone doesn't value your positive quality doesn't mean it's not a good asset to have. If your father thinks that math is the most important skill in the world, but you are fantastic at English, that doesn't mean your English skills are not of value.

In addition to strengthening your positive attributes it's also important to pay attention to how you talk to yourself *internally.* If you speak with yourself very negatively, you can expect that your mood and outlook will reflect that. Just for one minute, imagine being around someone who is chronically putting you down and saying negative things about you. How would you feel about this person? You probably wouldn't feel very good about them or yourself. What if that person was actually you? Replacing negative self-talk with positive self-talk intentionally and consistently can have a profound effect on how you view yourself. Nobody deserves to be put down constantly, especially by one's own self.

To improve your self-esteem *externally*, reflect on whether people around you are reinforcing negative feelings you have about yourself.

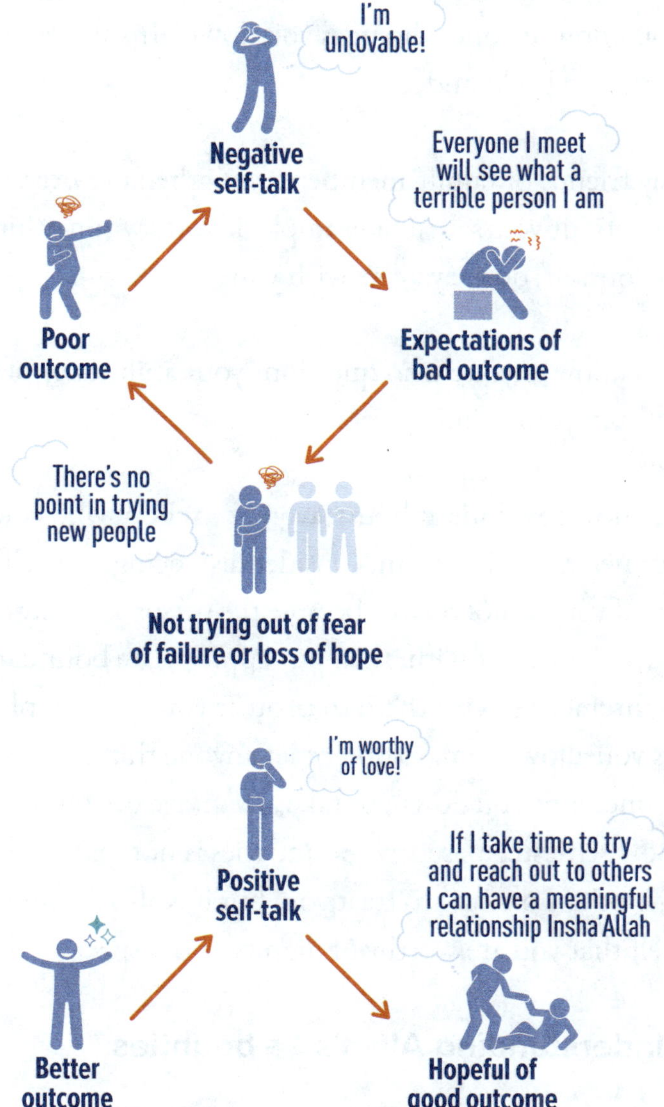

I'm unlovable!
Negative self-talk
Everyone I meet will see what a terrible person I am
Expectations of bad outcome
There's no point in trying new people
Not trying out of fear of failure or loss of hope
Poor outcome
I'm worthy of love!
Positive self-talk
If I take time to try and reach out to others I can have a meaningful relationship Insha'Allah
Hopeful of good outcome
I will invest time and effort in building a healthy relationship
Trying one's best
Better outcome

Do you know anyone who puts you down? Insults can be outright, or subtle and backhanded.

Do any friends or family members strengthen pre-existing negative feelings about yourself? For example, if you say something unkind about yourself, do they agree with you?

Do you know anyone who questions your abilities or plants seeds of doubt in your mind?

If you know someone at home, work, or school who contributes to your negative self-esteem, consider distancing yourself from that person. If you cannot do that because the person is family or someone you have to interact with, then put appropriate boundaries in place when interacting with them to protect yourself. People will treat you as you allow them, so do not let anyone think it's okay to call you names, put you down, or take advantage of you. For someone with low self-esteem, setting boundaries is not just important for guiding others on how to treat you, but it is also a reminder to yourself that you are worthy of dignity and respect.

Misunderstanding Allah's ﷻ bounties

Minimizing blessings is a sneaky way Shaytaan brings people down emotionally and spiritually without them realizing it. There is a regular kind of jealousy when you want what others have, and then a more sinister kind of jealousy when you want other people's blessings to be taken away. This latter form is dangerous because it involves a questioning of Allah's ﷻ Wisdom and perhaps even resenting Allah ﷻ for giving gifts to others and not you.

> *Why is my sister so beautiful and I'm so ugly? I wish my face looked different. What did she do to deserve the way she looks? Nothing.*

> *My friend is very intelligent and such a good test-taker. If only I was smarter than him. He doesn't even appreciate how easy he has it.*

> *Why do I have to work so hard to live paycheque to paycheque while this lazy* ammu *(uncle) at the* masjid *lives in a mansion and has all this generational wealth? I work way harder than him.*

At certain points in life, family and friends may *appear* to have more than us and that can be difficult to come to terms with, especially when it feels like blessings are outside our control. Sometimes blessings have nothing to do with how hard we work or desire something and that can make us feel powerless. It's important to note however that beauty, wealth, and success are not always blessings; beauty, wealth, and success can also be trials that take people further away from Allah ﷻ. They can sometimes even be the very things that lead people to Hell Fire when mismanaged or abused.

When we are on the outside looking in, it's important to not assume that others have *more* than us, or that what they have is *better* than what we have been given. Ultimately, Allah ﷻ has allotted a share for each person and questioning what He gives to whom indicates a lack of understanding and trust in His Wisdom. Allah ﷻ encourages, if not commands, us to be thankful, and tells us that if we are thankful, He will give us more:

> *And He gave you from all you asked of Him. And if you should count the favours of Allah, you could not enumerate them. Indeed, mankind is [generally] most unjust and ungrateful.*[6]

> *And if you should [try to] count the favours of Allah, you could not enumerate them. Indeed, Allah is Forgiving and Merciful.*[7]

6 Qur'an 14:34.
7 Qur'an 16:18.

So remember Me; I will remember you.
And be grateful to Me and do not deny Me.[8]

And [remember] when your Lord proclaimed, "If you
are grateful, I will surely increase you [in favour];
but if you deny, indeed, My punishment is severe."[9]

Then do you wonder that there has come to you
a reminder from your Lord through a man from
among you, that he may warn you? And remember
when He made you successors after the people of
Noah and increased you in stature extensively. So
remember the favours of Allah that you might succeed.[10]

If you feel that you are starting to go down the path of being ungrateful to Allah ﷻ, then seek refuge in Him from Shaytaan, as this tactic is an aggressive assault on both your emotional and spiritual well-being. It's one thing to lose faith in yourself, but never lose faith in Allah's ﷻ positive attributes and His ability to provide for you. Allah ﷻ is *Ar-Razzaq* (The Ever-Providing Sustainer), *Al-Fattah* (The Opener, the Victory Giver), *Al-Muqeet* (The Nourisher) and *Al-Karim* (The Generous, The Bountiful). When you ask and work hard, Allah ﷻ will give you what you are looking for, even though it may come in a different form than you anticipated. Allah ﷻ has no limitations on what He can give; if you see someone who has something you want, never fear that there isn't enough bounty left for you or that you cannot have the same.

---

8 Qur'an 2:152.
9 Qur'an 14:7.
10 Qur'an 7:69.

Abu Hurairah narrated that the Messenger of Allah ﷺ said:

> *There is not a man who calls upon Allah with a supplication, except that he is answered. Either it shall be granted to him in the world, or reserved for him in the Hereafter, or his sins shall be expiated for it according to the extent that he supplicated—as long as he does not supplicate for some sin, or for the severing of the ties of kinship, and he does not become hasty. They said: "O Messenger of Allah, and how would he be hasty?" He ﷺ said: "He says: 'I called upon my Lord, but He did not answer me.'"* [11]

Unrealistic expectations about how life works

If I was just a little wealthier, I know I would be happy.

If my spouse wasn't so lazy, my marriage would be better for sure.

If I were thinner or prettier, I would have more friends.

When we blame others (the world, *qadar*, society, parents, etc.) for things we want but can't have, we are creating unrealistic expectations for how the world works and giving those outside forces more power than they actually have. Blaming external factors

---

11 *Jami' al-Tirmidhi*, no. 3604d, bk. 48, hadith 238.

takes away from our own accountability and resourcefulness to find alternative means for our happiness. It's not what happens to you that dictates your life, it's how you choose to react and respond to those unexpected variables that affects your overall quality of life and happiness.

Lack of wealth is not preventing you from being happy; your thirst for more is clouding your ability to find contentment.

Your marriage could be better if your spouse wasn't lazy, but your marriage would also be better if you put more effort and positivity into it.

Perhaps your difficulties in making and keeping friends is from your negative attitude and not how you look.

Instead of focusing on things in your life outside of your control, focus on what is in your control:

- Your thoughts
- Feelings
- Attitude
- Appreciation
- Openness
- Flexibility
- Kindness
- Creativity
- Resourcefulness
- Resilience

The power you have to control and exercise these qualities can offset any circumstance; it's your outlook that determines if and how you bounce back from adversity.

> *You get to decide if something is important.*
>
> *You get to decide if something will persist in bothering you.*
>
> *You get to decide how you want to recover.*

Cognitive shifts needed in addressing comparing yourself to others

Once you have started to shift incorrect beliefs about yourself, you can begin to replace those erroneous thoughts with more empowering concepts and cognitions. It's not enough to just remove the old cognitions that were holding you back, you also need to utilize tools to improve how you relate to the world and those around you in a different way. Keeping perspective, self-improvement, making appropriate comparisons, and gratitude are great ways to do this.

1. **Keeping perspective:** In life there is always more to obtain, and there will always be someone who has more than you in one capacity or another. Chasing after these things, whether money, beauty, homes, cars, fame, etc. is never-ending and is very much like being a mouse running on a wheel. The mouse never gets anywhere running in place and achieves nothing but being tired. This is because oftentimes humans focus more on what they

don't have rather than what they do have. This is very eloquently narrated by Sahl ibn Sa'd who said:

> *I heard Ibn al-Zubayr who was on the pulpit at Makkah, delivering a sermon, saying, "O men! The Prophet used to say, 'If the son of Adam were given a valley full of gold, he would love to have a second one; and if he were given the second one, he would love to have a third, for nothing fills the belly of Adam's son except dust. And Allah forgives whoever repents to Him.' Ubayy said, "We considered this as a saying from the Qur'an till the* surah *(beginning with) 'The mutual rivalry for piling up of worldly things diverts you...' (102:1) was revealed."*[12]

We are reminded in the Qur'an, as well as the Sunnah, that possessions come and go, while good deeds last; so, amassing good deeds is far better than amassing goods. Good deeds increase us in rank and give us better provisions in the *akhirah* which is not only better, but permanent.

> *Wealth and children are [but an] adornment of the worldly life. But enduring good deeds are better [according] to your Lord for reward and better for [one's] hope.*[13]

> *Know that the life of this world is but amusement and diversion and adornment and boasting to one another*

12 *Sahih al-Bukhari*, no. 6438, bk. 81, hadith 27.

13 Qur'an 18:46.

and competition in increase of wealth and children—
like the example of a rain whose [resulting] plant
growth pleases the tillers; then it dries, and you see
it turned yellow; then it becomes [scattered] debris.
And in the Hereafter is severe punishment and
forgiveness from Allah and approval. And what is
the worldly life except the enjoyment of delusion?[14]

Focusing on long-term goals, such as trying to go to *jannah*, helps stabilize mental health when things don't go our way or when someone appears to have more than us. Factually, you don't know if someone truly has more than you, but even if they did, it wouldn't matter when you think about the Day of Judgement, *jannah*, and *jahannam* in light of this *hadith*:

Anas ibn Malik reported that Allah's Messenger ﷺ said,

One amongst the denizens of Hell who had led a life of ease and plenty amongst the people of the world would be made to dip in Fire only once on the Day of Resurrection and then it would be said to him: "O, son of Adam, did you find any comfort, did you happen to get any material blessing?" He would say: "By Allah, no, my Lord." And then that person from amongst the persons of the world will be brought who had led the most miserable life (in the world) from amongst the inmates of Paradise and he would be made to dip once in Paradise, and it would be said to him: "O, son of Adam,

14 Qur'an 57:20.

did you face any hardship? Or had any distress befallen you?" And he would say: "By Allah, no, O my Lord, never did I face any hardship or experience any distress." [15]

Furthermore, an increase in the blessings you seek results in an increase in accountability on the Day of Judgement. Ibn Mas'ud narrated that the Messenger of Allah ﷺ said:

The feet of the son of Adam shall not move from before his Lord on the Day of Judgement, until he is asked about five things: about his life and what he did with it, about his youth and what he wore it out in, about his wealth and how he earned it and spent it upon, and what he did with what he knew. [16]

Therefore, anyone who appears to have more than you at the moment may be questioned more extensively about it later—and perhaps to their detriment.

2. **Self-improvement for success:** One of the most destructive aspects of getting caught up in comparisons is that it takes away from working on oneself. Two hours a day checking out people's profiles on social media and feeling terrible about oneself, is two hours one could have used to read a book, volunteer, learn something new, or work on an important goal. Multiply two hours a day by seven days a week and that is fourteen hours a week that is being given up. Fourteen hours a week is a part-time job or approximately how many hours a student needs to be

15 *Sahih Muslim*, no. 2807, bk. 52, *hadith* 42.
16 *Jami' al-Tirmidhi*, no. 2416.

enrolled full-time at college. Multiply two hours a day by thirty days in a month and you will get sixty hours that could be used for bettering oneself. Sixty hours a month can do wonders: One could work on writing a book, memorize lots of Qur'an, create community programs, or get oneself in top physical shape. The travesty in spending your life looking at what others are doing is that you are completely overlooking what you could be doing yourself. Wasting time comparing yourself to others is bad enough, but the resulting poverty of your soul due to neglecting it and not taking care of it is far worse.

Abu Hurairah reported that the Messenger of Allah ﷺ said:

> ***Richness does not lie in the abundance of (worldly) goods, but richness is the richness of the soul (heart, self).***[17]

If you feel yourself caught up in thinking about how much more someone has than you, or how little you have, then put a cap on it. You may be thinking, "Well if I could stop thinking about it, I would." However, this technique works counterintuitively. Set a designated time for you to sit with your negative feelings for 5 or 10 minutes. Set a timer if you need to. Then when the time is up, make a conscious effort to shift gears to doing something productive. This is a way to compartmentalize your feelings and prevent your feelings from taking over your day. Giving yourself permission to feel bad for 5 minutes and then doing something beneficial for 2 hours is more useful than being distracted for

17 *Sahih Muslim*, no. 1051, bk. 12, hadith 157.

2 hours. Over time you will feel like sitting and being negative on purpose is a waste of time, and because it's now out of your system, you will no longer have a need for it.

3. **If you are going to compare, compare yourself to previous versions of who you were or to people who have less than you:** Everyone is born into a unique set of circumstances that will set them on an exclusive trajectory that nobody else will be able to experience. Some people have similar interests, values, and family dynamics as you, but nobody will ever have a life exactly like yours. Comparing your blessings to someone who you think has more than you will be of no benefit, whereas continually assessing your own growth to previous versions of yourself can increase your productivity and self-esteem. Comparing yourself to how you were 6 months ago, 2 years ago, and 5 years ago can give you concrete insights on how you may have improved or worsened in particular aspects of your life.

If you insist on comparing yourself to others, then look to those lower than you as demonstrated in this prophetic advice:

Abu Hurairah ﷺ narrated that the Messenger of Allah ﷺ said:

> ***Look at those who are lower than you (financially) but do not look at those who are higher than you, lest you belittle the favours Allah conferred upon you.***[18]

18 *Bulugh al-maram*, bk. 16, hadith 1482.

Looking to people who appear to have less than you can help foster appreciation for small blessings you may have not considered before. If you are worrying about having humiliated yourself in front of someone you respect, but then reflect on a friend's child who has a terminal illness, your problems may not seem as bleak anymore. Looking to those who have less than you is a useful way to develop a deeper appreciation for what you have.

4. **Gratitude:** One of the antidotes for dismissing positive things in your life is working on expressing thankfulness for what you have. It doesn't matter exactly how you practise gratefulness as long as you do it consistently. Research supports that gratitude lists, grateful contemplation (reflecting globally on things you are grateful for), and gratitude visits (writing a letter to someone who has done something good for you and reading it to them) are effective in improving well-being.[19]

   Consider the following exercises:

   A. Every day when you wake up, identify 3 things you are looking forward to and when you go to sleep, identify 3 things that you are grateful for. Blessings you are grateful for can be big or small, but the important thing is that the thankfulness should come from your heart. Examples of things you might look forward to include your morning coffee, your walk during lunchtime, hugging a family member, tending to your garden or making a new recipe for dinner. Examples of things you might be grateful for: That you snuck into a work meeting without anyone seeing you were late, that you made

19 Wood, Froh, and Geraghty, "Gratitude and Well-Being."

it to the gas station before your tank was empty, that your child did not have a tantrum when leaving the toy store, a delicious meal, or the chance to read a chapter from your favourite book.

B. When you are facing something traumatic or difficult, find three good things that can potentially come out of the situation. This exercise does not take away from the pain or hardship you are experiencing but can help you see that good can come from the worst of circumstances. The good thing might be a new relationship that was formed, an increase in patience, a new opportunity or strength you did not have before, or a chance to help others in a similar struggle. Many times, when reframing trauma, individuals find that in the long term the overall good outweighs the bad.

C. Volunteer to help those who have less than you. Scientific studies show that by helping others you actually feel better about yourself.[20] Places you can volunteer: a soup kitchen for the homeless, nursing homes where the elderly are away from their families, hospitals, social services agencies, etc. You can also visit sick people in your local community and get tremendous amounts of *ajr* that way.

It was narrated that 'Ali said: I heard the Messenger of Allah ﷺ say:

> ***Whoever comes to his Muslim brother and visits him (when he is sick), he is walking among the harvest of Paradise until he sits down, and when he sits down, he is covered with mercy. If it is morning, seventy thousand angels will send blessings upon him until evening, and if it is evening, seventy thousand angels will send blessings upon him until morning.***[21]

---

20 Tabassum, Mohan, and Smith, "Association of Volunteering"; Yeung, Zhang, and Kim, "Volunteering and Health Benefits."

21 *Sunan Ibn Majah*, vol. 1, bk. 6, *hadith* 1442.

Spiritual inspiration for reflection

"Allah extends provision for whom He wills and restricts [it]. And they rejoice in the worldly life, while the worldly life is only, compared to the Hereafter, a [brief] enjoyment."[22]

'Umar ibn al-Khāṭṭāb narrated that the Messenger of Allah ﷺ said:

"If you were to rely upon Allah with the required reliance, then He would provide for you just as a bird is provided for, it goes out in the morning empty, and returns full."[23]

Ibn Mas'ud reported that Umm Ḥabībah said:

"O Allah, enable me to derive benefit from my husband, Allah's Messenger ﷺ, and from my father Abu Sufyan, and from my brother Mu'awiya." Allah's Messenger ﷺ said to her: "Verily, you have asked Allah about the durations of life already set, and the steps which you would take, and sustenance the share of which is fixed. Nothing would take place earlier than its due time, and nothing would be deferred beyond that when it is due..."[24]

22 Qur'an 13:26.
23 *Jami' al-Tirmidhi*, no. 2344.
24 *Sahih Muslim*, no. 2663.

Practical exercises

A. Cultivating gratitude

Every morning, identify 3 things you are looking forward to:

1. ____

2. ____

3. ____

Every night before you go to sleep, identify 3 things that you are grateful for:

1. ____

2. ____

3. ____

B. Building your self-esteem and goals

Sometimes being distracted by what other people have is due to one's low self-esteem. What unique characteristics have you been blessed with?

1. ____

____

2. ____

____

3. ____

____

4. ____

____

5. ____

____

Pretend that you are older and reflecting back on your life. What are five long-term accomplishments you would like to have achieved? These goals should reflect values important to you, and not goals other people have for you or have for themselves. To increase well-roundedness, list goals in several different aspects of your life: familial, career, spiritual, philanthropic, etc.

1. ____

____

2. ____

____

3. ____

____

4. ____

____

5. ____

____

What are three short-term goals you can start to work on today to help meet your long-term goals?

1. ____

____

2. ____

____

3. ____

____

To work to become your best self, you will need to commit some time every day to work on your goals. Half an hour at a consistent time can do wonders for turning your life around. Pick the same time every day, preferably after *fajr* (since this is a blessed time) to work on your goals. If you are really committed to working on yourself, your focus on others and what they have will naturally decrease. When you are ready to pick a time, block off that time daily for 30 days and watch how both your outlook and life will change for the better *insha Allah*.

Case study revisited

One day Yaser felt he couldn't take how he felt anymore and knew that things had to change. Yaser understood that his mood was greatly affected by the amount of time he spent online so he started limiting social media use to one hour a day. He also realized that he was burnt out taking care of his mother and that if he was going to continue doing this long-term, he needed help. He asked extended family members for a loan to get his mother more in-home help. Having professionals assist him helped lift his spirits and allowed Yaser to be able to focus on himself, which was something he hadn't been able to do in a long time.

Yaser felt that he needed to adjust his outlook on life. His circumstances were different than his friends, but that didn't mean that his life was bad. Yaser owned a home, had good health, and was highly educated so it would be easy for him to get a new job. He also saw a great opportunity in taking care of his mother and was optimistic it would help him get to jannah insha Allah.

Yaser sat down and reflected on his life goals. He had wasted so much time on social media that he realized he really didn't have any long-term goals. Something that stood out right away was that he hadn't exercised in a long time and that always made him feel good. He joined a brothers' basketball team that met twice a month. The exercise and seeing old friends made him feel more like himself.

Regarding other long-term goals: Yaser knew he had no control over getting married or having children but understood that he could contribute to the ummah *in other ways. With his IT skills from college, he decided to create an online foundation for Muslims taking care of parents with chronic illness. His foundation would provide connections for other Muslims like himself to get support, learn about resources, and exchange helpful information.*

Focusing on long-term goals helped Yaser stop minimizing the good in his life and comparing it to others. Shifting attention to what Yaser could actually control empowered him and gave him a lot less time to sit around and compare his life to others. If Yaser ever felt like he was slipping into his old ways he would make sure to increase practising his gratefulness exercises (identifying things to look forward to in the morning and counting his blessings at night), and this would help him get back on track.

Chapter 10
"What Did I Do to Deserve This?"
Conquering the Assumptions that Hold You Back

When we can no longer change a situation, we are challenged to change ourselves... Everything can be taken from a human but one thing: the last of the human freedoms—to choose one's attitude in any given set of circumstances, to choose one's own way.

VIKTOR E. FRANKL
MAN'S SEARCH FOR MEANING

Case study

It all started in college. Ahmed couldn't remember the exact turning point but, little by little, anger and negativity began to overtake his daily life. He struggled to sleep due to his racing mind and also started to feel like getting out of bed each morning was an enormous task. Studying for exams became difficult after the shock of his first failing grade and he developed constant worries about further failures. Nearly every day was filled with dread and anger.

Ahmed had looked forward to becoming a pharmacist since he was a young boy, but as he struggled in his classes, he began to painfully realize this career path might not be for him. Slowly the goals, dreams, and life he had envisioned for himself began to disappear. He felt like a part of himself was fading away.

Friendships began to deteriorate as his struggles amplified and he complained about everything going on in his life each time he hung out with someone. He found himself getting angry over small things and noticed his friends stopped spending time with him, making him feel abandoned and resentful.

He began to miss prayers as he started to feel angry toward Allah for everything he was going through. He had done everything "right"—he was studious, worked hard, prayed and had been a good person—but he was still struggling in all aspects of his life and was lashing out with uncontrollable emotions. He thought to himself, "It doesn't matter what I do; I tried my best and turned out to be a failure. ***What did I do to deserve this?"***

What is happening to me?

Anger can feel like an ugly, unruly monster that rears its head at the worst times. It can make you feel like your emotions are all over the place and can result in reactions you instantly regret. When life takes a turn in a direction you did not anticipate, anger can completely take over, not just impacting your ability to function but also your ability to accept your new reality as well. The dreams you had so tenderly nurtured are suddenly burned to the ground only to be replaced by the scary realization that your life is not at all what you had pictured.

Coming to terms with a new reality involves the loss of a great deal in our lives. Every trauma involves some sort of loss—the loss of something tangible, such as a loved one, a job, a marriage, or one's health or the loss of something intangible, such as the dream we had once envisioned our lives would look like. No one expects that their pregnancy will end in miscarriage, that a dream job won't be nearly as fulfilling as anticipated, or that a marriage will end. Once reality hits, it can be difficult to cope.

When tough situations befall us, it is natural to experience pain and a sense of disappointment, shock, and anger. After all, you likely spent hours imagining what your life would look like only to realize it didn't pan out in the way you envisioned. You might find yourself thinking:

> ***I've been trying to get married for years and it hasn't happened. I'm so frustrated that nothing has been working.***

I keep having one financial mishap after another. Is Allah angry with me? I certainly feel angry with myself and those around me.

Parenting turned out to be way harder than I ever envisioned. I feel like I'm always on the brink of flying into a rage.

Anger is a challenging emotion because it feels so out of control and destructive. While anger can lay dormant and seep through everyday interactions with minimal damage for some people, it can be sudden and explosive for others. Bouts of anger don't just feel threatening to those around us but can threaten our own wellbeing as well. Just like a tornado, anger can descend suddenly and completely destroy relationships, opportunities, accomplishments, and even one's faith in a very short period of time.

Understanding your thoughts and emotions

When we experience strong emotions like anger, our minds often behave as though we possess a crystal ball, magic mirror, or a telepathic (mind-reading) ability. Our irrational thoughts override our reasoning capabilities and trick us into believing that we can predict what is going to happen next despite it being impossible to ascertain what the future is or what others are really thinking.

This "magical" ability we act as though our minds have is called **jumping to conclusions**. This type of cognitive distortion (unhealthy thought pattern) is defined as creating a negative interpretation of something even though there are no definitive facts that convincingly support that conclusion. Jumping to conclusions can occur in two ways: **mind-reading and fortune-telling.** "Mind-reading" involves a person thinking that others are negatively evaluating them or have bad intentions toward them. When a person is "fortune-telling," they are predicting a negative future outcome or deciding that situations will turn out badly before the situation has even occurred.

As human beings, our minds and our hearts search for meaning. When someone you care about hurts you or when a tragedy strikes, your brain makes assumptions about why this has happened. We tend to pick interpretations that fit with our existing view of the world. The problem with this is that traumatic experiences change our view of the world from one that is realistic to one that is fear-based and pessimistic. Every conclusion we come to, and every perception can be based on something inaccurate—pain, fear, and anger.

What started as one difficulty becomes something insurmountable because our minds perceive it to be so. Your mind begins to jump to conclusions to make sense of the situation, but these conclusions are often negative and self-destructive.

Consider these examples:

You are angry that your spouse is not spending enough time with you and think,

> ***"He doesn't care about me. We're growing more and more distant. This is the beginning of the end of our marriage."***

You've lost your job and so you begin to think,

> ***"I was fired because I can never do anything right. Nobody is going to hire me again."***

Your engagement has not come to fruition, and you think to yourself,

> ***"She must have found someone better because I was not good enough for her. No one will find me worthwhile or worthy of love."***

Using faith to soften the jumping to conclusions effect

Our lives do not always follow the trajectory that we hope for. The standards we often set for ourselves in order to be happy and content may not always be realistic. Likewise, the expectations that we have for Allah ﷻ— namely to decree everything we deem best for ourselves or that we have decided should be a part of our life plan—creates a very narrow view of our lives and, more importantly, our perception of Allah ﷻ.

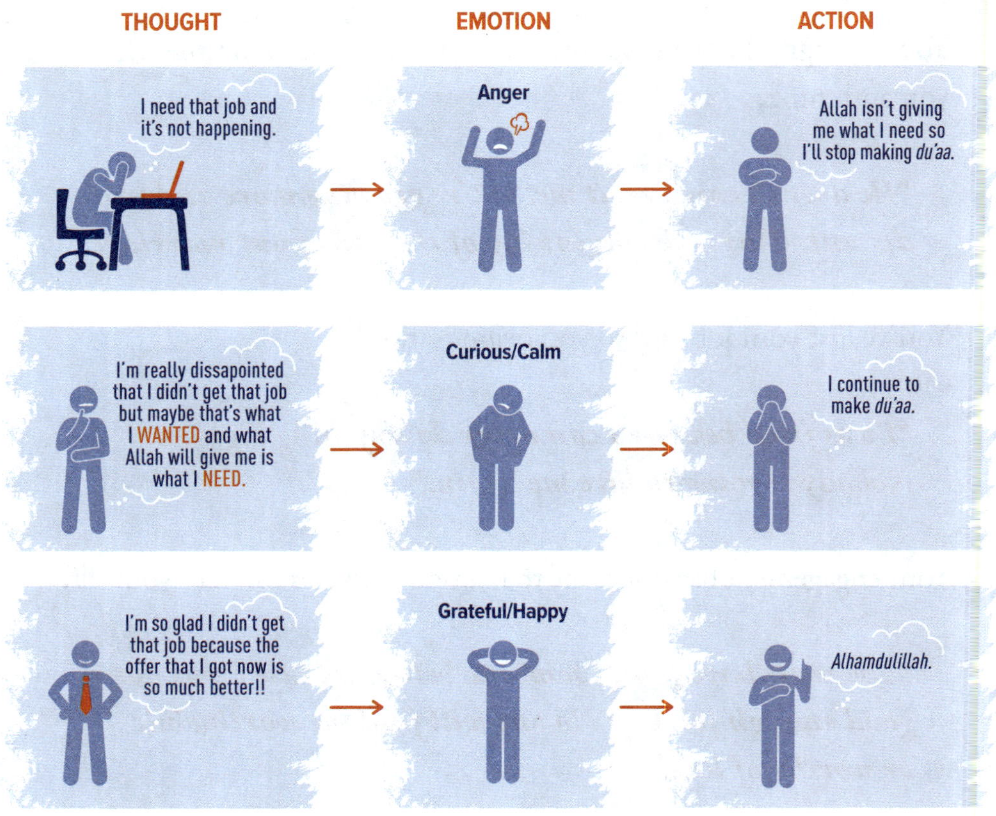

Rather than expecting that Allah ﷻ will grant us everything we want in the way we want it, shifting our understanding to realize that He ﷻ provides us with everything we **need** can improve both our mental and spiritual health. Have you ever thought you desperately needed something, were disappointed that it didn't happen and, after some time, learned that it wasn't what was best for you? We've all had experiences like that which serve as reminders of Allah's ﷻ limitless knowledge.

When we jump to conclusions about why certain tests were sent our way or why they shouldn't have been sent our way, we imagine, unwittingly, that we are capable of knowing what Allah ﷻ is thinking. However, consider the Name of Allah, *al-Hakim*: The One who is Most Knowing, Most Wise; the One who acts with perfect knowledge, wisdom, and comprehension of everything; the One who does the proper thing in the proper way in the proper place at the proper time.

Abū Bakr ﷺ used to say:

> ***O Allah! You know me more than I know myself.***[1]

The difference between Allah's ﷻ knowledge and human knowledge is that we must acquire our knowledge by what we see and experience around us. On the other hand, Allah's ﷻ knowledge has no beginning or end and is not based on trial and error. Allah ﷻ tells us in the Qur'an:

> ***And with Him are the keys of the unseen; none knows them except Him. And He knows what is on the land and in the sea. Not a leaf falls but that He knows it. And no grain is there within the darknesses of the earth and no moist or dry [thing] but that it is [written] in a clear record.***[2]

While we focus on the single thread we imagine is perfectly needed in our lives, Allah ﷻ sees the entire, beautiful tapestry that every single thread will eventually become.

---

1 Ibn Atheer, *Abū Bakr al-Ṣiddīq: The First Caliph*, 18.

2 Qur'an 6:59.

It takes humility to truly be able to embrace Allah's ﷻ Wisdom, especially when in a state of anger or pain. When our emotions tell us one thing, but the Word of Allah ﷻ tells us another, it takes humility to say, "I don't understand the full wisdom of Allah's decrees in this moment, but I trust Allah ﷻ and accept them."

The impact of anger during difficult times

Although we know many examples from our Islamic tradition that teach us that, spiritually, trials are good for us, we also know that they don't feel good in the moment. Difficult emotions naturally arise during times of struggle including frustration, sadness, disappointment, and anxiety. Every emotion serves the function of signalling to us that something is happening and needs our attention—including anger. Anger is a natural part of life as the Prophet Muhammad ﷺ describes,

> *Verily, anger is a burning ember in the heart of the son of Adam, as you see it in the redness of his eyes and the bulging of his veins. Whoever feels anything like that, let him lie down on the ground.*[3]

In order to get a better sense of control over this emotion, let's discuss how anger moves through the brain and body.

3 *Sunan al-Tirmidhī*, no. 2191.

The angry brain

Stress response: When something happens (a trigger), anger activates the amygdala in your brain before you're even aware that it's happening. The amygdala is the brain area responsible for emotional processing, particularly fear, anxiety, and aggression. When anger surges, the amygdala turns on the stress response system in your brain and body to prepare your body to respond to a threat. The adrenal glands secrete stress hormones (i.e., cortisol, adrenaline, and noradrenaline), which impact your brain and body quickly. This is why you may notice your heart racing and your muscles tensing when you feel angry.

Judgement reduction and pain amplification: When struggling with anger the brain regions that are responsible for good judgement and making new memories (prefrontal cortex and hippocampus) start to experience a loss of neurons which is why you might struggle with making good decisions or remembering what you wanted to say during an argument.[4] Along with neuron loss, too much cortisol also decreases serotonin, which is the hormone that makes you feel happy. With less serotonin, anger is amplified, as are physical and emotional pain.[5]

Jumping to conclusions and assuming the worst: Researchers have found that when something negative happens and you're not 100% sure what caused it to happen, you are more likely to jump to negative conclusions and to quickly associate two things together

4 Drevets et al., "Subgenual Prefrontal Cortex Abnormalities."
5 The National Institute for the Clinical Application of Behavioural Medicine, "How Anger Affects the Brain and Body."

that may not actually be linked.[6] When there is a lack of clarity, it's very easy for our brains to choose the worst possible explanation despite it being highly unlikely.

> ***When your spouse is late and not answering his phone, do you immediately start to wonder if he has been in a car accident?***

> ***When your friend seems a little distant, do you start to wonder if he's begun to tire of your friendship?***

> ***When your child is having a tantrum in the grocery store, do you wonder if you're failing as a parent?***

Our minds often jump to negative conclusions despite rationally knowing that a simpler conclusion (i.e., your husband's phone ran out of charge) is more likely.

Consider the way jumping to conclusions might progress after something like a miscarriage:

I've been hoping for a child for so long and now the chance has been snatched away from me.

↓

What did I do to deserve this? Allah ﷻ gives children to so many other people. He must think I'm unworthy of being a mother. (Mind-reading)

↓

6 Lee, O'Doherty, and Shimojo, "Neural Computations."

If I'm unworthy of being a mother, I'll never have children and my husband will hate me. (Fortune-telling and Mind-reading)

↓

My husband will divorce me, and I'll be alone forever. (Fortune-telling)

Now that we understand the impact that jumping to conclusions can have on your life and thought processes, let's explore how to change these thoughts.

Changing your mind, body, and heart

Jumping to conclusions depends on false evidence, fear, anger and distrust. People often have the misconception that "expecting the worst" will save them from disappointment. However, in reality, setting our sights on the worst possible outcome only sets us up for anger, anxiety, and depression. When we expect that people will mistreat us, we begin to harbour resentment toward them, leading us to pick fights, see the worst in them and within ourselves. When we expect to fail at something, we are much less likely to try our best due to our fears.

Jumping to conclusions can also impact your faith and can leave you feeling shaken. Consider how an initial thought might lead down this path:

I've always worked hard and been a good Muslim, but I still lost my job. Why did Allah ﷻ allow this to happen to me?

↓

Allah ﷻ didn't save my job, so He must not care about me. (Mind-reading)

I can't believe Allah ﷻ would do this to me. I do everything right and get nothing in return. Nothing is going to change so there's no point in trying. (Fortune-telling)

Our thoughts can drastically impact our emotions and behaviours. When anger floods our minds and hearts, it's easy for our thoughts to follow suit as well. However, as we see in the example above, allowing our angry thoughts to take root can be detrimental to our relationship with Allah ﷻ and can negatively impact our desire to connect with Him.

Ways to manage anger

We know that despite anger being a natural human emotion, it can also cause damage to our sense of self and our relationships with others, including Allah ﷻ. While we can never say it is "okay" or "permissible" to internalize anger or ill will toward Allah, it is important to know that having unwanted passive thoughts is a lot more common than you may think.

Abu Hurairah narrates that a Companion came to the Messenger of Allah ﷺ and asked:

> *Messenger of Allah! We have thoughts which we cannot dare talk about, and we do not like that we have them or talk about them. He said: Have you experienced that? They replied: Yes. He said: That is clear faith.*[7]

We see in this hadith that even some of the best people to walk this earth, our righteous predecessors, struggled with these fearful, confusing thoughts that led them to feel inadequate in their relationship with Allah ﷻ. These passing thoughts (not intentional or deliberate) say nothing about your faith in Allah ﷻ; rather, the discomfort you feel in experiencing these thoughts is indicative of how important your relationship with Allah ﷻ is to you.

Consider the emphasis of the Prophet Muhammad ﷺ when a man came to him asking,

> *"Advise me." The Prophet, peace and blessings be upon him, said, "Do not be angry." The man repeated his request and the Prophet said, "Do not be angry."*[8]

We all have experiences when certain situations or people push our buttons and set us off. Consider moments when you've received bad news, gotten a flat tire on the way to an important appointment, when your children are whining or throwing tantrums, or when

7 *Sunan Abi Dāwūd*, no. 5111.
8 *Ṣaḥīḥ al-Bukhārī*, no. 6116.

someone is being purposefully disrespectful toward someone you love. The intense anger that arises within you during these incidents can literally feel like a fire beneath your skin and it can feel almost impossible to handle. This is precisely why there is such a huge reward Islamically for controlling our responses when feeling angry.

> ***Those who spend (in Allah's cause) in prosperity and adversity, who repress their anger, and who pardon men. Verily, Allah loves those who do good.***[9]

> ***Abu Darda reported: I said, "O Messenger of Allah, tell me about a deed that will admit me into Paradise." The Messenger of Allah ﷺ said, "Do not be angry and you will enter Paradise."***[10]

Controlling your anger would not be something encouraged by Allah ﷻ if it was not something attainable. Knowing this, how can we begin to manage anger in healthier ways?

Physical shift

Creating a physical shift in moments of anger can be a powerful and transformative step in breaking the cycle of negative response patterns. Neuroanatomist Jill Bolte Taylor describes our ability to regulate our emotional reactions using what she calls the "90-second rule."[11] Whenever someone has a reaction to something that happens around them, a 90-second chemical process transpires.

---

9 Qur'an 3:134.
10 *Al-Mu'jam al-Awsaṭ*, 2411.
11 Taylor, *My Stroke of Insight.*

This means that it takes less than two minutes from the moment your anger is triggered to the moment the chemicals responsible for a stress response leave your body.

Once you realize this, it gives you the power to create a pause. Creating a pause between the moment a strong emotion is triggered and the moment you respond to the situation is one of the most transformative choices you can make. All of your power is in that window between the trigger and your reaction.[12]

When you expand that window, you acknowledge the following:

- No situation can force you to do anything.
- You always have a choice.
- While you cannot control your circumstances, you can control your response to them.
- You have the choice moment-to-moment in how you want to be in the world, in your relationships, and which version of yourself you want to show up as.

Creating a physical shift is one of the best ways to increase this pause, allow your "angry" chemicals to dissipate and allow your thinking brain to function more fully. Try some of these practical methods to relax your body during moments of anger:

---

12 Covey, *7 Habits of Highly Effective People.*

- Look at your watch to time yourself for 90 seconds. This way you are observing yourself having a bodily anger response rather than engaging with it.
- Take a few deep breaths until you feel your body beginning to relax.
- Muscle relaxation: Tense a part of your body (e.g., your hands), hold the tension for 5 seconds and then fully release the tension.
- Drink something cool.
- Use your 5 senses to ground yourself to give you a sense of stability (e.g., pay attention to the sounds you hear, pick out a few things you see around the room, feel the texture of something between your fingers, etc.)
- Change your posture:

> ***The Prophet ﷺ said, "If one of you is angry while he is standing, let him sit down so his anger will leave him; otherwise, let him lie down."*** [13]

- Make *wudu*:

> ***The Prophet ﷺ said, "When anyone of you gets angry, let him perform ablution because anger arises from fire."*** [14]

- Perform *sajdah*: When the Prophet ﷺ was distressed, Allah ﷻ comforted him in the Qur'an and encouraged prostration as one of the ways to help manage these difficult emotions saying,

13 *Sunan Abī Dāwūd*, no. 4782.
14 *Sunan Abī Dāwūd*, no. 4784.

We know how your heart is distressed at what they say. But celebrate the praises of your Lord and be of those who prostrate themselves in adoration.[15]

Mental shift

Once the physical shift has allowed some of the intensity of your emotions to dissipate, you're ready for a mental shift. This step is not fully effective when your anger response system is in overdrive so relaxing your body first will allow this step to be much more productive.

Anger is a secondary emotion, meaning that there are other emotions hidden beneath the surface. You can easily see your own or someone else's anger, but it can be difficult to see the underlying emotions beneath the outward manifestation of anger.

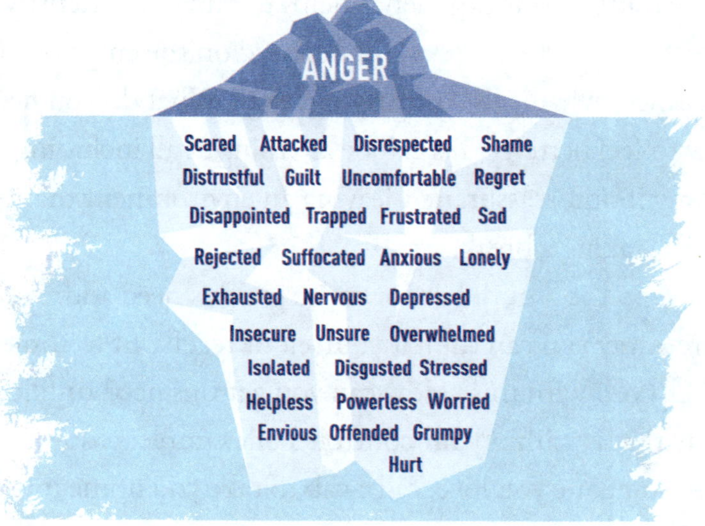

15 Qur'an 15:97–98.

Think of anger as the tip of an iceberg—the part you can see above the water. However, underneath our anger are the deeper emotions that trigger our outrage—feelings we may feel uncomfortable showing like hurt, humiliation, rejection, invisibility, disrespect, insecurity, and inadequacy. This is a really important distinction because in order to change our angry reactions, we have to understand why they happen. Identifying the underlying emotion—the root of why we feel so strongly in this situation—is essential.

Here are some key steps to begin this process:

1. **Identify the underlying emotion:** Take a look at the anger iceberg to identify which underlying emotion(s) you are actually experiencing that may be leading to the feeling of anger.
2. **Name it to tame it:**[16] Use a technique called "name it to tame it" by saying to yourself, "I'm feeling really ______ (hurt, ashamed, overwhelmed, etc.) right now." Acknowledging the emotion at the root of your experience helps to tame the intensity of it.
3. **Identify the underlying need:** Based on the emotion you've identified, what is the underlying need? What do you need right now to feel better? This can be anything at all including: a hug, talking it out, reassurance, leaving an environment that feels unsafe, taking a break, etc.
4. **Address the need:** Find a way to get this need addressed. Is there a way you can fulfil it yourself or reach out to someone to help you with this? How can you get this need fulfilled in a way that is within your control? For example: request a hug from someone you love; call a cab to take you home if you are

16 Siegel, *Brainstorm*.

uncomfortable; take a walk around your neighbourhood for a breather; call a friend you trust; etc.

Along with understanding and addressing your underlying emotions, changing your thoughts can also be a powerful way to curtail your anger. When a situation arises that leads you to feel the telltale signs of anger, your thoughts will likely amplify what you are feeling. For example:

"I can't believe my spouse just said that! This is another reason why we're probably headed toward divorce."

"My friends always treat me like a joke. They always look down on me."

"Allah just keeps sending disappointments my way. I'm sick and tired of this and I'm done trying."

Consider the following steps to transform your thought processes and help manage your reactions during moments of anger:

1. **Be aware of what you are saying to yourself.** Ask yourself: What are the thoughts running through my head right now?

2. **Challenge your thoughts.** Remember, just because you think something doesn't mean it's true. Ask yourself:
   A. What is a more helpful thought?

B. Can this situation be interpreted differently?
C. What story am I making up in my head right now?
D. How is *Shaytaan* trying to get me to think about this and is it accurate?

3. **Exercise gratitude.**
It's very hard to react in anger while also feeling grateful. This mindset shift can break the typical reaction pattern that tends to happen when something makes you feel upset. Ask yourself: Is there something I can be grateful for right now? Could this situation be even worse?

Spiritual shift

A final step in the process of managing feelings of anger is to create a spiritual shift to allow this experience to be a means of bringing you closer to Allah ﷻ and to assign meaning to the struggle you are enduring. The different triggers we face each day are all a part of the tests of this life. Allah ﷻ reminds us,

> *Do the people think that they will be left to say, "We believe," and they will not be tried? But We have certainly tried those before them, and Allah will surely make evident those who are truthful, and He will surely make evident those who are false.*[17]

One of the purposes of the tests we face is to propel us toward Allah ﷻ. When we experience difficult moments, the intensity

17 Qur'an 29:2–3.

of our emotions can be a way of connecting with Allah ﷻ. When we choose to do this, our experience can be transformed in a very powerful way.

Consider some of these steps to create a spiritual shift when you are feeling angry:

1. **Validate the emotion:** Just like Allah ﷻ reassured and validated the Prophet Muhammad's ﷺ emotional experience in the following *ayah*, realize that acknowledging your difficult emotion is an important step when trying to connect with Allah.

   > ***We know that you, [O Muḥammad], are saddened by what they say. And indeed, they do not call you untruthful, but it is the verses of Allah that the wrongdoers reject.***[18]

2. **Acknowledge that this emotion is a way through which your pain is manifested, and no pain goes unseen by Allah.** The Prophet ﷺ said,

   > ***Nothing afflicts a Muslim of hardship, nor illness, nor anxiety, nor sorrow, nor harm, nor distress, nor even the pricking of a thorn, but that Allah will expiate his sins by it.***[19]

18 Qur'an 6:33.

19 *Ṣaḥīḥ al-Bukhārī*, no. 5641; Sahih Muslim, no. 2573.

3. **Transform an uncomfortable emotion into *du'aa*.**
   Choose a Name of Allah ﷻ to call out to Him by and to request His help and support. Some powerful ones during moments of distress include: *al-Shaheed* (The Witness) who witnesses your pain; *al-Razzaq* (The Provider) who can provide you with anything you need right at the moment; and *al-Mu'min* (The Remover of Fear and the Giver of Tranquility) who can remove one's distress and bestow peace upon one. Example:

   "Yā Allah, you are al-Mu'min, the source of calm. I'm so overwhelmed and hurt right now. It almost feels like I can't control myself. Please help me through this. You are the source of all support and comfort. Please give me what I need to manage this."

4. **Choose an *ayah* or *du'aa* to recite when experiencing strong emotions.**
   Some suggestions include:

   - ***"I seek refuge with Allah from the accursed* Shaytaan."**

Sulaiman bin Surd narrated: *While I was sitting in the company of the Prophet ﷺ, two men abused each other and the face of one of them became red with anger, and his jugular veins swelled (i.e., he became furious).* On that the Prophet ﷺ said,

> ***"I know a word, the saying of which will cause him to relax, if he does say it. If he says: 'I seek Refuge with Allah from Satan,' then all his anger will go away."***[20]

---

20 *Ṣaḥīḥ al-Bukhārī*, no. 3282.

- *"Allah is sufficient for me. There is none worthy of worship but Him. I have placed my trust in Him, He is Lord of the Majestic Throne."* [21]

The Prophet ﷺ said,

> *"Allah will grant whoever recites this seven times in the morning or evening whatever he desires from this world or the next: 'Allah is sufficient for me. There is none worthy of worship but Him. I have placed my trust in Him, He is Lord of the Majestic Throne.'"* [22]

The *du'aa* of Musa عليه السلام:

- *"My Lord! I am indeed in need of any good You may send down to me!"* [23]

- *"There is no might nor power except with Allah."*

It was narrated that Abu Dharr said:

> *"The Messenger of Allah ﷺ said to me: 'Shall I not tell you of a treasure that is one of the treasures of Paradise?' I said: 'Yes, O Messenger of Allah.' He said:* **'La hawla wa la quwwata illa billah** *(There is no power and no strength except with Allah).'"* [24]

---

21 Quran 9:129.

22 *Ḥiṣn al-Muslim*, no. 83; *Sunan Abī Dāwūd*, 4/321; *Ibn al-Sunnī*, no. 71.

23 Qur'an 28:24.

24 *Sunan Ibn Mājah*, no. 3825.

You can choose the conclusion

The way we think is incredibly powerful and can either help us move forward or break us amidst difficulty. We naturally try to make sense of life by interpreting events and predicting what seems logical in the moment. However, we can *choose* which conclusion or interpretation we want. We may not be able to control the emotions we immediately feel upon receiving devastating news or witnessing a tragedy. We may not even be able to control the immediate passing thoughts that come to our minds in such a situation. However, we all have a choice: We can choose to dwell on thoughts that bring us closer to Allah ﷻ or on thoughts that push us further away from Him. And we can choose actions that either increase the strength of our connection with Allah or decrease it.

Consider the example of Musa عليه السلام when he was trapped with the army of Pharaoh on one side and the Red Sea on the other. In these verses we see the example of two different thought processes: One that would strengthen a relationship with Allah ﷻ and one that would diminish it:

> *When the two groups came face to face,*
> *the companions of Moses cried out, "We are*
> *overtaken for sure." Moses reassured [them],*
> *"Absolutely not! My Lord is certainly with me—*
> *He will guide me." So, We inspired Moses:*
> *"Strike the sea with your staff," and the sea*
> *was split, each part was like a huge mountain.*[25]

25 Qur'an 26:61–63.

During a difficult situation, the people of Musa jumped to the conclusion that they were doomed, which brought about feelings of fear and devastation. We see a very different response from Musa when he assumed the opposite. He expected good from Allah ﷻ and received a miracle that we still reflect on today. We find the evidence we search for, so search for the good and watch your thoughts and emotions transform.

Spiritual inspiration for reflection

> *"And He has granted you all that you asked Him for. If you tried to count Allah's blessings, you would never be able to enumerate them..."* [26]

> *"Satan threatens you with poverty and orders you to immorality, while Allah promises you forgiveness from Him and bounty. And Allah is all-Encompassing and Knowing."* [27]

> *"And will provide for him from where he does not expect. And whoever relies upon Allah—then He is sufficient for him."* [28]

The Prophet ﷺ advised his daughter, Fatima *radi Allahu anha*, to say in the morning and in the evening:

26 Qur'an 14:34.
27 Qur'an 2:268.
28 Qur'an 65:3.

> ***"O Allah, I have hope in Your Mercy, so do not leave me in charge of my affairs even for a blink of an eye and rectify for me all of my affairs. None has the right to be worshipped except You."*** [29]

Abdullah ibn 'Umar reported:
The Messenger of Allah ﷺ would supplicate saying,

> ***"O Allah, I seek refuge in you from a decline in your blessings, the transformation of the wellness You have provided, Your sudden retribution, and all things displeasing to you."*** [30]

Practical exercises

A. Choose the conclusion you want

Be aware of your thoughts:

We naturally try to make sense of life by interpreting events and predicting what seems logical in the moment. However, jumping to conclusions is based on false evidence, fear, anger, and distrust. What are the conclusions you tend to make about yourself, others, the world, and Allah ﷻ during distressing moments?

---

29 *Jami' al-Tirmidhi*, no. 3524.
30 *Sahih Muslim*, no. 2739.

1. **Example:** "I'm unlovable," "Allah doesn't care about me," "Life will never get better," etc.

2. ______________________________

3. ______________________________

Focus on the facts:

What are some observable and tangible facts about this situation? Do these facts match the thought you wrote above?

Example: "My friend called me to hang out over the weekend;" "Allah has provided me with a job, food, shelter, etc.;" "I've been through hard times before and things eventually got better," etc.

4. ______________________________

5. ______________________________

6. ______________________________

Change your conclusion:

Our minds create stories based on our emotions at the moment. However, you can choose the conclusion you want. What is an alternate conclusion to this situation? What is a more helpful thought? Can this situation be interpreted differently? What story are you making up in your head right now? How is Shaytaan trying to get you to think about this and is it accurate?

1. **Example:** "There are some struggles in my marriage, but we can work through them," "Allah tests those He loves," "Things are very difficult right now, but I know that Allah has promised ease with every hardship so ease will come," etc.
2. __________
3. __________
4. __________

B. What we need vs. What we want

Remember that Allah ﷻ gives us everything we need but not everything that we want.

Have you ever thought you desperately needed something, were disappointed that it didn't happen and, after some time, learned something that made you realize that it wasn't right for you?

Write about that experience and notice what thoughts and emotions come up.

____

____

____

____

____

____

C. Identifying anger patterns

Identifying your personal anger patterns is the first step to changing them. Self-awareness is powerful and is the starting point to any meaningful change.

What are situations that tend to lead to feelings of anger (triggers)? Write them below:

1. Example: when someone says something disrespectful, deadlines, child tantrums, arguments with loved ones, etc.
2. ____
3. ____
4. ____

What do you notice happening in your body during moments of anger? Write them below:

1. **Example:** racing heart, feeling overheated, shaking hands, tension in shoulders, etc.

2. ______________________________

3. ______________________________

4. ______________________________

Notice the thoughts that go through your mind during moments of anger. Write them below:

1. **Example:** "Everyone is out to get me," "I'm a monster," "No one ever listens to me," etc.

2. ______________________________

3. ______________________________

4. ______________________________

Managing anger

Our emotions can be very powerful but so can our thoughts and actions. When you notice yourself feeling angry, consider these different ways to navigate this difficult emotion.

D. Managing anger through a physical shift

Physical shift: To work on your anger through creating a physical shift, create a list of the different ways you can create a 90-second pause before reacting.

Examples: deep breathing, look at a clock, do jumping jacks, shake it out, sit down, make *wudu*, etc.

1. ______________________________
2. ______________________________
3. ______________________________
4. ______________________________
5. ______________________________
6. ______________________________

E. Managing anger through a mental shift

Identify the underlying emotion. What feeling are you actually experiencing underneath the surface that is leading to your anger?

Example: unappreciated, disrespected, overwhelmed, scared, exhausted, ashamed, etc.

Name the emotion to tame the intensity of it.

I am feeling really ______________ right now.

Identify the underlying need. Based on the emotion you've identified, what is the underlying need? What do you need right now to feel better?

Example: a hug, talking it out, reassurance, leaving an environment that feels unsafe, taking a break, etc.

Address the need. Find a way to get this need addressed. Is there a way you can fulfil it yourself or reach out to someone to help you with this? How can you get this need fulfilled in a way that is within your control?

Example: request a hug from someone you love; call a cab to take you home if you are uncomfortable; take a walk around your neighbourhood for a breather; call a friend you trust; etc.

____

____

____

F. Managing anger through a spiritual shift

Transform your anger into a *du'aa* to Allah ﷻ. Choose a Name of Allah ﷻ to call out to Him by and release whatever you're struggling with onto this page in a *du'aa* to Him.

Name of Allah ﷻ: ___________________________________

Meaning of this Name: _______________________________

Why does this Name of Allah ﷻ resonate with you right now? What are you asking of Allah ﷻ? What do you need right now?

____

____

____

Choose an *ayah* or *du'aa* to recite when experiencing strong emotions. Write it here:

____

____

____

Case study revisited

After realizing that his friends all hung out at their favourite spot without him over the weekend, Ahmed felt his anger bubble over once again. Ahmed was about to send angry text messages to his friends, but abruptly came to his senses and realized that he needed to get his anger under control, or he would lose the relationships that were so meaningful to him; he didn't need to make his life worse than it already was.

Ahmed began to reflect on the things that triggered his anger and realized that he felt most angry when he was left out or felt like a failure. Once he discovered the underlying emotions beneath his anger, he started to reflect on where these two feelings were showing up the most: with school and with friends.

Ahmed was feeling like a total failure because it was doubtful he was going to be able to fulfil his childhood dream of becoming a pharmacist. He decided to set up an appointment with an academic advisor to reevaluate this career path, explore options available, and get resources to help him do better in school. He also realized that jumping to conclusions was hurting him more than anything else and that he needed to focus on his accomplishments and strengths until he figured out what he was going to do next.

Ahmed also started to think more about his interactions with friends and it dawned on him that over the past few months he hadn't asked any of them how they were doing. Each time he spoke to someone, he complained about his own struggles. He started going through his friends' social media accounts and realized that at least two of them had been dealing with their own difficulties during this time. Instead of thinking, "My friends must hate me and that's why they aren't hanging out with me anymore," he began to think, "I've been really focused on my own struggles lately and haven't been as kind to my friends—this is something I'd like to work on."

As Ahmed worked on these negative thought patterns, his behaviours began to change. He started to identify the things that triggered his angry outbursts and was able to practise healthier ways of responding to them. He decided to exercise daily in order to release the adrenaline that was building up in his body. Ahmed felt a greater sense of overall calmness and began to feel proud of the way he was able to pause before reacting during situations that usually triggered his anger. He made it a point to ask his friends how they were doing and to journal about his own struggles to offer himself the ongoing release he needed.

Ahmed applied the same awareness to his thoughts about Allah ﷻ and the impact they had had on his relationship with Him. He realized that he had been thinking that Allah ﷻ didn't care for him due to all of the struggles he was enduring. When he realized that this was an example of mind-reading, Ahmed began to remind himself, "Allah tests those He loves, and I have to do my part to change my life as well." Ahmed began to consciously transform his angry moments into moments of connecting with Allah ﷻ through du'aa. As his thoughts toward Allah ﷻ improved, his connection through acts of worship also improved. Ahmed began to feel deserving of good and continued to take the initiative to increase the good in his life.

Coping Skills Toolbox

In previous chapters of this book, we discussed labeling unhealthy thoughts, modifying them, and then using coping skills to manage them. This section contains some of these **coping skills,** as well as some new ones, as individual segments.

The purpose of this section is to have an **easy-to-access collection of coping skills** that one can use on the go and long after the book has been finished. We've kept the coping skills short for easy reading, and simple so they can be used by anyone—even someone who hasn't read previous parts of this book.

All coping skills can be practised independently of each other; however, we recommend you start with the **Safe Place Exercise** because some of the other coping skills (like deep breathing) can be used in conjunction with it for maximum benefit. You can tell how effective a coping skill is by rating your level of stress on a scale of one to ten (one being the most relaxed and 10 being the most stressed) before and after the exercise for comparison.

Safe Place Exercise[1]

Trauma and anxiety can cause us to feel like we have no safe place for refuge. The Safe Place technique is a visualization exercise that one can use when feeling triggered. Developing a safe place in your mind that nobody has access to, or nobody can take away can bring oneself down from a heightened state of anxiety. Once you have practised this exercise a few times you may be able to close your eyes and do it without reading the script. This exercise is great to pair with deep breathing and aromatherapy.

1 Adapted from Ferentz, "Safe Place Induction."

Find a quiet place where you can sit comfortably without interruption. Close your eyes if you can.

Take a few seconds to breathe in deeply and out slowly. Breathe in and out intently. Breathe in and out slowly.

When you're ready, imagine that you are walking down a long, quiet hallway with a special door at the very end. This special door leads to your safe place where you can take shelter, relax, or regain your strength. It's a door that can transport you, in your mind, to a place that can be whatever you need it to be. Take a moment to visualize the colours and details of this hallway and you walking down it. In your mind, you might hear the sound of your feet stepping on the floor. Each step brings you closer to that door.

The closer you get to the door, the more a feeling of peace seems to come over you. You don't know exactly what awaits you on the other side, but you know this is a safe place for you. It's a place where nobody or nothing can harm you. What stands on the opposite side of the door is a place where you can exist freely without fear, judgement, or harm. This is a place where you can simply be.

As you put your hand on the doorknob, your heart looks forward to what awaits you. When you think it's time, slowly open the door and put one foot inside your safe place, while keeping your other foot in the hallway. Notice how it feels to have one foot on each side. Feel the calm start to overcome your body on the side that's in your safe place. Before you fully step in, look back at the door, and observe what it looks like. Notice all the colours and details so you can find it and come back to it easily when you are finished being in your safe space.

When you are ready, fully enter your safe place. Slowly shut the door behind you and hear the door as it softly closes.

When you look up, you might notice an image of what your safe space looks like. Take a few moments to see what image comes up for you in your mind. Take as long you need for a full image to appear. This may be a place you have visited in real life or a place you have never been before.

To get a closer look you may want to take a few steps into your safe place. What do you see all around you? What are the colours like? Are the colours sharp or soft? Take a moment to let a clear picture develop in your mind as you scan the environment from right to left. Take a deep breath and scan again from left to right. Take in a deep breath and exhale slowly.

As you take a few more steps inside, continue to take notice of all the sights around you, including above you... and below you. What do you see above your head, and what do you see beneath your feet? What do you see directly in front of you and behind you?

While you continue to take in full, deep breaths notice how the air feels around you, going into your lungs as you inhale and then exhale. Note what the air smells like. Gently concentrate on that scent as it drifts to the back of your nose. Is the scent floral? Or perhaps it smells like spices, wood, or the ocean. Breathe deeply.

As you get settled in your safe space, walk around and touch some of the objects you see. Are these objects heavy or light? Smooth or rough? Feel the details beneath your fingertips as you pick objects up and put them back down. Notice if these objects feel cool or warm in your hands.

As you continue to experience this place with all your senses, notice if there are any tastes in your safe place. The taste might be sweet or salty, or something completely from your imagination.

As you continue to immerse yourself in your safe space, you may want to shift your attention to the sounds of this place. Are there any noises? The sounds might be close by or far away. The sounds might be clear or muffled, or perhaps you hear nothing at all.

As you relax in your safe place, glance back at the door and know that you can leave any time you wish. In the meantime, however, take as long as you need being present where you are and absorbing whatever comforting, uplifting, or calming energy you need from your special place.

Notice how it feels in your body being in this place. Imagine all your anxiety and sadness slowly leaving your body starting with the top of your head... neck... shoulders... back... chest... arms... fingers... torso... thighs... knees... calves... feet and then toes. Take a few seconds focusing on each body part, letting your worries and sorrow drain onto the floor and disappear into the ground. Take all the time you need to fully experience this.

When you are ready to go back to your day-to-day life, slowly begin to walk back to the door. You can walk as quickly or slowly as you would like. Take a last look at your safe place knowing that everything will stay the same and be here whenever you want to return. When you are ready to leave, slowly open the door and exit. Close the door gently behind you and slowly walk away down the hallway. Each footstep brings you closer to the present. When you are ready, open your eyes and take a few seconds to reorient yourself in the here and now.

Containment Exercise[2]

Processing trauma can be cathartic, but sometimes might also cause feelings of overwhelm, sadness, and anxiety afterwards. These feelings can be especially bothersome when they come up unexpectedly—like at work, when we are with our children, or when we are trying to go to sleep. Suppressing feelings of trauma doesn't work and sometimes can make them more intense. Containment is a visualization technique that can be used to compartmentalize unruly feelings so that they are healthily put away until a more appropriate time, like in therapy or during journal writing.

2 Adapted from Ferentz, Trauma Certificate Program.

Directions:

Step 1: Close your eyes. Using your imagination, collect and gather all the difficult feelings you are currently experiencing in your mind and in your body, and visually place them in front of you on the floor. Visualize that your feelings are tangible objects that you can transfer from your body to a spot in front of you.

Step 2: Visualize condensing the difficult feelings you just removed from your body into one object. Imagine what this object might look like. What is the shape of this object? What colours does your object have? Is it opaque or transparent? Is it solid or some other form? How big or small is it? What does it smell like? Keep your object at a distance while making mental notes of all its details.

Step 3: Imagine a safe container or vault that you can put your difficult feelings inside. Use all your senses to visualize a secure object to put the thoughts and feelings into. What kind of container or vault is it? What colour is it and what is it made out of? Is it a thick metal, wood, or something else that is impenetrable? How does the container open and close? Does it have a lock? What is the lock like? The more you can visualize details of your container, the better. Imagine what the vault looks, feels, and smells like.

Step 4: Put all your difficult feelings into the container until they feel distant from you. You can drop them in or pour them. Take all the time you need. For some people this may take a few minutes and for others the process can take much longer. When all your feelings are inside, imagine locking or sealing the container in whatever manner you choose. Take your time and really experience what it feels like to put away your feelings.

Step 5: Assess if you feel like your thoughts and emotions are contained. Remember this exercise is not to make your sadness and anxiety go away—but to safely store them until another time. If you feel like your emotions are safely stored then visualize where you would like to keep this container until you are ready to retrieve it again (like in your therapist's office, the bottom of the ocean, your closet, etc.). Visualize the process of putting the container away.

Step 6 (if needed): If your emotions do not feel contained, visualize putting your container in another container or vault using the same visualization techniques. Continue to do this until you feel secure. When you are finished, put away the container wherever you would like until you are ready to retrieve it again.

Du'aa Exercise

Having someone to talk to that completely understands you is invaluable. Many times, we seek this comfort out from family and friends, completely overlooking that we also have a more trustworthy, dependable, and strong ally: Allah ﷻ.

And when My servants ask you, [O Muhammad], concerning Me—indeed I am near. I respond to the invocation of the supplicant when he calls upon Me. So let them respond to Me [by obedience] and believe in Me that they may be [rightly] guided.[3]

In this exercise, you are tapping into the relationship you have with your One and Only Creator, who not only hears you, but knows exactly what you need.

What are some of the benefits of speaking with Allah ﷻ?

1. Sometimes when you speak with family members or friends, they simply do not understand what you are experiencing, while Allah ﷻ knows everything you are going through. He knows the level of your excruciating pain and also knows about all the circumstances contributing to what ails you. He knows about all the injustices being done to you, and the struggles weighing you down.

2. Allah ﷻ has the power to change your circumstances even when solving your problems seems impossible, or the odds are not in your favour. Your free will and what others can do for you *may* be able to solve some problems in your life, but Allah ﷻ has power over all things and can change factors that are apparent as well as hidden.

3. Connecting with Allah ﷻ helps you realize that you are not alone. Even when the whole world seems to have turned against you, Allah ﷻ is always there to listen, no matter what you have done or what has been done to you.

---

3 Qur'an 2:186.

Directions:

Find a quiet and comfortable place where you can make *du'aa*.

Believe in the power of the *du'aa* and feel in your heart that your *du'aa* will be answered.

Put your hands up as though you are asking for something.

Begin by praising Him, thanking Him for what He has given you and sending *salaam* on Prophet Muhammad ﷺ.

Pour out your heart to Allah ﷻ by telling Him all the things that are bothering you. Feel the *du'aa* coming from your heart and soul.

Tell Him that you need guidance and help, and that nobody has the power to change things except Him.

Ask Allah ﷻ for what you want help with, to make it easy for you, and to rectify your affairs.

End by asking Allah ﷻ to forgive you for your sins, glorifying Him, thanking Him, and sending *salaam* on Prophet Muhammad ﷺ.

Abu Hurairah narrated that the Messenger of Allah ﷺ said:

There is not a man who calls upon Allah with a supplication, except that he is answered. Either it shall be granted to him in the world, or reserved for him in the Hereafter, or his sins shall be expiated for it according to the extent that he supplicated—as long as he does not supplicate for some sin, or for the severing of the ties of kinship, and he does not become hasty. They said: "O Messenger of Allah, and how would he be hasty?" He ﷺ said: "He says: 'I called upon my Lord, but He did not answer me.'"[4]

4 *Jamiʿ al-Tirmidhi*, no. 3604.

Mantra Repetition

Mantra repetition is the practise of repeating an uplifting, usually spiritual, phrase to yourself. When one thinks of mantras, one might think of Hinduism, but Prophet Muhammad ﷺ repeated dhikr *throughout the day, every day. Research indicates that mantra repetition can significantly improve wellbeing for individuals who have PTSD.*

One Islamic mantra supported by secular research is "*Bismillāh al-Raḥmān al-Raḥīm*" (In the name of Allah, the Merciful, the Compassionate); however, you can use whatever phrase you wish that brings up positive feelings for you.[5] At first saying the mantra will feel mechanical, but over time it will become habitual and internalized.

Picking your mantra might be the toughest part. You can think about this for a period of time or use a few until you figure out which one suits you the best. A few examples might be:

> ***Do not grieve; indeed, Allāh is with us.***[6]
>
> ***We belong to God and to Him we shall return.***[7]
>
> ***Lā ilāha illā Allāh, Muhammadun rasulu Allāh.***

Once you pick your mantra, repeat it to yourself throughout the day, especially when faced with uncomfortable feelings. Use it intentionally to reconnect with Allah ﷻ and ground yourself. When we get overwhelmed, we tend to flee to the past or to the future; allow your mantra to recalibrate you back to the present and your purpose in life. Try this for a few weeks until it feels like second nature. You can combine this with other coping skills like when practising mindfulness or doing breathing exercises. If you are artistically inclined, you can draw, paint, or create something related to your mantra.

---

5 Bormann and Abraham, "Evaluation of the Mantram Repetition Program."
6 Qur'an 9:40.
7 Qur'an 2:156.

Note: If using an *ayah*, be sure to be respectful of how you use it and store it.

Grounding

Memories of traumatic experiences and worrisome thoughts can cause our body and brain to perceive a threat where there is currently none. This results in an increase in anxiety and feeling physically and emotionally overwhelmed. Grounding is a technique that breaks this cycle by shifting your mind away from stressful thoughts and into the present moment. Grounding helps to reorient a person to the here-and-now to regain mental focus from an intensely emotional state.

This grounding technique is called the 5-4-3-2-1 method in which you will use all your five senses to help redirect you back to the present moment.

Directions:

Step 1: Sit comfortably, close your eyes, and take a few deep breaths in through your nose and out through your mouth.

Step 2: Open your eyes and look around you. Find:

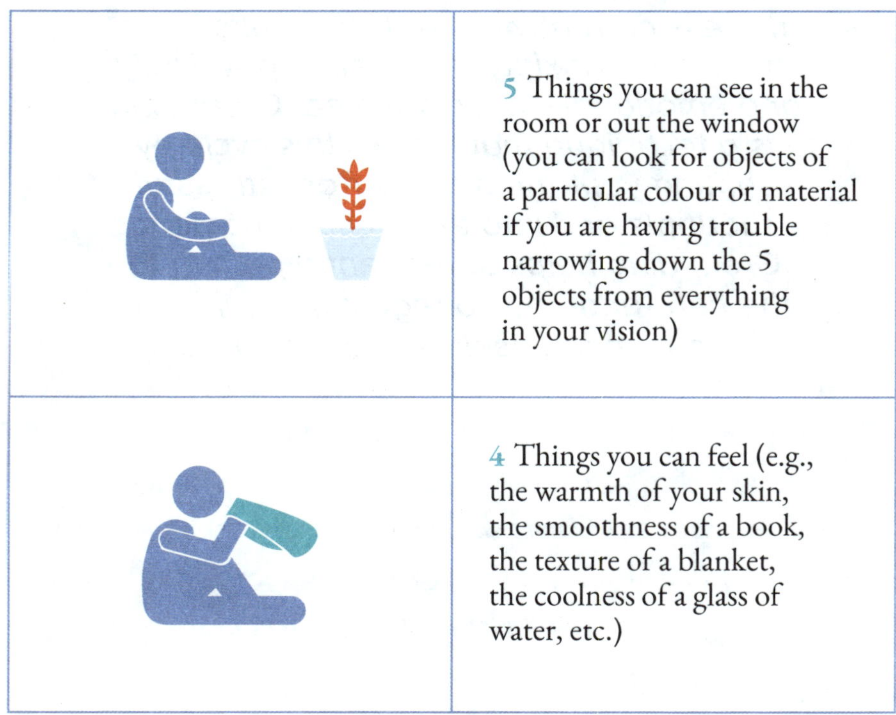

5 Things you can see in the room or out the window (you can look for objects of a particular colour or material if you are having trouble narrowing down the 5 objects from everything in your vision)

4 Things you can feel (e.g., the warmth of your skin, the smoothness of a book, the texture of a blanket, the coolness of a glass of water, etc.)

	3 Things you can hear (e.g., traffic noise, birds chirping, the sound of your breathing, a clock ticking, etc.)
	2 Things you can smell or smells that you enjoy if no smells are clearly present
	1 Things you can taste (your morning coffee, a refreshing sip of water, or something you can allow to rest in your mouth [like chocolate or fruit] for a few seconds to savor the flavour).

Step 3: Take a deep, encompassing breath to end and as you exhale, slowly say "*Alhamdulillah*" aloud to thank Allah ﷻ for the ability to experience your fully functioning senses.

Paced Breathing

Trauma activates our sympathetic nervous system, which makes us feel anxious, agitated, and overwhelmed. If we can counteract this unpleasant stress response by activating the parasympathetic nervous system, we can calm down quickly and effectively. Simple, deep breathing is one of the most effective ways to lower our heart rate, relax our muscles, and refocus our minds. A relaxed body yields a relaxed mind and a heart that is open to healing.

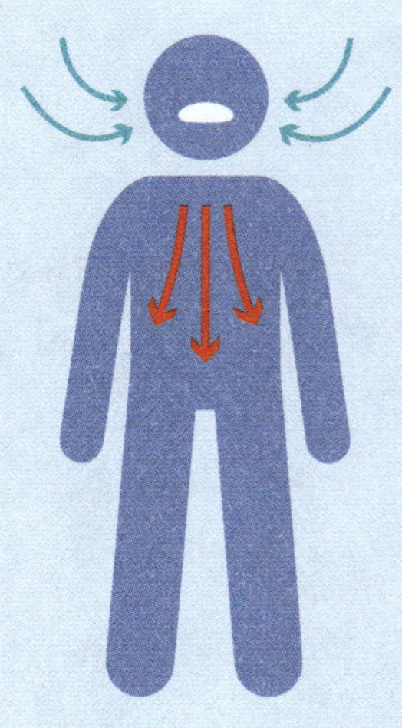

Directions for paced breathing:

Sit upright and comfortably in a chair with your arms supported on the chair or in your lap.

Take a slow, deep breath in through your nose imagining your lower belly inflating like a balloon. Do this for 4 counts.

Hold your breath for 2 seconds.

Exhale slowly through your mouth, feeling your belly move inward toward your spine as you push out the air. Do this for 5 to 6 counts.

The longer the exhale, the greater the relaxation response so ensure that the exhale breath is at least one to two counts longer than the inhale breath.

Wait a few seconds before repeating this exercise. It is often helpful to repeat this exercise 5–10 times to decrease feelings of anxiety.

Try to practise this technique during times when you are calm in order to reap the full benefits during times of stress and anxiety.

Progressive Muscle Relaxation[8]

Progressive muscle relaxation is one of the easiest and most effective relaxation techniques to learn. It teaches you to relax your mind and relieve stress by learning to progressively tense and release different muscle groups in your body—allowing an increase in awareness of the physical manifestation of difficult emotions.

8 Adapted from Cohen, "Progressive Muscle Relaxation."

The script below is a guide, which you can modify as needed. Most people find that holding tension in a muscle group for 5 to 10 seconds works best. If you experience any pain when tensing a particular muscle group, that step can be omitted.

Progressive muscle relaxation script

Begin by finding a comfortable position, either sitting or lying down, in a location where you will not be interrupted.

Allow your attention to focus only on your body. If you begin to notice your mind wandering, bring it back to the muscle you are attending to. It is perfectly natural if your mind wanders during this exercise. Just bring it back to the muscles you're addressing when you realize you're thinking about something other than this exercise.

Take a deep breath through your abdomen, hold for a few seconds, and exhale slowly.

As you breathe, notice your stomach rising and your lungs filling with air. Take your time and just spend a minute or two breathing and noticing your breathing.

As you exhale, imagine the tension in your body being released and flowing out of your body.

And again, inhale and exhale 

Feel your body already relaxing.

As you go through each step of this exercise, visualize the muscles tensing. Then it can be helpful to imagine a wave of relaxation flowing over the muscle group as you release that tension. It is important that you keep breathing normally throughout the exercise and not hold your breath.

Now let's begin. Tighten the muscles in your forehead by raising your eyebrows as high as you can. Hold for about five seconds. Then, abruptly release, feeling that tension fall away.

Pause for 5–10 seconds and breathe.

Now smile widely, feeling your mouth and cheeks tense. Hold for about 5 seconds, and release, appreciating the softness in your face.

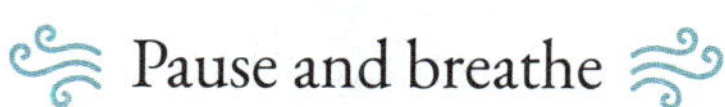

Next, tighten your eye muscles by squinting your eyelids tightly shut. Hold for about 5 seconds, and release.

Gently pull your head back as if to look at the ceiling.

Hold for about 5 seconds, and release, feeling the tension melting away.

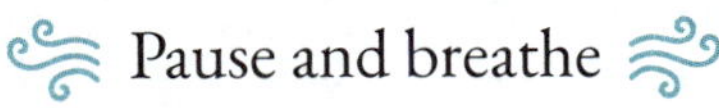

Now feel the weight of your relaxed head and neck sink. Breathe in and breathe out.

Now, tightly, but without straining, clench your right fist and hold this position for about 5 seconds… and release.

Pause and breathe

Now, feel the tension in your right forearm and hand. Feel that buildup of tension. You may even visualize that set of muscles tightening.

Hold for about 5 seconds… and release, enjoying that feeling of limpness. Breathe in and breathe out.

Now, feel the tension in your entire right arm. Feel that buildup of tension. Tense your entire right arm. Hold for about 5 seconds, and release.

Pause and breathe

Now, tightly, but without straining, clench your left fist and hold this position for about 5 seconds… and release.

Pause and breathe

Now, feel the tension in your left forearm and hand. Feel that buildup of tension. You may even visualize that set of muscles tightening.

Hold for about 5 seconds... and release, enjoying the feeling of limpness. Breathe in and breathe out.

Now, feel the tension in your entire left arm. Feel that buildup of tension. Tense your entire left arm, feeling the tension. Hold for about 5 seconds, and release.

Pause and breathe

Now lift your shoulders up as if they could touch your ears. Hold for about 5 seconds, and quickly release, feeling their heaviness.

Pause and breathe

Tense your upper back by pulling your shoulders back trying to make your shoulder blades touch. Hold for about 5 seconds, and release.

Pause and breathe

Tighten your chest by taking a deep breath in, hold for about 5 seconds, and exhale, blowing out all the tension.

Pause and breathe

Now tighten the muscles in your stomach by sucking it in. Hold for about 5 seconds, and release.

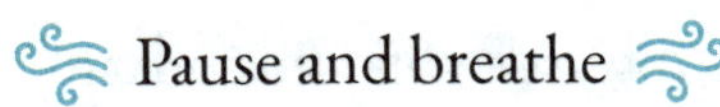
Pause and breathe

Gently arch your lower back. Hold for about 5 seconds... and relax.

Pause and breathe

Tighten your buttocks. Hold for about 5 seconds... and release, imagine your hips falling loose.

Pause and breathe

Feel the tension in your entire right leg and thigh. Hold for about 5 seconds... and relax. Feel the tension melting away from your leg.

Pause and breathe

Now flex your right foot, pulling your toes towards you and feeling the tension in your calves. Hold for about 5 seconds... and relax, feel the weight of your legs sinking down.

Pause and breathe

Feel the tension in your entire left leg and thigh. Hold for about 5 seconds... and relax. Feel the tension melting away from your leg.

Pause and breathe

Now flex your left foot, pulling your toes towards you and feeling the tension in your calves. Hold for about 5 seconds... and relax, feel the weight of both of your legs sinking down.

Pause and breathe

Curl your toes under, tensing your feet. Hold for about 5 seconds, and release.

Pause and breathe

Now imagine a wave of relaxation slowly spreading through your body beginning at your head and going all the way down to your feet. Each wave feels warm and comforting. Your body is completely relaxed.

Feel the weight of your relaxed body. Breathe in and breathe out.

As you breathe, notice your stomach rising, and your lungs filling with air. Spend a moment or two breathing and noticing your breathing.

As you exhale, imagine the tension in your body being released and flowing out of your body.

And again, inhale and exhale

Slowly open your eyes and savour the sensation of a fully relaxed body.

Mindfulness

Mindfulness prioritizes conscious living through avoiding unconscious or mechanical activity, tuning into the present moment, and becoming fully aware of your inner sensations and the world around you. Over the past several decades, researchers have found increasing evidence of the benefits of mindfulness practises. They have been found to reduce stress, depression, and anxiety and have also been used to heal trauma.

This particular mindfulness guided meditation script uses the metaphor of a mountain, one of the majestic signs of Allah ﷻ, to create a sense of calm and stability. It can be used during both times of ease and distress.

"Be the Mountain" guided meditation script:[9]

Breathe deeply. Bring your awareness to the sensations of your breath, and the gentle rhythm it is creating within you. Letting it be, just as it is.

Expand your awareness to the sensations of your body. Sitting upright and with dignity reminding yourself that Allah ﷻ told us,

> ***And We have certainly honoured the children of Adam...***[10]

and you are one of the honoured children of Adam.

Bring your attention to the surface beneath you and the support it provides. Root your body into its strength and become aware of your connection to it—complete, whole, and in this moment, you are grounded by its unwavering resolve.

As you sit there, visualize a grand mountain, imagining the words of Allah ﷻ, marvelling,

9 Adapted from Kabat-Zinn, *Wherever You Go, There You Are.*
10 Qur'an 17:70.

...at the mountains, how they
are rooted and fixed firm?[11]

Visualize a mountain whose peaks pierce smoky clouds and continue upward where the air is clear, and the view is endless. A mountain with slopes that are both jagged and gentle; supported by a vast foundation, rooted deep in the bedrock of the earth. This mountain is a monument to all that is solid, grand, unmoving, and beautiful—a sign of Allah ﷻ, The Creator, The Magnificent.

Take a moment and look: Are there trees? Does snow blanket its lofty heights? Perhaps waterfalls cascade and send mist into an open sky? However it is, let it be as it is: a perfect creation.

Imagine yourself as this mountain and share in its stillness.

Grounded in your posture, your head its skyward peak, supported by the rest of your form, granting you an awe-inspiring perspective of the landscape before you, behind you, and around you, which flows from your centre into the distant horizon.

Be this mountain.

And take on its stability as your own. From the top of your crown, down your neck, and into the balance of your shoulders, like cliffs, descending into your arms and forearms, and coming to rest in the valley of your hands.

---

11 Qur'an 88:19.

Be the mountain. Your feet, legs, and hips its base—solid and rooted beneath you—a foundation, extending up your spine and abdomen: a core of stability.

The rhythm of your breath is all that moves you. A living mountain: alive and aware, yet unwavering in inner stillness grounded in the strength given to you by The Almighty.
As Allah ﷻ says,

Allah is He who created you in (a state of) weakness, then gave you strength after weakness...[12]

A mountain that witnesses the sun traveling across the sky, casting light and shadows and colours as it remains solid, unmoving. Moment by moment, in the mountain's stillness, the surface teems with life and activity. Snows melt, streams run down its face, trees and flowers bloom, and die and bloom again as the wildlife returns and departs with the seasons.

Be the mountain that sits and sees how night follows day and back again. That knows the sun by the warmth it brings on rising, and the stars by the way they show in a darkened sky. That knows the closeness of its Creator who says,

Indeed, I am near.[13]

12 Qur'an 30:54.
13 Qur'an 2:186.

Through it all, the mountain sits. Aware of the changes that each moment brings, around it and to it. Yet it remains itself. True to itself and to its Creator. Still, as the seasons flow one into the other, and the air swirls from hot and cold, and the weather turns from tame to turbulent.

Still, none of this concerns the mountain, whose serenity is housed within, and cannot be disturbed by fleeting turmoil. Knowing that after turbulent winds will come peaceful breezes due to the promise of its Lord,

For indeed, with hardship will be ease.
Indeed, with hardship will be ease.[14]

Like the mountain, you will experience the changing nature of your mind and body, and of the world around you. You will have periods varying in intensity—of darkness and light, of activity and inactivity, and moments that fill your life with colour.

Through it all, be the mountain, and call on the patient strength and stability Allah ﷻ has given you.

Let it empower you to encounter each moment with mindful composure and compassionate clarity.

---

14 Qur'an 94:5–6.

What Now?

Getting help beyond this book

Congratulations on completing this book. We hope you found the individual chapters, and the book as a whole, beneficial in understanding more about trauma and how to begin your healing journey. This last section is about cultivating supports beyond the book.

Tips for healing

Now that you have read all the sections of this book you might be wondering what to do next. Ideally you have completed the exercises in the various chapters and have begun to incorporate some of the techniques in your day-to-day life. Strategies for healing take practice and patience. Keep in mind that if you have been holding on to trauma for years, the impact of it is not going to go away in a short period of time.

In addition to working on your trauma, it's important to take care of your whole self in the recovery process. The trauma you experienced is just one part of your mental health and it's important to nurture other parts of your well-being, including your physical health and interpersonal relationships. The next section offers some quick tips and suggestions on how you can enhance your healing process in a more comprehensive way.

Functional tips

It's difficult to address the symptoms of trauma if you are constantly in a state of crisis. Everyday stressors may include running late to appointments, missing deadlines, mediating conflict between family members and having to complete large amounts of work (at home, school, work, etc.). Stress is an unavoidable part of life but can be drastically reduced by being proactive instead of reactive. Small strategies can make a big difference in decreasing stress so you can get out of survival mode (which many people who have endured trauma get stuck in), and into thriving mode. A person cannot flourish without the proper free time to reflect, be forward thinking, creative, and well-rested.

Consider learning about time-management skills such as prioritization, short-term and long-term goal setting, and effective communication to be more proactive. The time it will take you to read about these strategies is minimal when you consider how much time you will get back after implementing them. There is an abundance of free articles, books, podcasts, and webinars that can easily be accessed online or at your local library.

Physical tips

In addition to treating trauma in the body, it will enhance your healing process to work toward good physical health. Sleep, for example, is very important, and lack of it can exacerbate mental health symptoms.[1]

Every person is different, but in general 7–9 hours of sleep is ideal for most people. Additionally, good nutrition and adequate exercise are beneficial to mental health.[2] It may sound overly simplistic, but having a well-balanced and nutritious diet, as well as getting regular exercise, can actually make you feel better.

---

1 Mental Health Foundation, *Sleep Matters*.

2 Lim et al., "Nutritional Factors Affecting Mental Health"; Swan and Hyland, "Review of the Beneficial Mental Health Effects."

Psychological tips

Self-care is important for regulating mood and keeping stress at bay. Good self-care is the consistent practice of making your mental, physical, and spiritual health a priority. There is a misconception amongst some Muslims that good time management is filling every moment of your day with something useful, so that on the Day of Judgement you will be able to say you used your time effectively.

Human beings are not meant to operate this way. Even if you think about how the body is designed, human beings need to take breaks to pray, eat, use the bathroom, and sleep. Good self-care is intentional rest to keep your mind and body running at optimal levels. If you are chronically overworked, you will likely have ebbs and flow of productivity—good progress alternating with debilitating crashes that come afterward. If you prioritize self-care, through scheduling consistent rest periods throughout your day or week, your ability to steadily progress towards your goals will more likely be successful long-term. Intentional rest can include writing in a journal, getting some fresh air, doing a creative project, reading, doing *dhikr*, and reflecting on your relationship with Allah ﷻ.

Interpersonal tips

The people in your everyday environment make a big difference in your trauma management. If you have friends, family members, or colleagues who treat you with disrespect, or hostility, you may be reminded of the trauma that you experienced; these kinds of interactions can exacerbate your symptoms. It helps to surround yourself with people who are supportive, have similar values as you, and treat you with respect. The quality of friends is much more important than the quantity.

It's useful to know what type of boundaries to put in place when there is a toxic person in your life. If the toxic person is not a family member or coworker, consider removing that person from your life altogether. You don't need to tell the person you are ending the relationship, or that they are unhealthy for you- just distance yourself slowly over time while being cordial if you do run into them. If the toxic person is someone you must deal with, learn effective communication skills, limit the frequency of interaction with them, and be assertive (respectful but firm) when you need to. Through additional reading about coping with difficult people and ways to create healthy boundaries, whether online or your local library, you can find ways to protect yourself without severing the ties that can't be broken.

Spiritual tips

The spiritual interventions in this book will help with your trauma healing journey insha Allah, but there are spiritual activities beyond the scope of this book that can make a big difference. Working on your spirituality is paramount for your well-being in this world and the next, and therefore your connection to Allah should take precedence in your day-to-day activities and goals. Prioritize your life by putting Allah ﷻ and what He commands first, like *salah*.

Keep in mind that daily activities such as work, caring for children, and doing schoolwork can feel mundane, but can also be done for His sake. By making the intention to please Allah ﷻ through these everyday tasks, one gets the opportunity to accumulate more good deeds while feeling closer to Him. When we make a conscious choice to be practising Muslims, living our lives in accordance with Islamic principles can alleviate a lot of our stress and improve many of our relationships.

Abu Hurairah (May Allah be pleased with him) reported that the Prophet ﷺ said,

When Allah loves a servant, He calls Gabriel and He says: "Verily, I love this person so you should love him." Then Gabriel loves him and makes an announcement in the heavens, saying: "Allah loves this person, and you should love him." Thus, the dwellers of the heavens love him, and he is honoured on the earth.[3]

Those are upon [right] guidance from their Lord, and it is those who are the successful.[4]

...And whoever fears Allah—He will make for him a way out.[5]

3 *Sahih al-Bukhari*, no. 3037; *Sahih Muslim*, no. 2637.

4 Qur'an 2:5.

5 Qur'an 65:2.

This book is not the end

As stated in the beginning of this book, this publication is not meant to be a substitute for therapy so if you are feeling that your trauma is still unresolved, we highly recommend getting additional support. Stigma in the Muslim community about seeking psychotherapy is decreasing, but there are still some prevalent myths about counselling. We will address some of these myths briefly here:

Counselling is haraam

We are not quite sure where this myth originated from, but we suspect it has something to do with the fact that some concepts in Western psychology are not congruent with Islamic principles, and so people without knowledge of what psychology really is began discouraging friends and family from seeking help, fearing it would hurt them spiritually. The field of psychology is immense and, while some theories are not Islamically sound, this does not make the whole field of psychology worthless. This is the same with Islam—there are some deviant views of Islam and people who practise Islam incorrectly, but this does not affect the importance or validity of the religion itself. In fact, research indicates that Muslim scholars contributed to the field of psychology as early as 800 AD, way before modern-day psychology was developed.[6]

Additional concerns about the permissibility of counselling come from questions about complaining and backbiting. Discussing problems with the intention of fixing them is not being ungrateful to Allah ﷻ and conversing with a trusted advisor about problems you have with other people for the sake of fixing those issues is not backbiting.

Counselling is expensive

Psychotherapy is a medical service from a licensed professional and can be costly if you don't have insurance. Here are a few things to consider about the myth of counselling being too expensive:

1. What are the long term emotional, physical, and interpersonal costs of not seeking counselling to heal your trauma? Will you miss many days of work, not be able to finish school, or pay a lot of money to doctors and specialists for psychosomatic complaints? When you do the math this way, perhaps seeking counselling might be less expensive. Also keep in mind the long-term emotional cost to your soul and your relationships with loved ones. We live in this *dunya* for a very short period of time and being consumed with trauma can prevent us from meeting our full potential in this world and the next.

6 Haque, "Psychology from Islamic Perspective."

2. Some people have very limited funds, and it is almost impossible for them to pay full fee for services; however if you are like the average person, you likely have the money to pay for counselling but are choosing other comforts over your mental health. If you say you cannot afford counselling, but spend $200 a month on take-out food, you are prioritizing eating out over your mental health. If you need counselling, but every year during Black Friday spend $1500 on the latest tech gadgets, then you are prioritizing your love of electronics over your mental health. We are not saying that people should avoid eating out or buying nice things, but to be honest with themselves that the issue at hand is choosing not to spend on mental wellness, versus not having the money to spend on mental wellness.

3. There are many ways to get counselling at a reduced cost if you cannot afford it. The most popular way is to use health insurance and see an in-network therapist. Another method is to get counselling through your work's Employee Assistance Program (EAP); many places of employment will pay on your behalf for a certain number of sessions from an approved provider. If you are a student, ask your university counselling centre about therapy, as many colleges and universities will provide a certain number of sessions for free. Lastly, you can look into reduced cost therapy from organizations that offer pro bono services in which therapists donate some of their time. It might take a little bit of work upfront, but affordable counselling is available.

Counselling doesn't work

You may have heard from a family member or friend that counselling does not work. Perhaps therapy didn't work for that individual, but you may not know all of the reasons why. Therapist-client fit, the individual's motivation to get better, unrealistic expectations of therapy, and the complexity of the situation or the specific mental health problem are all potential reasons why therapy may have turned out poorly for that individual. In general, however, if the therapist-client relationship is good, the therapist has effective tools to help the client, and the client is motivated to work toward change in their life, therapy almost always provides some benefit.

Counselling will bring shame to my family

Counselling is completely confidential unless your therapist has reasonable cause to think you are going to hurt yourself or someone else, or if a vulnerable person is being or has been abused. Other than these circumstances, the contents of your therapy sessions are completely private by law. If you are concerned about someone seeing you at a therapist's office, then seek online counselling from the comfort of your own home. You can also pay for services without using your insurance if you want added privacy.

Finding the right therapist

If you are now interested in counselling, but have no idea where to start, you are not alone. Searching for and choosing a therapist might feel daunting at first when you don't know what you are looking for. Below is some information to consider and characteristics to look for in a potential therapist:

Types of mental health professionals

There is a lot of confusion for people outside the field of mental health about what types of professionals offer what kind of mental health services. Below are short and simple definitions of each profession. Please keep in mind that these definitions are not comprehensive, and may be defined differently depending on the state or country you live in.

Psychiatrist: A medical doctor who prescribes medicine for mental health symptoms. Some psychiatrists offer counselling, but many do not.

Nurse practitioner: Similar to a psychiatrist, these medical professionals can prescribe psychotropic medication, but do not provide therapy. Some nurse practitioners specialize in the field of mental health, but most do not.

Psychologist: Unbeknownst to many, psychologists specialize in different services and not all are trained in providing counselling. Clinical psychologists are qualified to provide psychotherapy, whereas some other types of psychologists are only trained in administering psychometric testing or conducting research.

Social worker: Licensed clinical social workers are trained and qualified to engage in psychotherapy but cannot prescribe medication. Non-clinical social workers are helping professionals and work in many settings including schools, hospitals, and government offices, but do not provide therapy.

Professional counsellors, mental health counsellors, marriage and family therapists: These professionals are trained and qualified to provide psychotherapy to clients when licensed, but cannot prescribe medication.

Coaches: Most coaches have no clinical training and are not qualified to give psychotherapy. Coaches are good for psychoeducation, problem-solving, consultation, and mentoring. Some coaches are also psychotherapists, but most of the time they are not.

Questions to ask when choosing a provider

In searching for the right medical professional for you, make sure you understand the type of help you are looking for in order to find the best fit. Also keep in mind that just because someone graduated from a university with a mental health degree doesn't mean they are licensed and legally allowed to provide counselling.

Here are some basic questions you can ask a potential mental health professional when you begin to look for services:

1. Are you licensed to practise therapy? What states and countries are you licensed to practise in?
2. What types of mental health services do you provide? Individual, family, group? Online or in-person?
3. Do you prescribe medication or work with someone who does?
4. Do you have any counselling specialties (children, trauma, marriage, etc.)?
5. What is your personal approach to therapy?
6. What is your experience in this field and how long have you been in it?

Deciding whether to begin therapy or medication

If you have mild symptoms of anxiety, depression, or trauma, our personal recommendation is to start therapy first for at least 3–6 months consistently before trying other options like psychotropic medication or alternative medicine.

Psychiatric medication is very important and useful but can have unintended side effects. Many people will find relief with just psychotherapy and won't need medication, which is why we recommend this route first. If you attend therapy sessions consistently (every week or every two weeks) for 3–6 months and treatment is not working, then explore the idea of medication with your provider.

If you have severe mental health symptoms, cannot function, are psychotic (seeing and hearing things that are not there), suicidal, or homicidal, then medication should be considered alongside your therapy immediately. Each individual case is different so be sure to speak with your mental health provider(s) about all your symptoms and treatment options.

In-person counselling vs. online counselling

When looking for a therapist you may want to reflect on if you prefer seeing someone in-person or online. Some people prefer in-person therapy because of the direct face-to-face experience while others prefer online therapy because there is no commute, and they have more provider options if they are looking for a specific type of treatment. Drawbacks for online therapy include that it's not recommended for everyone (clients with severe symptoms) and that occasional technical difficulties are inevitable over time. If you see a therapist online, make sure your mental health provider is using a secure telehealth platform and that they are licensed to provide services in the locality in which you reside.

Personality and theoretical orientation

When you are looking for a therapist, you want to find a provider that has a personality that is compatible, but not necessarily similar, with yours. If you are very cerebral, a cognitive behavioural therapist may be a better fit for you than someone who specializes in expressive therapies like art. If you are laidback and want to explore who you are as a person in a very causal and open-ended way, then a therapist with a very directive approach might not be a good fit. There is no way to guarantee who will be a good fit for you, but most therapists offer free consultations in which you can get a feel for their personality. If you go to a few therapy sessions and feel like the fit isn't right, don't get disheartened. The person you saw is not a bad therapist, and you are not a bad client for wanting to try someone else. Be honest with your therapist and tell them that you are not sure it's a good fit. Your therapist might try a different approach with you or may refer you to someone else.

Spirituality

By default, licensed therapists are not supposed to give counselling from a spiritual perspective unless the client expresses interest in that. While every therapist has their own spiritual biases (no human being is truly neutral), you can expect counselling to be secular whether your therapist is Muslim or of another faith. If you are looking for someone to give you counselling from an Islamic perspective, then naturally you need to seek this out and communicate that to your potential therapist.

Some Muslim therapists provide counselling congruent with Islamic values, but may not use Islamic interventions, so inquire about whether and, if so, how your potential therapist incorporates Islam into their practice. If you are considering a therapist who is of a different faith than yours (because no Muslim therapist is available, you must use someone who takes your insurance, etc.), then make sure they are culturally and spiritually competent and don't look down upon your values. This is especially important if you are taking your child for counselling, as you do not want a therapist who promotes different values than your own.

Ending *du'aa*

As this book comes to an end, we pray that you will find the relief that you are looking for in your mind, body, and heart. We ask Allah ﷻ to comfort you in your journey and give you complete healing. We beseech Allah ﷻ to give you the strength, wisdom, and courage to put the destructive parts of your trauma to rest, and to use the good that's left to propel yourself into a better emotional, interpersonal, physical, spiritual, and functional state than you have ever experienced before.

O Allah, You are the source of healing so heal me. O Allah, You are the source of peace so fill every aspect of my life with peace, contentment, and tranquility. O Allah, expand my heart and fill it with ease and closeness to You. Please alleviate my hardships and allow all of the struggles I'm enduring to be a means of gaining closeness to You. Please reward me immensely for everything I'm going through and protect me from ever falling into despair or giving up hope. O Allah, please bless my healing journey and grant me goodness in this life and the next. O Allah, please allow me to grow into the best possible version of myself as I attempt to navigate all of the different roles you have given me. I am trying and only You can truly see all of my effort. Oh Allah, You are al-Shahīd *(The All- and Ever-Witnessing) and You are* al-Shakūr *(The Most Appreciative)—only You can truly acknowledge and appreciate all of my efforts. My Lord, I am truly in need of whatever good You will send down to me, so please send down good to me. O Allah, You know what I need more than I know myself, so set my affairs aright and grant me everything that is good for me. Thank You for all You have given me and bringing me to these first steps towards healing. Please don't ever let me think for a second that You have forsaken me. Oh Allah, please guide me, shower me with Your Mercy, and heal me in the most beautiful of ways.* Allahumma Āmīn.

About the authors

Najwa Awad, LCSW-C, PMH-C is a psychotherapist, certified perinatal mental health specialist and organizational mental health consultant who is passionate about helping Muslims heal, grow, and thrive after adversity. She has a private practice and has been providing services to individuals, families, schools, and nonprofits in the Baltimore-Washington metropolitan area for over 15 years. Najwa enjoys giving workshops to destigmatize mental illness, address current mental health issues within the community, and promote psychological health from an Islamic perspective.

Sarah Sultan, LPC, LMHC is a licensed professional counsellor who strives to empower her clients through achieving healthier, more fulfilling lives and relationships while reconnecting with Allah during the healing process. Sarah obtained a master's degree in Mental Health Counselling and has practiced therapy for over 10 years. She is also an instructor with Mishkah University and AlMaghrib Institute, where she teaches courses about the intersections between Islam, psychology, and counselling.

Bibliography

Aifuwa, Soloman. "Effects of Child-Parent Attachment and God Attachment on Depression in Adolescent Christians." PhD diss., Liberty University, 2016. Doctoral Dissertations and Projects. https://digitalcommons.liberty.edu/cgi/viewcontent.cgi?article=2408&context=doctoral.

Al-Nawawi, Abū Zakariyyā Yaḥyā ibn Sharaf. *Riyad as-salihin*. The Book of Miscellany, book 1, hadith 27. https://sunnah.com/riyadussaliheen/1/27.

Al-Qarni, 'Aaidh ibn Abdullah. *Don't Be Sad*. Riyadh: International Islamic Publishing House, 2005.

Avants, Brian B., Daniel A. Hackman, Laura M. Betancourt, Gwendolyn M. Lawson, Hallam Hurt, and Martha J. Farah. "Relation of Childhood Home Environment to Cortical Thickness in Late Adolescence: Specificity of Experience and Timing." *PLoS ONE* 10, no. 10 (2015). https://doi.org/10.1371/journal.pone.0138217.

Badri, Malik. *Abu Zayd al-Balkhi's Sustenance of the Soul: The Cognitive Behavior Theory of a Ninth Century Physician*. Washington: The International Institute of Islamic Thought, 2013.

Beck, Aaron. *Love Is Never Enough: How Couples Can Overcome Misunderstandings, Resolve Conflicts and Solve Relationships through Cognitive Therapy*. New York: Harper & Row Publishers, 1989.

Bennett, Edward L., Marian C. Diamond, David Krech, and Mark R. Rosenzweig. "Chemical and Anatomical Plasticity of the Brain," *Science* 146, no. 3644 (1964): 610–19.

Boag, Simon. "Psychodynamic Approaches to Borderline Personality Disorder." *The ACPARIAN* 9 (1994): 25–28.

Bormann, Jill E., and Traci H. Abraham. "Evaluation of the Mantram Repetition Program for Health Care Providers." *Federal Practitioner* 36, no. 5 (2019): 232.

Boser, Ulrich, Megan Wilhelm, and Robert Hanna. "The Power of the Pygmalion Effect: Teachers' Expectations Strongly Predict College Completion." Center for American Progress, 2004. https://files.eric.ed.gov/fulltext/ED564606.pdf.

Bowlby, John. *Attachment and Loss* Vol. 1, *Attachment*. New York: Basic Books. 1969.

Brach, Tara. *True Refuge: Finding Peace and Freedom in Your Own Awakened Heart*. New York: Bantam Books, 2013.

Brown, Brené. *Daring Greatly: How the Courage to Be Vulnerable Transforms the Way We Live, Love, Parent, and Lead*. New York: Gotham, 2012.

Brown, Brené. *The Gifts of Imperfection: Let Go of Who You Think You're Supposed to Be and Embrace Who You Are*. Center City, MN: Hazelton Publishing, 2010.

Buades-Rotger, Macià, Frederike Beyer, and Ulrike M. Krämer. "Avoidant Responses to Interpersonal Provocation Are Associated with Increased Amygdala and Decreased Mentalizing Network Activity." *eNeuro* 4, no. 3 (2017). https://doi.org/10.1523/ENEURO.0337-16.2017.

Burns, David D. *Feeling Good: The New Mood Therapy*. New York: Penguin Books, 1981.

Caine, Christine. "Sometimes when you're in a dark place." Facebook, January 9, 2016. https://www.facebook.com/theChristineCaine.

Camus, Albert. "Return to Tipasa." In *Summer*. New York: Penguin, 1995.

Cashwell, Craig S., Paige B. Bentley, and J. Preston Yarborough. "The Only Way Out Is Through: The Peril of Spiritual Bypass." *Counseling and Values* 51 (2007): 139–48. https://doi.org/10.1002/j.2161-007X.2007.tb00071.x.

Chartier, Isabelle S. and Martin D. Provencher. "Behavioural Activation for Depression: Efficacy, Effectiveness and Dissemination." *Journal of Affective Disorders* 145, no. 3 (2013): 292–99. https://doi.org/10.1016/j.jad.2012.07.023.

Cohen, Harold. "Progressive Muscle Relaxation." Psych Central, 2018. https://psychcentral.com/lib/progressive-muscle-relaxation/.

Cornah, Deborah. *The Impact of Spirituality on Mental Health: A Review of the Literature*. Mental Health Foundation, 2006. https://www.mentalhealth.org.uk/sites/default/files/impact-spirituality.pdf.

Covey, Stephen R. *The 7 Habits of Highly Effective People: Restoring the Character Ethic*. New York: Free Press, 2004.

Dickie, Jane R., Amy K. Eshleman, Dawn M. Merasco, Amy Shepard, Michael Vander Wilt, and Melissa Johnson. "Parent-Child Relationships and Children's Images of God." *Journal for the Scientific Study of Religion* 36, no. 1 (1997): 25–43.

Drevets, Wayne C., Joseph L. Price, Joseph R. Simpson, Richard D. Todd, Theodore Reich, Michael Vannier, and Marcus E. Raichle. "Subgenual Prefrontal Cortex Abnormalities in Mood Disorders." *Nature* 386 (1997): 824–27.

Dunphy, Kim, Sue Mullane, and Marita Jacobsson. "The Effectiveness of Expressive Arts Therapies: A Review of the Literature." *Psychotherapy and Counselling Journal of Australia*, 2013. http://pacfa.org.au/wp-content/uploads/2012/10/expressiveartsreviewnov20131.pdf.

Emler, Nicholas. "Self Esteem: The Costs and Causes of Low Self Worth." *Youth Studies Australia*, no. 21 (2001).

Engel, George L. "Is Grief a Disease? A Challenge for Medical Research." *Psychosomatic Medicine* 2, 1961, 18–22.

Falconer, Caroline J., Aitor Rovira, John A. King, Paul Gilbert, Angus Antley, Pasco Fearon, Neil Ralph, Mel Slater, and Chris R. Brewin. "Embodying Self-Compassion within Virtual Reality and Its Effects on Patients with Depression," *British Journal of Psychiatry Open* 2, no. 1 (2016): 74–80.

Felitti, Vincent J., Robert F. Anda, Dale Nordenberg, David F. Williamson, Alison M. Spitz, Valerie Edwards, Mary P. Koss, and James S. Marks. "Relationship of Childhood Abuse and Household Dysfunction to Many of the Leading Causes of Death in Adults: The Adverse Childhood Experiences (ACE) Study." *American Journal of Preventive Medicine* 14, no. 4 (1998): 245–58. https://doi.org/10.1016/S0749-3797(98)00017-8.

Ferentz, L. "Safe Place Induction, Adapted from Milton Erikson." Trauma Certificate Program Level II. Baltimore, MD, 2013.

Ferentz, L. Trauma Certificate Program, Level I. Baltimore, MD, 2011.

Frankl, Viktor. *Man's Search for Meaning*. Boston: Beacon Press, 2006.

Gilbert, Josiah Hotchkiss. *Dictionary of Burning Words of Brilliant Writers*. New York: W. B. Ketcham, 1895.

Haque, Amber. "Psychology from Islamic Perspective: Contributions of Early Muslim Scholars and Challenges to Contemporary Muslim Psychologists." *Journal of Religion and Health* 43, no. 4 (2013): 357–77t.

Hassanpour, Mahlega S., Lirong Yan, Danny J. J. Wang, Rachel C. Lapidus, Armen C. Arevian, W. Kyle Simmons, Jamie D. Feusner, and Sahib S. Khalsa. "How the Heart Speaks to the Brain: Neural Activity During Cardiorespiratory Interoceptive Stimulation." *Philosophical Transactions of The Royal Society B: Biological Sciences* 371, no. 1708 (2016). https://doi.org/10.1098/rstb.2016.0017.

Hofmann, Stefan G., Anu Asnaani, Imke J.J. Vonk, Alice T. Sawyer, and Angela Fang. "The Efficacy of Cognitive Behavioral Therapy: A Review of Meta-Analyses." *Cognitive Therapy and Research* 36, no. 5 (2012): 427–40. https://doi.org/10.1007/s10608-012-9476-1.

Holahan, Charles J., Rudolf H. Moos, Carole K. Holahan, Penny L. Brennan, and Kathleen K. Schutte. "Stress Generation, Avoidance Coping, and Depressive Symptoms: A 10-Year Model." *Journal of Consulting and Clinical Psychology* 73, no. 4 (2005): 658–66.

Hussein, Asmaa. *A Temporary Gift: Reflections on Love, Loss, and Healing*. Toronto: Ruqaya's Bookshelf, 2015.

Ibn al-Qayyim al-Jawzīyah, Muḥammad ibn Abī Bakr. *Kitab al-fawaid al-mushawwiq ilá ulum al-Qur'an wa-ilm al-bayan talif al-Imam ibn al-Qayyim al-Jawziyah*. Kujranwalah: Dar Nashr al-Kutub al-Islamiyah, n.d.

Ibn al-Qayyim al-Jawzīyah, Muḥammad ibn Abī Bakr. *Al-Fawā'id*. N.p.: Dār al-Salām, 2019.

Ibn al-Qayyim al-Jawzīyah, Muḥammad ibn Abī Bakr. *Shifā al-'alīl fī masāil al-qaḍā wa-al-qadar wa-al-ḥikmah wa-al-ta'līl*. Cairo: Dār at-Turāth, 1978.

Ibn Atheer, Rida M. *Abu Bakr al-Seddeq: The First Caliph*. Beirut: Dar al-Kotob al-Ilmiyah, 2008.

Ibn Ḥanbal, Aḥmad ibn Muḥammad. *Al-Zuhd*.

Ibn Kathīr, Ismā'īl ibn 'Umar, and Ṣafī al-Raḥmān al-Mubārakfūrī. *Tafsīr Ibn Kathīr* (abriged edition). Riyadh: Darussalam, 2000.

Ibn Rajab, Abd al-Rahman ibn Ahmad. *Jami' al-ulum wa al-hikam*.

John-Steiner, Vera, Carolyn P. Panofsky, and Larry W. Smith, eds. *Sociocultural Approaches to Language and Literacy: An Interactionist Perspective*. Cambridge: Cambridge University Press, 1994. https://doi.org/10.1017/CBO9780511897047.

Joseph Rowntree Foundation. *The Costs and Causes of Low Self-Esteem*. Joseph Rowntree Foundation, 2001. https://www.jrf.org.uk/sites/default/files/jrf/migrated/files/n71.pdf.

Kabat-Zinn, Jon. *Wherever You Go, There You Are: Mindfulness Meditation in Everyday Life*. New York: Hyperion, 1994.

Kaur, Rupi. *Milk and Honey*. Kansas City: Andrew McMeel Publishing, 2015.

King, Laura A. "The Health Benefits of Writing about Life Goals." *Personality and Social Psychology Bulletin*, no. 27 (2001): 798–807.

King, Laura A., and Joshua A. Hicks. "Detecting and Constructing Meaning in Life Events." *The Journal of Positive Psychology* 4, no. 5 (2009): 317–30. https://doi.org/10.1080/17439760902992316.

Knapp, Paulo, and Aaron T. Beck. "Cognitive Therapy: Foundations, Conceptual Models, Applications and Research." *Brazilian Journal of Psychiatry*, 2008. http://www.scielo.br/pdf/rbp/v30s2 /en_a02v30s2.pdf.

Koscik, Timothy R., and Daniel Tranel. "The Human Amygdala Is Necessary for Developing and Expressing Normal Interpersonal Trust." *Neuropsychologia* 49, no. 4 (2011): 602–11. https://doi.org/10.1016/j.neuropsychologia.2010.09.023.

Kross, Ethan, Marc G. Berman, Walter Mischel, Edward E. Smith, and Tor D. Wager. "Social Rejection Shares Somatosensory Representations with Physical Pain." Proceedings of the National Academy of Sciences of the United States of America, 108 (2016): 6270–75.

Kübler-Ross, Elisabeth, and David Kessler. *Life Lessons: Two Experts on Death and Dying Teach Us about the Mysteries of Life and Living*. New York: Scribner, 2000.

Lazar, Sarah W., Catherine E. Kerr, Rachel H. Wasserman, Jeremy R. Gray, Douglas N. Greve, Michael T. Treadway, Metta McGarvey, Brian T. Quinn, Jeffery A. Dusek, Herbert Benson, Scott L. Rauch, Christopher I. Moore, and Bruce Fischld. "Meditation Experience Is Associated with Increased Cortical Thickness." *NeuroReport* 16 (2005): 1893–97.

Lee, Jia-In, Ming-Been Lee, Shih-Cheng Liao, Chia-Ming Chang, Suz-Chieh Sung, Hung-Chi Chiang, and Chuan-Wan Taid. "Prevalence of Suicidal Ideation and Associated Risk Factors in the General Population." *Journal of the Formosan Medical Association* 109, no. 2 (2010): 138–47.

Lee, Sang Wan, John P. O'Doherty, and Shinsuke Shimojo. "Neural Computations Mediating One-Shot Learning in the Human Brain." *PLoS Biology* 13, no. 4 (2015).

Leman, Joseph, Will Hunter III, Thomas Fergus, and Wade Rowatt. "Secure Attachment to God Uniquely Linked to Psychological Health in a National, Random Sample of American Adults." *The International Journal for the Psychology of Religion* 28, no. 3 (2018): 162–73. https://doi.org/10.1080/10508619.2018.1477401.

Li, Xingyi. "Treating Complex Trauma with Art Therapy from a Neurobiological Viewpoint." Master's thesis, Hofstra University, 2015. https://doi.org/10.13140/2.1.4365.3925.

Lim, So Young, Eun Jin Kim, Arang Kim, Hee Jae Lee, Hyun Jin Choi, and Soo Jin Yang. "Nutritional Factors Affecting Mental Health." *Clinical Nutrition Research* 5, no. 3 (2016):143–52.

Lincoln, Lawrence J. *Reclaiming Banished Voices: Stories on the Road to Compassion*. Bloomington, IN: Balboa Press, 2017.

Linehan, Marsha M. *DBT Skills Training Manual*. 2nd ed. New York: The Guilford Press, 2015.

Linehan, Marsha M., Linda Dimeff, Kelly Koerner, and Erin M. Miga. "Research on Dialectical Behavior Therapy: Summary of Non-RTC studies." Behavioral Tech, 2013. https://behavioraltech.org/downloads/Research-on-DBT_Summary-of-Data-to-Date.pdf.

Lundahl, Brad, and Brian L. Burke. "The Effectiveness and Applicability of Motivational Interviewing: A Practice-Friendly Review of Four Meta-Analyses." *Journal of Clinical Psychology* 65, no. 11 (2009): 1232–45.

Maier, Steven F., and Martin E. P. Seligman. "Learned Helplessness: Theory and Evidence." *Journal of Experimental Psychology: General* 105, no. 1 (1976): 3–46.

Matos, Marcela, José Pinto Gouveia, and Cristiana Duarte. "Constructing a Self Protected against Shame: The Importance of Warmth and Safeness Memories and Feelings on the Association between Shame Memories and Depression." *International Journal of Psychology and Psychological Therapy* 15, no. 3 (2015): 317–35.

McDonald, Angie, Richard Beck, Steve Allison, and Larry Norsworthy. "Attachment to God and Parents: Testing Correspondence vs. Compensation Hypotheses." *Journal of Psychology and Christianity* 24 (2005): 21–28.

Mental Health Foundation. *Sleep Matters: The Impact of Sleep on Health and Wellbeing*. Mental Health Foundation, 2011. https://www.mentalhealth.org.uk/sites/default/files/MHF-Sleep-Report-2011.pdf.

Mujtaba, Bahaudin G. "Interpersonal Change through the 'Inside-Out-Approach': Exercising the Freedom to Choose Our Responses during Conflict and Stressful Situations." *RU International Journal* 2, no. 1 (2008): 1–12.

National Institute for the Clinical Application of Behavioral Medicine. "How Anger Affects the Brain and Body." The National Institute for the Clinical Application of Behavioral Medicine. https://www.nicabm.com/how-anger-affects-the-brain-and-body-infographic/.

Newberg, Andrew, Michael Pourdehnad, Abass Alavi, and Eugene d'Aquili. "Cerebral Blood Flow during Meditative Prayer: Preliminary Findings and Methodological Issues." *Perceptual and Motor Skills* 97, no. 2 (2003): 625–30. https://doi.org/10.2466/pms.2003.97.2.625.

O'Dea, Meghan. "Transcript: Sheryl Sandberg at the University of California at Berkeley 2016 Commencement." *Fortune*, May 14, 2016. http://fortune.com/2016/05/14/sandberg-uc-berkley-transcript/.

O'Rourke, Justin J. F., Benjamin Tallman, and Elizabeth Altmaier. "Measuring Post-Traumatic Changes in Spirituality/ Religiosity." *Mental Health, Religion, & Culture* 1 (2008): 719–28.

Otsuka, Yumiko. "Face Recognition in Infants: A Review of Behavioral and Near-Infrared Spectroscopic Studies." *Japanese Psychological Research* 56, no. 1 (2014): 76–90.

Panagioti, Maria, Patricia Gooding, and Nicholas Tarrier. "Post-Traumatic Stress Disorder and Suicidal Behavior: A Narrative Review." *Clinical Psychology Review* 29, no. 6 (2009): 471–82.

Parrott, Justin. *Daily Hadith Online* (blog). https://www.abuaminaelias.com/

Preminger, Son. "Transformative Art: Art as Means for Long-Term Neurocognitive Change." *Frontiers in Human Neuroscience* 6, no. 96 (2012). https://doi.org/ 10.3389/fnhum.2012.00096.

Rakic, Pasko. "Neurogenesis in Adult Primate Neocortex: An Evaluation of the Evidence." *Nature Reviews Neuroscience* 3, no. 1 (January 2002): 65–71.

Riley, Theo, Gerald R. Adams, and Elwin Nielsen. "Adolescent Egocentrism: The Association among Imaginary Audience Behavior, Cognitive Development, and Parental Support and Rejection." *Journal of Youth and Adolescence* 13, no. 5 (1984): 401–17.

Riva, Federica, Chantal Triscoli, Claus Lamm, Andrea Carnaghi, and Giorgia Silani. "Emotional Egocentricity Bias across the Life-Span." *Frontiers in Aging Neuroscience* 8, no. 74 (April 26, 2016). https://www.ncbi.nlm.nih.gov/pmc/articles/PMC4844617/.

Roozendaal, Benno, Bruce S. McEwen, and Sumantra Chattarji. "Stress, Memory and the Amygdala." *Nature Reviews Neuroscience* 10, no. 6 (2009): 423–33. https://doiorg/10.1038/nrn2651.

Rosenthal, Robert, and Lenore Jacobson. "Teachers' Expectancies: Determinants of Pupils' IQ Gains." *Psychological Reports* 19 (1966): 115–18.

Sajjadi, Fatemah, Yadolla Zargar, Leila Zare, and Fakhri Tajikzadeh. "The Predictive Role of Early Trauma Dimensions on Self-Esteem in 11–13-Year-Old Students: Controlling the Role of Maladaptive Schema," *Razavi International Journal of Medicine* 4, no. 3 (2016).

Semple, William E., Peter F. Goyer, Richard McCormick, Beverly Donovan, Raymond F. Muzic Jr., Loreen Rugle, Kevan McCutcheon, Colleen Lewis, David Liebling, Sean Kowaliw, Ken Vapenik, Mary Ann Semple, Christy R. Flener, and S. Charles Schulz. "Higher Brain Blood Flow at Amygdala and Lower Frontal Cortex Blood Flow in PTSD Patients with Comorbid Cocaine and Alcohol Abuse Compared to Controls." *Psychiatry Interpersonal and Biological Processes* 63, no. 1 (2000): 65–74. https://doi.org/10.1080/00332747.2000.11024895.

Sheikh, Alia I. "Posttraumatic Growth in Trauma Survivors: Implications for Practice." *Counselling Psychology Quarterly* 21, no. 1 (2008): 85–97. https://doi.org/10.1080/09515070801896186.

Sheldon, Kennon M., and Sonja Lyubomirsky. "How to Increase and Sustain Positive Emotion: The Effects of Expressing Gratitude and Visualizing Best Possible Selves." *The Journal of Positive Psychology* 1, no. 2 (2006): 73–82.

Shelquist, Richard. "The Beautiful Names of Allah: Al-Latif." Wahiduddin's Web, n.d. https://wahiduddin.net/words/99_pages/latif_30.htm.

Shelquist, Richard. "The Beautiful Names of Allah: Al-Wali." Wahiduddin's Web, n.d. https://wahiduddin.net/words/99_pages/walee_55.htm.

Shin, Lisa M., Scott L. Rauch, and Roger K. Pitman. "Amygdala, Medial Prefrontal Cortex, and Hippocampal Function in PTSD." *Annals of the New York Academy of Sciences* 1071 (2006): 67–79. https://doi.org/ 10.1196/annals.1364.007.

Shin, Lisa M., Scott P. Orr, Margaret A. Carson, Scott L. Rauch, Michael L. Macklin, Natasha B. Lasko, Patricia Marzol Peters, Linda J. Metzger, Darin D. Dougherty, Paul A. Cannistraro, Nathaniel M. Alpert, Alan J. Fischman, and Roger K. Pitman. "Regional Cerebral Blood Flow in the Amygdala and Medial Prefrontal Cortex during Traumatic Imagery in Male and Female Vietnam Veterans with PTSD." *Archives of General Psychiatry* 61 (2004): 168–76.

Siegel, Daniel J. *Brainstorm: The Power and Purpose of the Teenage Brain.* New York: Penguin, 2015.

Spertus, Ilyse L., Rachel Yehuda, Cheryl M. Wong, Sarah Halligan, and Stephanie V. Seremetis. "Childhood Emotional Abuse and Neglect as Predictor of Psychological and Physical Symptoms in Women Presenting to Primary Care Practice." *Child Abuse & Neglect* 27, no. 11 (2003): 1247–58.

Stamm, B. Hudnall, ed. *Secondary Traumatic Stress: Self-Care Issues for Clinicians, Researchers, and Educators*. Baltimore, MD: The Sidran Press, 1995.

Swan, James, and Philip Hyland. "A Review of the Beneficial Mental Health Effects of Exercise and Recommendations for Future Research." *Psychology & Society* 5, no. 1 (2012): 1–15.

Tabassum, Faiza, John Mohan, and Peter Smith. "Association of Volunteering with Mental Well-Being: A Lifecourse Analysis of a National Population-Based Longitudinal Study in the UK," *BMJ Open* 6, no. 8 (2016).

Taylor, Jill Bolte. *My Stroke of Insight*. London: Hachette, 2009.

Tedeschi, Richard G., and Lawrence G. Calhoun. "The Posttraumatic Growth Inventory: Measuring the Positive Legacy of Trauma." *Journal of Traumatic Stress* 9, no. 3 (1996): 455–72.

Tedeshi, Richard G., and Lawrence G. Calhoun. "Posttraumatic Growth: Conceptual Foundations and Empirical Evidence." *Psychological Inquiry* 15 (2004): 1–18.

The National Institute for the Clinical Application of Behavioral Medicine. *Guilt vs. Shame*. The National Institute for the Clinical Application of Behavioral Medicine, April 2018. https://www.nicabm.com/guilt-vs-shame/.

The Qur'ān: Arabic Text with Corresponding English Meanings. [Al-Qur'ān al-Karīm ma'a tarjamat al-ma'ānī bi-al-lughah al-injilizīyah.] Jeddah: Abul-Qasim Publishing House, 1997. http://www.qur'an.com.

Therapist Aid. *Deep Breathing*. Therapist Aid, 2017. https://www.therapistaid.com/worksheets/deep-breathing-worksheet.pdf.

Todd, Rebecca M., Daniel J. Müller, Daniel H. Lee, Amanda Robertson, Tayler Eaton, Natalie Freeman, Daniela J. Palombo, Brian Levine, and Adam K. Anderson. "Genes for Emotion-Enhanced Remembering Are Linked to Enhanced Perceiving." *Psychological Science* 24, no. 11 (2013): 2244–53.

Van der Kolk, Bessel A. "The Body Keeps the Score: Memory and the Evolving Psychobiology of Posttraumatic Stress." *Harvard Review of Psychiatry* 1 (1994): 253–65. https://doi.org/10.3109/10673229409017088.

Wahbeh, Helané, Angela Senders, Rachel Neuendorf, and Julien Cayton. "Complementary and Alternative Medicine for Post-Traumatic Stress Disorder Symptoms: A Systematic Review." *Journal of Evidence-Based Integrative Medicine* 19, no. 3 (2014): 161–75.

Wong, Albert. "Somatic Approaches to Healing Trauma." Online Course, 2019. https://www.somatopia.com.

Wood, Alex M., Jeffrey J. Froh, and Adam W. A. Geraghty. "Gratitude and Well-Being: A Review and Theoretical Integration." *Clinical Psychology Review* 30, no. 7 (2010): 890–905. https://doi.org/10.1016/j.cpr.2010.03.005.

Wood, Alex M., Jeffrey J. Froh, and Adam W. A. Geraghty. "Gratitude and Well-Being: A Review and Theoretical Integration." *Clinical Psychology Review* 30, no. 7 (2010): 890–905. https://doi.org/10.1016/j.cpr.2010.03.005.

Worden, J. William. *Grief Counseling and Grief Therapy: A Handbook for the Mental Health Practitioner*. 4th ed. New York: Springer Publishing Company, 2009.

Wright, Eric R., William P. Gronfein, and Timothy J. Owens. "Deinstitutionalization, Social Rejection, and the Self-Esteem of Former Mental Patients." *Journal of Health and Social Behavior* 41, no. 1 (2000): 68–90.

Yeung, Jerf W. K., Zhuoni Zhang, and Tae Yeun Kim. "Volunteering and Health Benefits in General Adults: Cumulative Effects and Forms." *BMC Public Health* 18, no. 8 (2018).

Ziglar, Tom. "The Gratitude Journey." *Ziglar* (blog). https://www.ziglar.com/articles/the-gratitude-journey/.

Zoellner, Tanja, and Andreas Maercker. "Posttraumatic Growth in Clinical Psychology: A Critical Review and Introduction of a Two-Component Model." *Clinical Psychology Review* 26, no. 5 (2006): 626–53. https://doi.org/10/1016/j.cpr.2006.01.008.